THE AMERICAN PRESIDENCY

Clinton Rossiter is John L. Senior Professor of American Institutions at Cornell University, and has also been Pitt Professor of American History at Cambridge University. His books include *The Supreme Court and the Commander in Chief, Constitutional Dictatorship, The American Presidency, Parties and Politics in America, Marxism: The View from America, Conservatism in America,* and *Seedtime of the Republic,* for which he received the Bancroft Prize, the Woodrow Wilson Foundation Award, and the prize of the Institute of Early American History and Culture.

Mr. Rossiter has been a consultant to the Ford and Rockefeller Foundations, is general editor of the series of books on "Communism in American Life" sponsored by the Fund for the Republic, and was a contributor to *Goals for Americans,* the Report of the President's Commission on National Goals (1960).

THE
AMERICAN
PRESIDENCY

by Clinton Rossiter

Revised Edition

Harcourt, Brace

& World, Inc.

New York

14220

Library of Congress Catalog Card Number: 60-5436

Printed in the United States of America

ISBN 0-15-605598-8

Twelfth Printing

To My Students, Past and Present, in
The American Presidency (Government 216)
Cornell University

"Methought I heard a voice cry, 'Sleep no more!' "
—*Macbeth*, II, i, 36

Preface to the First Edition

This book is a revised version of six lectures given on the Charles R. Walgreen Foundation at the University of Chicago, April 23–May 3, 1956. I am grateful to the officers of the Foundation for giving me this opportunity to rethink the thoughts of fifteen years on the Presidency. I am also grateful to James M. Burns, Edward S. Corwin, Arch Dotson, Richard P. Longaker, Alexander J. Morin, Richard E. Neustadt, J. Francis Paschal, John P. Roche, and, most of all, Mary Crane Rossiter, for their help and advice.

CLINTON ROSSITER

Ithaca, New York
March, 1956

Preface to the Second Edition

This book is a revised version of the revised lectures of 1956. In addition to strewing second thoughts all through these pages, I have tried to bring fresh materials, drawn largely from the conduct of the Presidency in the past four years, into chapters 1, 2, 4, and 8. I have added new passages on such topics as the process of impeachment and the President's responsibility in the broad field of science, and two new chapters on the currently agitated questions of election and succession to the Presidency. Least important to my own purposes but probably most interesting to readers and reviewers of this book, I have made a second attempt (based on seven years of observation rather than just three) to assess the performance of Dwight D. Eisenhower and to predict his place in the history of the Presidency. In all this I have been helped by the comments—some friendly, some critical, and some explosive—of hundreds of persons who took the trouble to write me about the first edition. To them, to Gladys Kessler, and once again to Mary Crane Rossiter I am genuinely grateful.

CLINTON ROSSITER

Ithaca, New York
December, 1959

CONTENTS

THE AMERICAN PRESIDENCY

CHAPTER **1**

THE POWERS OF THE PRESIDENCY

Sometimes the stranger outside the gates has a clearer vision of an American institution than we who have lived with it all our lives. John Bright, best friend in all England of the embattled Union, paid this tribute to the Presidency in 1861:

I think the whole world offers no finer spectacle than this; it offers no higher dignity; and there is no greater object of ambition on the political stage on which men are permitted to move. You may point, if you will, to hereditary rulers, to crowns coming down through successive generations of the same family, to thrones based on prescription or on conquest, to sceptres wielded over veteran legions and subject realms,—but to my mind there is nothing more worthy of reverence and obedience, and nothing more sacred, than the authority of the freely chosen magistrate of a great and free people; and if there be on earth and amongst men any right divine to govern, surely it rests with a ruler so chosen and so appointed.

My purpose is to confirm Bright's splendid judgment by presenting the American Presidency as what I honestly believe it to be: one of the few truly successful institutions created by men in their endless quest for the blessings of free government. This great office, like even the greatest men who have filled it, displays its fair share of warts, and I shall try to paint them as large as life. Yet I would be less than candid were I not to make clear at the outset my own feeling of veneration, if not

15

exactly reverence, for the authority and dignity of the Presidency.

This book is very far from a detailed or definitive portrait of this astounding institution. It is at best an impressionistic rendering of the main dimensions, and I beg early forgiveness for all the things I cannot possibly find room to say about it. My hope is simply that those who read these chapters may come to a sharper understanding of the position the Presidency occupies in the annals of our past and the hopes of our future.

This presentation must begin with a careful accounting of those tasks we call upon the President to perform, for if there is any one thing about him that strikes the eye immediately, it is the staggering burden he bears for all of us. Those who cherish Gilbert and Sullivan will remember Pooh-Bah, the "particularly haughty and exclusive person" in *The Mikado* who filled the offices of "First Lord of the Treasury, Lord Chief Justice, Commander-in-Chief, Lord High Admiral, Master of the Buckhounds, Groom of the Back Stairs, Archbishop of Titipu, and Lord Mayor, both acting and elect." We chuckle at the fictitious Pooh-Bah; we can only wonder at the real one that history has made of the American President. He has at least three jobs for every one of Pooh-Bah's, and they are not performed with the flick of a lacquered fan. At the risk of being perhaps too analytical, let me review the functions of the modern President. These, as I interpret them, are the major roles he plays in the sprawling drama of American government.

First, the President is Chief of State. He remains today, as he has always been, the ceremonial head of the government of the United States, and he must take part with real or apparent enthusiasm in a range of activities that would keep him running and posing from sunrise to bedtime if he were not protected by a cold-blooded staff. Some of these activities are solemn or even priestly in nature; others, through no fault of his own, are flirtations with vulgarity. The long catalogue of public duties that the Queen discharges in England, the President of the Republic in France, and the Governor-General in Canada is the President's responsibility in this country, and the catalogue is even longer because he is not a king, or even the agent of one, and is therefore expected to go through some rather undignified paces by a people who think of him as a combination of scoutmaster, Delphic oracle, hero of the silver screen, and father of the multitudes.

As figurehead rather than working head of our government, he greets distinguished visitors from all parts of the world, lays wreaths on the tomb of the Unknown Soldier and before the statue of Lincoln, makes proclamations of thanksgiving and commemoration, bestows medals on flustered pilots, holds state dinners for the diplomatic corps and the Supreme Court, lights the nation's Christmas tree, buys the first poppy from the Veterans of Foreign Wars, gives the first crisp banknote to the Red Cross, throws out the first ball for the Senators (the harmless ones out at Griffith Stadium), rolls the first egg for the Easter Bunny, and in the course of any month greets a fantastic procession of firemen, athletes, veterans, Boy Scouts, Campfire Girls, boosters, hog callers, exchange students, and heroic school children. The annual United Fund Drive could not possibly get under way without a five-minute telecast from the White House; Sunday is not Sunday if the President and his lady skip church; a public-works project is not public until the President presses a silver key in Washington and explodes a charge of dynamite in Fort Peck or Hanford or the Tennessee Valley.

The President is not permitted to confine this sort of activity to the White House and the city around it. The people expect him to come to them from time to time, and the presidential grand tour, a precedent set conspicuously by George Washington, is an important aspect of the ceremonial function. Nor is this function, for obvious political and cultural reasons, untainted with commercialism. If it isn't one "Week" for him to proclaim or salute, it's another, and what President, espe-

cially in an election year, would turn away the Maid of Cotton
or the Railroad Man of the Year or, to keep everybody happy,
the Truck Driver of the Year from the White House door?

The President, in short, is the one-man distillation of the
American people just as surely as the Queen is of the British
people; he is, in President Taft's words, "the personal embodiment and representative of their dignity and majesty." (Mr.
Taft, it will be remembered, was uniquely shaped by nature's
lavish hand to be a personal embodiment of dignity and majesty.) Or as Attorney General Stanberry argued before the
Supreme Court in 1867 in the case of *Mississippi* v. *Johnson:*

> Undoubtedly so far as the mere individual man is concerned there
> is a great difference between the President and a king; but so far as
> the office is concerned—so far as the great executive office of this
> government is concerned—I deny that there is a particle less dignity
> belonging to the office of President than to the office of King of
> Great Britain or of any other potentate on the face of the earth. He
> represents the majesty of the law and of the people as fully and as
> essentially, and with the same dignity, as does any absolute monarch
> or the head of any independent government in the world.

The role of Chief of State may often seem trivial, yet it cannot be neglected by a President who proposes to stay in favor
and, more to the point, in touch with the people, the ultimate
source of all his power. It is a conspicuous thief of his precious
time, yet more than one President, most notably Harry S Truman, has played it in such a way as to gain genuine release
from the routine tasks and hard decisions that filled the rest of
his day. And whether or not he enjoys this role, no President
can fail to realize that all his powers are invigorated, indeed are
given a new dimension of authority, because he is the symbol
of our sovereignty, continuity, and grandeur. When he asks a
Senator to lunch in order to enlist his support for a pet project,
when he thumps his desk and reminds the antagonists in a
labor dispute of the larger interests of the American people,
when he orders a general to cease caviling or else be removed

from his command, the Senator and the disputants and the general are well aware—especially if the scene is laid in the White House—that they are dealing with no ordinary head of government. The framers of the Constitution took a momentous step when they fused the dignity of a king and the power of a prime minister in one elective office. And, if they did nothing else, they gave us a "father image" that should satisfy even the most demanding political Freudians.

The second of the President's roles is that of Chief Executive. He reigns, but he also rules; he symbolizes the people, but he also runs their government. "The true test of a good government is its aptitude and tendency to produce a good administration," Hamilton wrote in *The Federalist,* at the same time making clear that it would be the first duty of the proposed President to produce this "good administration." For reasons that I shall touch upon later, the President (and I mean any President, no matter how happily he may wallow in the details of administration) has more trouble playing this role successfully than he does any of the others. It is, in fact, the one major area of presidential activity in which his powers are simply not equal to his responsibilities. Yet the role is an important one, and we cannot savor the fullness of the President's duties unless we recall that he is held primarily and often exclusively accountable for the ethics, loyalty, efficiency, frugality, and responsiveness to the public's wishes of the two and a third million Americans in the national administration.

Both the Constitution and Congress have recognized his authority to supervise the day-to-day activities of the executive branch, strained and restrained though this supervision may often be in practice. From the Constitution, explicitly or implicitly, he receives the twin powers of appointment and removal, as well as the primary duty, which no law or plan or circumstance can ever take away from him, to "take care that the laws be faithfully executed." He alone may appoint,

with the advice and consent of the Senate, the several thousand
top officials who run the government; he alone may remove,
with varying degrees of abruptness, those who are not executing the laws faithfully—or, in the case of all those Secretaries
and generals and attorneys directly under his command, not
executing them in a manner consistent with his own policies.

It is the power of removal—the "gun behind the door"—
that makes it possible for the President to bend his "team"
to his will. More to the point, this power is the symbol and
final sanction of his position as Chief Executive, and no official
in the administration, not even the most nonpartisan chairman
of the most independent regulatory commission, is entirely
immune to a fatal attack of presidential displeasure. A member
of the Federal Trade Commission or Interstate Commerce
Commission is protected by statute and judicial decision against
the kind of arbitrary removal the President may visit upon a
Secretary of the Army or Director of the Budget, but if he
has stepped out of line in a way for all the world to see—if,
to take a crude example, he has been drunk on the job for
weeks on end—then he cannot hope to stand up to the man
who has been commanded by the Constitution to see to the
faithful execution of the laws of the United States. His official
life would be forfeit; a veiled threat of removal, especially if
the threat were fortified by "pressure from the White House,"
would be enough to force the surrender of even the most thick-
skinned wrong-doer. The "voluntary" resignation of Richard
A. Mack from the Federal Communications Commission in
1958 is the most recent case in point. The disclosure by a committee of Congress of an apparent conflict of interest between
Mack the Commissioner and Mack the Friend of National Air-
lines, Inc. was enough to set the White House (more precisely, Sherman Adams) in motion, and Mr. Mack gave up
his post without a struggle. Occasionally, to be sure, the President must come right out and remove an official—because the
official has sinned too grievously to be allowed to resign, or,

as is more likely, because he is so proud of his record and convinced of his rectitude that he refuses to resign. Hard cases, Justice Holmes once said, make bad law, yet I doubt that there has ever been a more forceful vindication of the President's authority "to produce a good administration" than Mr. Roosevelt's cashiering of Dr. A. E. Morgan from the chairmanship of the Tennessee Valley Authority in 1938. Frustrated in his attempts to secure Dr. Morgan's co-operation in clearing up a nasty clash of personalities that had brought the activities of T.V.A.'s governing board to a standstill, the President removed him peremptorily, made a new appointment to the position, and sent T.V.A. about its business. There were screams of anguish and prophecies of dictatorship, but there was no effective challenge to the President's contention that, although he could not construe Morgan's duties for him nor substitute his own judgment for that of a board rendered independent by statute and custom, he could and must act to keep T.V.A. in operation.

From Congress, through such legislative mandates as the Budget and Accounting Act of 1921 and the succession of Reorganization Acts, the President has received further acknowledgment of his administrative leadership. Although independent agencies such as the Interstate Commerce Commission and the National Labor Relations Board operate by design outside his immediate area of responsibility, most of the government's administrative tasks are still carried on within the fuzzy-edged pyramid that has the President at its lonely peak. The laws that are executed daily in his name and under his general supervision are numbered in the hundreds. One task illustrates the scope of the President's administrative responsibility: the preparation and execution of the federal budget. One program attests the power he wields over the public's servants: the loyalty standards instituted by President Truman's Executive Order 9835 of March 21, 1947, and tightened by President Eisenhower's Executive Order 10450 of April 29, 1953. One passage from the *United States Code* makes clear that Congress itself expects much of him:

> The President is authorized to prescribe such regulations for the admission of persons into the civil service of the United States as may best promote the efficiency thereof, and ascertain the fitness of each candidate in respect to age, health, character, knowledge, and ability for the branch of service into which he seeks to enter; and for this purpose he may employ suitable persons to conduct such inquiries, and may prescribe their duties, and establish regulations for the conduct of persons who may receive appointment in the civil service.

It might be useful to hear the opinion of the acknowledged experts in this field. I take these paragraphs from the report of the sixth American Assembly, which met at Arden House in October 1954 to consider the "character, prestige, and problems" of the public service:

> *The President* has the responsibility for leadership of the Executive Branch of the Federal Government service. Constitutional principles, the necessities of our national life and the example of successful corporate enterprise all underscore the indispensability of executive responsibility for the personnel policies and the personnel management of the Federal Government.
>
> This leadership must be acknowledged and supported by the heads and employees of executive departments, by the party leaders and by the members of the Congress. This leadership must be accepted and exercised by the President, if the business of the National Government is to be efficiently performed.

Whether it is his letters or his taxes the ordinary citizen wants more efficiently collected, he looks first of all to the President as business manager of the administration. There was a time when Presidents could and did pay strict attention to matters such as these, and about a hundred million people still do not seem to realize that the time has long since passed.

The President's third major function is one he could not escape if he wished, and several Presidents have wished it mightily.

The Constitution designates him specifically as "Commander-in-Chief of the Army and Navy of the United States, and of the militia of the several States when called into the actual service of the United States." In peace and war he is the supreme commander of the armed forces, the living guarantee of the American belief in "the supremacy of the civil over military authority."

In time of peace he raises, trains, supervises, and deploys the forces that Congress is willing to maintain, and he has a great deal to say about the size and make-up of these forces. With the aid of the Secretary of Defense, the Secretaries of the three services, the Joint Chiefs of Staff, and the members of the National Security Council—every one of these men his personal choice—he looks constantly to the state of the nation's defenses. He is never for one day allowed to forget that he will be held accountable by people, Congress, and history for the nation's readiness to meet an enemy assault. There is no more striking indication of the present latitude of the President's military power than these matter-of-fact words in the Atomic Energy Act of 1946:

Sec. 6(a) Authority. The *Commission* is authorized to—

(1) conduct experiments and do research and development work in the military application of atomic energy; and

(2) engage in the production of atomic bombs, atomic bomb parts, or other military weapons utilizing fissionable materials; except that such activities shall be carried on only to the extent that the express consent and direction of the President of the United States has been obtained, which consent and direction shall be obtained at least once each year.

The President from time to time may direct the Commission (1) to deliver such quantities of fissionable materials or weapons to the armed forces for such use as he deems necessary in the interest of the national defense or (2) to authorize the armed forces to manufacture, produce, or acquire any equipment or device utilizing fissionable material or atomic energy as a military weapon.

It should be added that, despite the wounded protests of Senator Bricker, most citizens agreed with Mr. Truman's brisk assertion in 1950 that it was for the President to decide whether the H-bomb should be built. Congress might have refused to grant funds for such an undertaking, but this would not have stopped the President from pushing ahead as best he could with the other resources at his command. And, as the same doughty man demonstrated in 1945, it is for the President to decide in time of war when and where and how the H-bomb or A-bomb or any other bomb should be dropped.

In such time, "when the blast of war blows in our ears," the President's power to command the forces swells out of all proportion to his other powers. All major decisions of strategy, and many of his tactics as well, are his alone to make or to approve. Lincoln and Franklin Roosevelt, each in his own way and time, showed how far the power of military command can be driven by a President anxious to have his generals and admirals get on with the war. No small part of his time, as we know from Lincoln's experience, can be spent searching for the right generals and admirals.

But this, the power of command, is only a fraction of the vast responsibility the modern President draws from the Commander in Chief clause. The framers of the Constitution, to be sure, took a narrow view of the authority they had granted. "It would amount," Hamilton wrote offhandedly in *The Federalist*, "to nothing more than the supreme command and direction of the military and naval forces, as first General and Admiral of the Confederacy." This view of presidential power as something purely military foundered on the hard facts of the first of our modern wars. Faced by an overriding necessity for harsh, even dictatorial action, Lincoln used the Commander in Chief clause, at first gingerly, in the end boldly, to justify an unprecedented series of measures that cut deeply into the accepted liberties of the people and the routine pattern of government. Wilson added another cubit to the stature of the wartime Presidency by demanding that Congress give him those powers over the economy about which there was any constitutional doubt, and Franklin Roosevelt, who had read about Lincoln and lived with Wilson, carried the wartime Presidency to breath-taking heights of authority over the American economy and social order. The creation and staffing of a whole array of emergency boards and offices, the seizure and operation of more than sixty strike-bound or strike-threatened plants and industries, and the forced evacuation of 70,000 American citizens of Japanese descent from the West Coast are three startling and prophetic examples of what a President can do as Commander in Chief to stiffen the home front in support of the fighting forces. It is important to recall that Congress came to Roosevelt's aid in each of these series of actions by passing laws empowering him to do what he had done already or by fixing penalties for violating the orders of his subordinates. Congress, too, likes to win wars, and Congressmen are more likely to needle the President for inactivity and timidity than to accuse him of acting too swiftly and arbitrarily.

Now that total war, which ignores the old line between battlefield and home front, has been compounded by the absolute weapon, which mocks every rule we have ever tried to honor, we may expect the President to be nothing short of a "constitutional dictator" in the event of war. The next wartime President, who may well be our last, will have the right, of which Lincoln spoke with feeling, to take "any measure which may best subdue the enemy," and he alone will be the judge of what is "best" for the survival of the republic. We have placed a shocking amount of military power in the President's keeping, but where else, we may ask, could it possibly have been placed?

Next, the President is Chief Diplomat. Although authority in the field of foreign relations is shared constitutionally among three organs—President, Congress, and, for two special purposes, the Senate—his position is paramount, if not indeed dominant. In 1799 John Marshall, no particular friend of executive power, spoke of the President as "the sole organ of the nation in its external relations, and its sole representative with foreign nations." In 1936 Justice Sutherland, no particular friend of executive power and even less of Franklin D. Roosevelt, put the Court's stamp of approval on "the very delicate, plenary and exclusive power of the President as the sole organ of the government in the field of international relations."

The primacy of the executive comes under vigorous attack from time to time, chiefly from those who object to a specific policy even more strongly than to a President's pursuit of it, and it is true that he acts more arbitrarily and independently than the framers of the Constitution ever intended him to act. Yet the growth of presidential authority in this area seems to have been almost inevitable, and hardly the outcome of a shameful conspiracy by the three Democratic Presidents of the twentieth century. Constitution, laws, custom, the practice of other nations, and the logic of history have combined to place the President in a dominant position. Secrecy, dispatch, unity, continuity, and access to information—the ingredients of successful diplomacy—are properties of his office, and Congress, I need hardly add, possesses none of them. It is a body with immense power of its own in the field of foreign relations—a fact perfectly symbolized by the unprecedented conference between Prime Minister Macmillan and the leaders of Congress in March 1959—but the power is essentially negative in character and application. And as if all this were not enough to insure the President's dominance, he is also, as we have just noted, Commander in Chief, the man who controls and directs the armed might of the United States in a world in which force, real or threatened, is the essence of diplomacy.

The field of foreign relations can be conveniently if somewhat inexactly divided into two sectors: the formulation of policy and the conduct of affairs. The first of these is a joint undertaking in which the President proposes, Congress disposes, and the wishes of the people prevail in the end. The President's leadership is usually vindicated. Our most ancient and honored policy is significantly known as the *Monroe* Doctrine; our leading policies of recent years have been the *Truman* Doctrine and the *Eisenhower* Doctrine. From Washington's Proclamation of Neutrality in 1793 to Eisenhower's decision to stand fast in Berlin in 1959, the President has repeatedly committed the nation to decisive attitudes and actions abroad, more than once to war itself. Occasionally Congress has compelled him to abandon a policy already put forward, as it did in the case of Grant's plans for Santo Domingo, or has forced distasteful policies upon him, as it did upon Madison in 1812 and McKinley in 1898. Nevertheless, a stubborn President is hard to budge, a crusading President hard to thwart. The diplomatic lives of the two Roosevelts are proof enough of these assertions. Mr. Truman was not exaggerating much when he told an informal gathering of the Jewish War Veterans in 1948: "I make American foreign policy."

The transaction of business with foreign nations is, as Jefferson once wrote, "executive altogether," and Congress finds it difficult to exercise effective control or to deliver constructive criticism, not that Congress can be accused of lack of trying. The State Department carries on its many activities in the name of the President, and he is or ought to be in command of every procedure through which our foreign relations are carried on from one day to the next: negotiation of treaties and executive agreements, recognition of new governments and nations, selection and supervision of diplomatic personnel, adjustment of tariff barriers within statutory limits, direction of our delegation to the United Nations, and communications with foreign powers. As Commander in Chief he deploys our armed forces abroad and occasionally supports our policies with what is known as "presidential warmaking." The conduct of foreign relations as a short-range proposition is a presidential prerogative, and short-range actions—the recognition of a revolutionary re-

gime in Cuba, the reception of a Burmese prime minister, the
raising of the duty on Swiss watches—can have long-range
consequences.

In recent years, the role of Chief Diplomat has become the
most important and exacting of all those we call upon the
President to play. Indeed, when one thinks of the hours of
"prayerful consideration" President Eisenhower devoted each
week to briefing sessions with the Dulles brothers, conferences
with the National Security Council, lunches with Senators
Fulbright and Wiley, chats with Nehru or Macmillan or Diefen-
baker or whoever else might be in town, explanatory and in-
spirational speeches to the nation, and lonely wrestling bouts
with appointments and reports and messages to Congress—not
to mention his correspondence with Khrushchev, Zhukov, and
Bulganin—it is a wonder that he had a moment's time for any
of his other duties.

The President's duties are not all purely executive in nature.
He is also intimately associated, by Constitution and custom,
with the legislative process, and we may therefore consider him
to be the Chief Legislator. Congress has a wealth of strong and
talented men, but the complexity of the problems they are
asked to solve by a people who assume that all problems are
solvable has made *external* leadership a requisite of effective
operation. The President alone is in a political, constitutional,
and practical position to provide such leadership, and he is
therefore expected, within the limits of constitutional and political propriety, to guide Congress in much of its lawmaking
activity. Indeed, since Congress is no longer organized to guide
itself, not even under such tough-minded leaders as Senator
Johnson and Speaker Rayburn, the refusal or inability of the
President to point out the way results in weak or, at best,
stalemated government.

Success in the delicate area of executive-legislative relations
depends on several variables: the political complexion of Presi-

dent and Congress, the state of the Union and of the world around us, the vigor and tact of the President's leadership, and the mood of Congress, which is generally friendly near the beginning of a President's term and rebellious near the end. Yet even the President whose announced policy is to "restore our hallowed system of the separation of powers" and leave Congress strictly alone (Coolidge is a capital example, one not likely to be repeated) must exercise his constitutional option to veto or not to veto about a thousand times each session, must discourse once a year on the state of the Union and occasionally recommend "such measures as he shall judge necessary and expedient," must present the annual budget, and must make some effort to realize at least the less controversial promises in his party's platform. "After all," Mr. Eisenhower told a press conference in 1959, "the Constitution puts the President right square into the legislative business." In the hands of a Wilson or a Roosevelt, even at times in the hands of an Eisenhower, the Presidency becomes a sort of prime ministership or "third House of Congress," and the chief concern of the President is to push for the enactment of his own or his party's legislative desires.

Upon many of our most celebrated laws the presidential imprint is clearly stamped. Each of these was drafted in the President's offices, introduced and supported by his friends, defended in committee by his aides, voted through by a party over which every form of discipline and persuasion was exerted, and then made law by his signature. The signature, of course, was affixed with several dozen fountain pens, which were then passed out among the beaming friends and aides. Among the "ploys and gambits" the President may have used in the process were the White House breakfast with his chief lieutenants, or perhaps with his chief obstructionists; the fireside chat with his constituents, some of whom were also constituents of the obstructionists; the press conference, in which he proclaimed his astonishment at the way Congress was dragging its feet; the dangled patronage or favor, which brought a wavering or even hostile Senator to his side; and the threat of a veto, which he brandished like the Gorgon's head to frighten the mavericks into removing objectionable amendments to the bill he had first sent over.

Even the President who lacks a congressional majority must go through the motions of leadership. The Republicans in the Eightieth Congress always waited politely for Mr. Truman's proposals on labor, taxes, inflation, civil rights, and education, however scant the regard they intended to pay them. The Democrats, if we may believe the protests of Speaker Rayburn and Senator Johnson, were impatient to hear President Eisenhower's proposals and to feel the lash of his leadership. In any case, the chief responsibility for bridging the constitutional gulf between executive and legislature now rests irrevocably with the President. His tasks as leader of Congress are difficult and delicate, yet he must bend to them steadily or be judged a failure. The President who will not give his best thoughts to guiding Congress, more so the President who is temperamentally or politically unfitted to "get along with Congress," is now rightly considered a national liability.

Chief of State, Chief Executive, Commander in Chief, Chief Diplomat, Chief Legislator—these functions make up the strictly constitutional burden of the President. As Mr. Truman himself allowed in several of his folksy sermons on the Presidency, they form an aggregate of power that would have made Caesar or Genghis Khan or Napoleon bite his nails with envy. Yet even these are not the whole weight of presidential responsibility. I count at least five additional functions that have been piled on top of the original load.

The first of these is the President's role as Chief of Party, one that he has played by popular demand and to a mixed reception ever since the administration of Thomas Jefferson. However sincere Washington's abhorrence of "factions" may have been, his own administration and policies spawned our first two parties, and their arrival upon the scene altered the character of the Presidency radically. No matter how fondly or how often we may long for a President who is above the heat of political strife, we must acknowledge resolutely his right and duty to be the leader of his party. He is at once the least political and most political of all heads of government.

The value of this function has been attested by all our first-rate Presidents. Jackson, Lincoln, Wilson, and the two Roosevelts were especially skillful party leaders. By playing the politician with unashamed zest the first of these gave his epic administration a unique sense of cohesion, the second rallied doubting Republican leaders and their followings to the cause of the Union, and the other three achieved genuine triumphs as catalysts of congressional action. That elegant amateur, Dwight D. Eisenhower, played the role with devotion if not exactly zest. It would have astonished George Washington, but it cannot even ruffle us, to learn that the President devoted breakfast and most of the morning of June 20, 1955—a day otherwise given over to solemn celebration of the tenth birthday of the United Nations—to mending a few fences with Republican leaders of California. He was demonstrating only what close observers of the Presidency know well: that its incumbent must devote an hour or two of every working day to the profession of Chief Democrat or Chief Republican. The President dictates the selection of the national chairman and other top party officials, reminds his partisans in Congress that the legislative record must be bright if victory is to crown their joint efforts, delivers "fight talks" to the endless procession of professionals who call upon him, and, through the careful distribution of the loaves and fishes of federal patronage, keeps the party a going concern. The loaves and fishes are not so plentiful as they were in the days of Jackson and Lincoln, but the President is still a wholesale distributor of "jobs for the boys."

It troubles many good people, not entirely without reason, to watch their Chief of State dabbling in politics, smiling on party hacks, and endorsing candidates he knows to be unfit for anything but immediate delivery to the county jail. Yet if he is to persuade Congress, if he is to achieve a loyal and cohesive administration, if he is to be elected in the first place (and re-elected in the second), he must put his hand firmly to the plow of politics. The working head of government in a constitutional democracy must be the nation's number-one boss, and most Presidents have had no trouble swallowing this truth.

Yet he is, at the same time if not in the same breath, the Voice of the People, the leading formulator and expounder of public opinion in the United States. While he acts as political leader of some, he serves as moral spokesman for all. Well before Woodrow Wilson had come to the Presidency, but not before he had begun to dream of it, he expressed the essence of this role:

His is the only national voice in affairs. Let him once win the admiration and confidence of the country, and no other single force can withstand him, no combination of forces will easily overpower him. His position takes the imagination of the country. He is the representative of no constituency, but of the whole people. When he speaks in his true character, he speaks for no special interest. If he rightly interpret the national thought and boldly insist upon it, he is irresistible; and the country never feels the zest for action so much as when its President is of such insight and calibre.

Throughout our history there have been moments of triumph or dedication or frustration or even shame when the will of the people—would it be wrong to call it the General Will?—demanded to be heard clearly and unmistakably. It took the line of Presidents some time to grasp the meaning of this function, but since the day when Andrew Jackson thundered against the Nullifiers of South Carolina no effective President has doubted his prerogative to speak the people's mind on the great issues of his time, to act, again in Wilson's words, as "the spokesman for the real sentiment and purpose of the country."

The coming of the radio, and now of television, has added immeasurably to the range and power of the President's voice, offering the man who occupies this "bully pulpit" (as Theodore Roosevelt described it) an opportunity to preach the gospel of America in every home and, indeed, in almost every land. Neither Steve Allen nor Ed Sullivan, neither Bishop Sheen nor Edward R. Murrow—not even, I would insist, the men of the mythical West who fill every channel with the sound of their guns—can gain access to so many millions of American homes. Indeed, the President must be especially on his guard not to pervert these mighty media that are his to command. It is one thing for a huckster to appeal to the people to buy a mouthwash; it would be quite another for a President to appeal to them to stampede the Senate. I like to think that our sales resistance would be as dogged in the second case as in the first, but there is no denying that, even in defeat, a President could do a great deal of damage to our scheme of representative government.

Sometimes, of course, it is no easy thing, even for the most sensitive and large-minded of Presidents, to know the real sentiment of the people or to be bold enough to state it in defiance of loudly voiced contrary opinion. There are definite limits to presidential free speech, as Mr. Eisenhower learned in 1959 when he was egged into a few plaintive comments on the size and shape of American automobiles. Yet the President who senses the popular mood and spots new tides even before they start to run, who practices shrewd economy in his appearances as spokesman for the nation, who is conscious of his unique power to compel discussion on his own terms, and who talks the language of Christian morality and the American tradition, can shout down any other voice or chorus of voices in the land. There have been times, to be sure, when we seemed as willing to listen to an antagonist as to the President—to Senator Taft in 1950, General MacArthur in 1951, Clarence Randall of Inland Steel in June 1952—but in the end, we knew, and the antagonist knew, too, that the battle was no Armageddon, that it was a frustrating skirmish fought between grossly ill-matched forces. And if we learned anything from Senator Johnson's speech of January 6, 1958, to his Democratic colleagues, it was that two addresses on the state of the Union are one too many.

The President is the American people's one authentic trumpet, and he has no higher duty than to give a clear and certain sound. "Words at great moments of history are deeds," Clement Attlee said of Winston Churchill on the day the latter stepped down in 1945. The strong and imaginative President can make with his own words the kind of history that Churchill made in 1940 and 1941. When the events of 1933 are all but forgotten, we shall still recall Roosevelt's words, "The only thing we have to fear is fear itself."

In the memorable case of *In re Neagle* (1890), which still makes good reading for those who like a touch of horse opera in their constitutional law, Justice Samuel Miller spoke with feeling of the "peace of the United States"—a happy condition, it would appear, of domestic tranquillity and national prosperity that is often broken by violent men and forces and just as often restored by the President. Perhaps the least known of his functions is the mandate he holds from the Constitution and the laws, but even more positively from the people of the United States, to act as Protector of the Peace. The emergencies that can disturb the peace of the United States seem to grow thicker and more vexing every year, and hardly a week now goes by that the President is not called upon to take forceful steps in behalf of a section or city or group or enterprise that has been hit hard and suddenly by disaster. Generally, it is for state and local authorities to deal with social and natural calamities, but in the face of a riot in Detroit or floods in New England or a tornado in Missouri or a railroad strike in Chicago or a panic in Wall Street, the people turn almost instinctively to the White House and its occupant for aid and comfort.

And he, certainly, is the person to give it. No man or combination of men in the United States can muster so quickly and authoritatively the troops, experts, food, money, loans, equipment, medical supplies, and moral support that may be needed in a disaster. Are thousands of homes flooded in the Missouri and Ohio Valleys?—then the President will order Coast Guardsmen and their boats to be flown to the scene for rescue and patrol work, and he will go himself to bring cheer to the homeless. Are cattle starving on the snow-bound western plains? —then the President will order the Air Force to engage in Operation Haylift. Are the farmers of Rhode Island and Massachusetts facing ruin in the wake of a September hurricane?— then the President will designate these states as disaster areas and order the Secretary of Agriculture to release surplus foods and make emergency loans on easy terms. Is Maine scourged by forest fires? Is Texas parched with drought? Is Kansas invaded by grasshoppers? Is Little Rock soiled with the blood of men and tears of children?—then in every instance the President must take the lead to restore the normal pattern of existence.

Or are we having a March 1933 all over again, and are we caught up in the first dreadful moments of a financial panic?— then the President will issue the necessary orders on the authority of two laws that have been waiting quietly on the books since the first years of the New Deal:

Section 4 of the Emergency Banking Act of 1933:

In order to provide for the safer and more effective operation of the National Banking System . . . during such emergency period as the President of the United States by proclamation may prescribe, no member bank of the Federal Reserve System shall transact any

banking business except to such extent and subject to such regulations, limitations and restrictions as may be prescribed by the Secretary of the Treasury, with the approval of the President.

Section 19 (a) of the Securities Exchange Act of 1934:

The Commission is authorized . . . if in its opinion the public interest so requires, summarily to suspend trading in any registered security on any national securities exchange for a period not
exceeding ten days, or with the approval of the President, summarily
to suspend all trading on any national securities exchange for a
period not exceeding ninety days.

If I may reduce the meaning of these two laws to simple
terms, they empower the President to meet the challenge of
any future panic like that of March 1933 by declaring a state
of financial martial law. At the same time, he remains constitutionally, we might even say extraconstitutionally, empowered
to respond to an atomic attack by declaring straight-out martial
law through all the land. This, be it noted for future reference,
is exactly what President Eisenhower pretended to do in the
simulated hydrogen-bomb attack of June 1955. One of the remarkable events of that three-day test of our readiness for
atomic war was the startled discovery by Mr. Eisenhower and
his staff that "the inherent powers of the Presidency," something about which Republicans usually maintain uneasy silence,
would be the nation's chief crutch in the aftermath of the
ultimate disaster. This fact, and thus his status as Protector of
the Peace, had already been recognized by a group of Senators
who called on Mr. Eisenhower to "assume personal responsibility" for creating an adequate program of civil defense,
something he shortly proceeded to do within the limits of his
budget and our expectations.

There is at least one area of American life, the economy, in
which the people of this country are no longer content to let
disaster fall upon them unopposed. They now expect their
government, under the direct leadership of the President, to
prevent a depression or panic and not simply to wait until one

has developed before putting it to rout. Thus the President has a new function, which is still taking shape, that of Manager of Prosperity.

The origin of this function can be fixed with unusual exactness. The Employment Act of 1946 was the first clear acknowledgement by the federal government of a general responsibility for maintaining a stable and prosperous economy:

Sec. 2. The Congress hereby declares that it is the continuing policy and responsibility of the Federal Government to use all practicable means consistent with its needs and obligations and other essential considerations of national policy, with the assistance and cooperation of industry, agriculture, labor, and State and local governments to coordinate and utilize all its plans, functions, and resources for the purpose of creating and maintaining, in a manner calculated to foster and promote free competitive enterprise and the general welfare, conditions under which there will be afforded useful employment opportunities, including self-employment, for those able, willing, and seeking to work, and to promote maximum employment, production, and purchasing power.

The significant feature of this law from our point of view is the deliberate manner in which, in section after section, the President is singled out as the official who is "to foster and promote free competitive enterprise, to avoid economic fluctuations or to diminish the effects thereof, and to maintain employment, production, and purchasing power." He is granted the handsome gift of the Council of Economic Advisers; he is requested to make the annual Economic Report and such supplementary reports as may be advisable; he is expected to propose "a program for carrying out the policy declared in section 2, together with such recommendations for legislation as he may deem necessary or desirable." There is apparently no doubt in Congress's collective mind that one of the President's prime duties is to watch like a mother hen over all the eggs in all our baskets. As for the American people, it is a notorious fact that we give our President small credit for prosperity and full blame for hard times.

Yet even if the Employment Act had never been passed, he would have this duty and most of the powers that go with it. We have built some remarkable stabilizing devices into our political economy since 1929, and the men who control them —in the Federal Reserve System, the Securities and Exchange Commission, the Federal Security Agency, the countless credit organizations, the Federal Deposit Insurance Corporation— are wide open to suggestions, even directions from the President. There are limits, both strategic and physical, to what can be done in the White House, but certainly the alert President stands always ready to invite the managers of a sick industry or the leading citizens of a city plagued by chronic unemployment to come together and take counsel under his leadership. Of course, it is not his counsel but a well-placed government contract or a hike in the tariff or a dramatic recommendation to Congress for which they have come. Fortunately for the President, his position as overseer of the entire economy is obvious to even the most embittered spokesmen for special interests, and he can take refuge from their pleas for relief by insisting that he must consider the whole picture before deciding on action in their behalf.

The very notion of the President as Manager of Prosperity strikes many people as an economic and political heresy, especially those who still swear allegiance to the tattered doctrine of the self-healing economy. Most of us, however, now accept the idea of a federal government openly engaged in preventing runaway booms and plunging busts. We need only think of Mr. Eisenhower's creditable performance in the slack days of 1954—or, for that matter, of his uninspired performance in the harder days of 1958-1959—to recognize the central position of the Presidency in this new kind of government. Lest there be any doubt how the President himself felt about the new dimension of government responsibility, let me quote from his message to Congress accompanying the Economic Report for 1953:

The demands of modern life and the unsettled status of the world require a more important role for government than it played in earlier and quieter times. . . .

Government must use its vast power to help maintain employment and purchasing power as well as to maintain reasonably stable prices.

Government must be alert and sensitive to economic developments, including its own myriad activities. It must be prepared to take preventive as well as remedial action; and it must be ready to cope with new situations that may arise. This is not a start-and-stop responsibility, but a continuous one.

The arsenal of weapons at the disposal of Government for maintaining economic stability is formidable. It includes credit controls administered by the Federal Reserve System; the debt-management policies of the Treasury; authority of the President to vary the terms of mortgages carrying Federal insurance; flexibility in administration of the budget; agricultural supports; modification of the tax structure; and public works. We shall not hesitate to use any or all of these weapons as the situation may require.

And this from a Republican President dedicated to the glories of free enterprise! Thus far have we and the Presidency moved in a generation of welfare and warfare.

In order to grasp the full import of the last of the President's roles, we must take him as Chief Diplomat, Commander in Chief, and Chief of State, then thrust him onto a far wider stage, there to perform before a much more numerous and more critical audience. For the modern President is, whether we or our friends abroad like it or not, marked out for duty as a World Leader. The President has a much larger constituency than the American electorate: his words and deeds in behalf of our own survival as a free nation have a direct bearing upon the freedom and stability of at least several score other countries.

The reasons why he, rather than the British Prime Minister or French President or an outstanding figure from one of the smaller countries, should be singled out for supranational leadership are too clear to require extended mention. Not only are we the richest and most powerful member of any coalition we may enter, not only are we the chief target of the enemy and thus the most truculent of the powers arrayed against him, but the Presidency, for the very reasons I have dwelled upon in this chapter, unites power, drama, and prestige as does no other office in the world. Its incumbent sits, wherever he sits, at the head of the table. Winston Churchill, an A-plus student of our system of government, recognized this great truth with unerring eye when he insisted that not he, the elder statesman, but Mr. Eisenhower, the American President, take the chair in the middle at the Big Three conference in Bermuda in 1953. No British Prime Minister would ever be likely to forget that the President with whom he must deal every week of the year is a head of state as well as a head of government, a king and a prime minister rolled into one.

This role is not much more than a decade old, although there was a short rehearsal of it in late 1918 and the first few months of 1919. Whether it will continue to grow in the years of tension ahead depends, of course, on just how high the tension remains. It does seem probable that the President will have no choice but to act consciously for and speak openly to the nations with whom we are associated in defense of freedom—to act as Truman did in the North Korean aggression of June 1950, to speak as Eisenhower did in his proposal for an international atomic-energy pool delivered to the Assembly of the United Nations in December 1953, to act and speak together as Eisenhower did in the Berlin crisis of 1959. If the British Prime Minister often seemed to be the most influential figure in the Atlantic coalition during the first part of that nerve-racking year, this could be ascribed to the reluctance of the President rather than to any decline in the stature of the Presidency. Whoever the incumbent of our first office may be, its stature in the world grows mightier with every passing year. For some time to come the President of the United States will also be the "President of the West."

Having engaged in this piecemeal analysis of the Presidency, I hasten to fit the pieces back together into a seamless unity. For that, after all, is what the Presidency is, and I hope this exercise in political taxonomy has not obscured the paramount fact that it is a single office filled by a single man. I feel something like a professor of nutritional science who has just ticked off the ingredients of a wonderful stew. The members of the audience may be clear in their minds about the items in the pot, but they have not the slightest notion of what the final product looks like or tastes like or will feel like in their stomachs. The Presidency, too, is a wonderful stew whose unique flavor cannot be accounted for simply by making a list of its ingredients. It is a whole greater than and different from the sum of its parts, an office whose power and prestige are something more than the arithmetical total of all its functions. The President is not one kind of official during one part of the day, another kind during another part—administrator in the morning, legislator at lunch, king in the afternoon, commander before dinner, and politician at odd moments that come his weary way. He is all these things all the time, and any one of his functions feeds upon and into all the others. He is a more exalted Chief of State because he is also Voice of the People, a more forceful Chief Diplomat because he commands the armed forces personally, a more effective Chief Legislator because the political system forces him to be Chief of Party, a more artful Manager of Prosperity because he is Chief Executive.

At the same time, several of these functions are plainly in competition, even in conflict, with one another, and not just in terms of their demands on the President's time and energy. The roles of Voice of the People and Chief of Party cannot both be played with equal fervor, as Mr. Truman proved on

several occasions that had best be forgotten, while to act as
Chief Diplomat but to think as Chief of Party, as he was apparently persuaded to do in the Palestine crisis of 1948, can
throw our foreign relations into indelicate confusion. Mr. Eisenhower certainly had his periods in which, despite perfect health,
he reigned too much and thus ruled too little, and one can think
of several competent Presidents—Cleveland and Taft and
Hoover, to name three out of the last hundred years—who tried
much too hard to be faithful Chief Executives.

There is no easy formula for solving this problem inherent
in the nature of the office. If the Presidency is a chamber
orchestra of ten pieces, all played by the leader, he must learn
for himself by hard practice how to blend them together,
remembering always that perfect harmony is unattainable, remembering, too, with Whitman, to "resist anything better than
my own diversity." The only thing he can know for certain
before he begins to make presidential music is that there are
several parts, notably those of Chief of Party and Chief Executive, that he must not play too long and loud lest he drown
out the others.

The burden of these ten functions is monstrous, and the
President carries it as well as he does only because a remarkable array of administrative machinery has been invented
to help him in his daily tasks, because

> Thousands at his bidding speed,
> And post o'er land and ocean without rest.

Yet the activities of this train of experts, the Executive
Office and the Cabinet and all their offshoots and auxiliaries,
must not draw our final attention away from the man all alone
at the head. The Presidency, as I shall try to show in Chapter
4, has been converted into an institution during the past quarter-
century, and we can never again talk about it sensibly without
accounting for "the men around the President." Yet if it has
become a thousand-man job in the budget and in the minds of

students of public administration, it remains a one-man job in the Constitution and in the minds of the people—a truth of which we were dramatically reminded when the President fell ill in September 1955. Since it is a one-man job, the one man who holds it can never escape making the final decisions in each of the many areas in which the American people and their Constitution hold him responsible.

Mr. Truman, so it is said, used to keep a sign on his desk that read: "The buck stops here." That, in the end, is the essence of the Presidency. It is the one office in all the land whose occupant is forbidden to pass the buck.

CHAPTER **2**

THE LIMITS OF THE PRESIDENCY

The American Presidency is not universally admired. Most of us may think of it as a choice instrument of constitutional government, but there are loud dissenters in this country, especially in deep right field, and sharp dissenters abroad, especially in those happy lands where the parliamentary system is counted a success. If the opinions of the former are generally too mixed up with politics to demand serious attention, the opinions of the latter deserve a hearing and rebuttal. The particulars of their bill of indictment against the Presidency read as follows:

1) The President and Congress, thanks chiefly to the independence that each enjoys under the Constitution, are set perennially at odds with one another. Antagonism is built into the system, and the President is forced willy-nilly to choose between meek withdrawal, which leaves the government leaderless, or bold aggression, which throws it into turmoil.

2) The President, thanks chiefly to his fixed term and his exemption from the final penalty of a vote of no confidence by the legislature, is held neither continuously responsible for his general conduct of office nor ever responsible for specific acts and policies. He feels not at all the kind of day-to-day, act-to-act accountability that compels the working head of

44

government in a parliamentary system to mind every important step.

3) The Presidency, thanks to the whole of Article II of the Constitution, combines power and independence to a dangerous degree. It is, indeed, a "matrix for dictatorship," as the Swiss took pains to point out while writing their Constitution of 1848. The sad history of the Presidency south of Florida and Texas is a warning to Americans that they had better think of reducing either the power or independence of the original model at home.

The American rebuttal to the case against the Presidency makes three general points: that all these criticisms add up to a caricature of the real office, that they ignore the broad pattern of constitutional morality into which this office fits, and that their contempt for history is so flagrant as to raise laughs rather than doubts in the minds of all reasonable men. More specifically, we reject the first particular by answering that the founding fathers "planned it that way," preferring imperfect safety to perfect efficiency, and that we their descendants are coming more and more to suspect that they wrought more shrewdly than they knew in separating the executive and legislative powers. Would this giant democracy of ours—spread over an entire continent, undisciplined by the sanctions of a clear-cut class structure, assaulted daily by the massed voices of vulgarity and unreason—make as safe and sane a success of parliamentary government as it seems to be making of our divided system? This is a question to which even the most perceptive of our resident and visiting critics have yet to address themselves at all persuasively.

We reject the second particular not quite so confidently, for it would have been rather healthy, I think, to have held Roosevelt accountable for the "Court-packing" scheme, Truman for his proposed draft of the railroad strikers in 1946, and Eisenhower for the debacle over the Salk polio vaccine. But we cannot have the best of both great systems, and this, the too easy manner in which Presidents escape paying any real penalty for their blunders, is part of the minimum price we must meet in return for the benefits of the independent Presidency. And, after all, how do we know which kind of executive we would get if we were to adopt the parliamentary system in order to secure the blessings of continuous, piece-meal responsibility: the British Prime Minister, who operates just about as freely as an executive should, or the French Premier under the Fourth Republic, who was harassed at every step?

To the last criticism, that the Presidency blends too much power with too much independence, we can only make answer by inviting its critics to look back over the whole sweep of American political and constitutional history. Whatever gro-tesque shapes the Presidency may have assumed in Latin America, it has not been a matrix for dictatorship here in the United States; and I hardly think it an act of bravery, even an act of faith, to predict that it will not become one for a very long time, if ever. The Presidency, like every other instrument of power we have created for our use, operates within a grand and durable pattern of private liberty and public morality, which means that it operates successfully only when the Presi-dent honors the pattern by selecting ends and means that are "characteristically American." I may well be accused of begging the question of dictatorship by saying that the American system simply would not permit it, but I know of no better way to underline the impossibility of our spawning and then succumb-ing to a Perón or a Batista than to point to the history and people and climate of opinion of the United States and let it go at that.

The Presidency, be it noted, presents a most convincing argument in its own behalf and in that of the American people: 170-odd years and thirty-three Presidents—and still no despot or profligate or scoundrel has made the grade. In my opinion, no despot or profligate, and no scoundrel except Aaron Burr, ever made a good race, and perhaps the Presidency would have sobered even that "damaged soul." It was then and it is now the most thoroughly American of institutions, and I trust I will be excused from any further laboring of the plain historical and sociological truth that it is not a standing invitation to counterrevolution.

Yet, if we should not lose sleep over the possibility of a presidential *coup d'état,* we do have a right to worry about occasional abuses of power. The President is in a position to do serious damage, if not irreparable injury, to the ideals and methods of American democracy. Power that can be used decisively can also be abused grossly. No man can hold such a concentration of authority without feeling the urge, even though the urge be honest and patriotic, to push it beyond its usual bounds. We must therefore consider carefully the various safeguards that are counted upon to keep the President's feet in paths of constitutional righteousness. I have already discussed the powers of the President, as most writers on the subject delight to do, and now I think it proper to discuss the limits on him, as most do not. Blended together in judicious amounts, powers and limits make up a constitution, and the Presidency is nothing if not a constitutional office. Its powers are huge, but they are of no real effect unless exercised through constitutional forms and within constitutional limits.

The search for limitations begins with the written and unwritten law, and thus with the Constitution. Like the good constitution it is, it grants spacious authority in a few frugal words (for which we must be ever grateful to the one-legged man who polished them so brightly) and then clamps on limitations with equal economy of detail. Restrictions on the President are sprinkled all through the Constitution. One has only to think of the rigid four-year term of office, the qualifications on the power of veto, and, to prove that we are not yet entirely content with the bounds fixed by the framers, the

flat ban on a third term established in the Twenty-second
Amendment. Perhaps even more important than these specific
restrictions are the powers the Constitution withholds silently
from the President or bestows bountifully on other organs
over which he has no control. The prime constitutional limit
on the Presidency is the existence of Articles I and III.

The laws of Congress are full of implicit or explicit limitations. For one example, they rarely extend the President substantial authority today without requesting him to report to
Congress annually or semiannually on his use thereof, or at
even briefer intervals. For another, appropriations are more
often than not made in such painful detail that he and his
lieutenants are left with scant discretion to spend them with
any flexibility. For a third, he is limited sharply in his power
of appointment by the many qualifications—as to citizenship,
loyalty, political affiliations, professional attainments, residence,
and the like—that the laws fix in varying degrees on "offices
under the United States." The laws, like the Constitution, are
full of indirect checks on the President, especially those statutes
which set up agencies and commissions independent of his
direction.

Like Congress and the Justices themselves, the President can
show eye-opening ingenuity in bypassing decisions of the
Supreme Court. Yet no President can fail to recognize the
restrictions set upon the free play of his executive will in such
famous cases as *Humphrey's Executor* v. *U.S.* (1935), which
upheld the power of Congress to protect certain administrative
officials against arbitrary removal from office, and *Youngstown
Sheet and Tube Co.* v. *Sawyer* (1952), which denied Mr.
Truman authority to seize and operate the steel industry.
Custom, too, can be ignored in unimportant matters and for
short periods, but it has a way of asserting itself against the
most strong-willed President. The ancient custom of senatorial
courtesy, which appears to have burst full-grown from the
heads of the Senators from Georgia in the first year of Wash-

ington's administration, puts narrow limits on the President's power of appointment to hundreds of offices.

Most of these restrictions are fine and welcome, and they should be studied more thoughtfully by students of American government. Yet they exist on paper, and paper limitations, even those in the Constitution, need the support of living people and going institutions if they are to be of any force. We must therefore look further, into the political and social system all about us, if we are to learn what really puts the brakes on the President who has a mind to wander too far afield. "Brakes" is perhaps not the happiest word to use in this instance, because I am concerned with persons and institutions and centers of power that not only block the President's way, convincing him that a course of action is more trouble than it is worth or even frustrating him flatly, but often force him to take a course of action that he does not want to take at all. What are some of these, and how do they operate to restrain or persuade him?

The first and most vigorous is the Congress of the United States —a concourse of self-willed persons, a venerable institution, a fiercely independent center of power. Some of the weapons with which it may check or persuade the President are bright with use; others have not been hauled out and brandished for many years. Yet all must be reckoned with by the President who sets out upon an extraordinary line of conduct, or even, for that matter, by the President who simply tends quietly to his legitimate business. Let me list them briefly and add one or two comments.

The power of legislation is one that I have already touched upon sufficiently by indicating some of the ways in which the President is limited by statute. I would add only the observation that this power is a great deal easier for Congress to wield over future Presidents than over the President of the moment. Yet the Humphrey-Stennis joint resolution of July 1955, which

set up the Wright Commission to investigate and report on the
loyalty and security program, shows that pressure can sometimes be applied by law to an incumbent President. This
shrewdly designed statute persuaded Mr. Eisenhower much
against his stated will to join in re-examining a program for
which he was primarily responsible. The Senate and the House,
acting separately or concurrently, can also exert strong pressure
on the President through the agency of a resolution, even though
such a resolution is nothing more than an expression of opinion.
No President is likely to help Communist China take a seat in
the United Nations so long as Congress keeps on resolving
unanimously that "such admission would gravely injure the
United Nations and impair its effective functioning." It may be
argued that such resolutions have only moral force, but ours is
a system of government in which moral force is often the only
kind that really counts.

Another check, whose potentialities (and constitutionality)
have yet to be fully explored, is the provision occasionally inserted in broad delegations of emergency power that permits
the power to be recaptured by concurrent resolution, that is,
without the President's consent. A variation on this check is
the provision in the Reciprocal Trade Act of 1958 that permits
Congress, by a two-thirds vote in both houses, to overrule presidential objections to decisions of the Tariff Commission. Many
grants of power, of course, are made for limited periods; some
of the most important wartime statutes named specific terminal
dates. And there is always the "rider" placed artfully in a bill
the President cannot afford to veto. Rutherford B. Hayes, I am
told by residents of Fremont, Ohio, still shakes in his grave
every time a President is forced to protest against this practice.
No President was ever more beset by "riders," nor ever flung
them back more boldly at the gamesmen in Congress.

The power of investigation, which includes the power to ask
questions if not always to get answers from the President's chief
lieutenants, calls for even less comment. The excellent uses and

disgraceful abuses of this power over the past generation are etched sharply in our memories, and it is scarcely necessary to point out that in many of the leading investigations of this period (those, for example, conducted by Senator McCarthy in 1953 and Senator Kefauver in 1955) the real target was the President himself. While these men were engaged in high theater, other Congressmen, less ambitious and more merciful, were plodding quietly ahead with the routine inquiries into administrative purposes, methods, and shortcomings that do much to keep the Chief Executive and his helpers in touch with democratic realities. Hardly less effective as a limit upon the strong-minded President is the vast web of informal contacts and friendships and understandings between the old hands in Congress and the old hands in the civil service. Many of these relationships, which are rarely publicized, are maintained in blithesome disregard of the stated policies of the President—but he, after all, is only passing through.

The power of the purse was once upon a time considered the most formidable of Congress's weapons, and there are those who persist in talking about it as did Madison in *The Federalist:*

This power over the purse may, in fact, be regarded as the most complete and effectual weapon with which any constitution can arm the immediate representatives of the people, for obtaining a redress of every grievance, and for carrying into effect every just and salutary measure.

I am afraid we must enter a dissent to this much too mechanical evaluation of a power more vaunted than viable. Instances in which Congress slapped a President, and hurt him, by withholding funds from schemes in which he had an intense personal interest do not come to mind in bunches. Perhaps the most notable use of this weapon in recent years was the senseless murder of the National Resources Planning Board in 1943 by the Seventy-eighth Congress. In the same year, however, Mr. Roosevelt sent in a budget of $100,000,000,000, and Congress fell all over itself trying to give the Commander in Chief every-

thing he needed to win the war—everything, that is, but the
National Resources Planning Board. In the warfare-welfare
state, which Madison could hardly have foreseen, the power of
the purse exists more in rhetoric than in fact. Indeed, the evidence is rather convincing that in time of emergency, when
controls on expenditures are most needed, Congress itself takes
the lead in loosening them. In this permanent emergency
through which we seem to be living, the annual defense budget
makes a cruel mockery of all claims for the power of the purse.

The power of impeachment is the "extreme medicine" of the
Constitution, so extreme—and so brutally administered in the
one instance in which it was prescribed for a President—that
most observers now agree with Jefferson that it is a "mere scare-
crow" and with Henry Jones Ford that it is a "rusted blunderbuss, that will probably never be taken in hand again." The one
instance, of course, was the audacious attempt of the Radical
Republicans in Congress to have done once and for all with
Andrew Johnson. Johnson was impeached by the House of
Representatives in March 1868 on eleven counts. The key
charge was his alleged violation of the Tenure of Office Act of
1867 in insisting on his right to remove the faithless Edwin M.
Stanton from his position as Secretary of War, but in point of
fact the whole attack was vengefully political in motivation and
purpose. In the trial before the Senate—with Chief Justice Chase
presiding in keeping with the Constitution and with the President absenting himself in keeping with the dignity of his office
—he was thrice saved from removal by a margin of one vote.
The votes of thirty-six Senators were necessary to convict under
the two-thirds rule laid down in the Constitution, and on three
counts the vote to convict was 35 to 19. This fact, coupled with
the arguments of Johnson's counsel and the wording of the
charges, made clear for all time that impeachment is not an
"inquest of office," a political process for turning out a President whom a majority of the House and two-thirds of the Senate simply cannot abide. It is certainly not, nor was it ever

intended to be, an extraordinary device for registering a vote of no confidence. Yet, rusted though the blunderbuss may be, it still endures, stacked away defiantly in the Constitution, and it could yet be used to bring down a President who engages openly in "treason, bribery, or other high crimes and misdemeanors." If it is not, as Professor Edward S. Corwin has written, "an effective weapon in the arsenal of liberty," this must be largely due "to the fact that Presidents have in the past kept pretty clear of courses which might make people think seriously of so extreme a discipline." I predict confidently that the next President to be impeached will have asked for the firing squad by committing a low personal rather than a high political crime—by shooting a Senator, for example. Lest someone take the phrase "firing squad" seriously, I invite my readers to turn to Appendix II and read for themselves in the Constitution what penalties can be inflicted upon a wrongdoing President by an outraged Senate.

Congress, or either house, also retains the power of "soft impeachment," although this, too, has been used on a President only about once a century. The Senate's censure of Andrew Jackson in 1834 for "the late executive proceedings in relation to the public revenue" was the most drastic exercise of this extraordinary power. It cannot be said to have had much influence on Jackson's subsequent conduct; rather, it proved to be one of the most deadly boomerangs in American political history. An interesting variation on the power of censure was the resolution of the Republican conferences in the House and Senate in December 1950 demanding the removal of Secretary of State Acheson. This unprecedented "vote of no confidence" by the minority party may have hurt Mr. Acheson's prestige at the Brussels parley, but it, too, proved a boomerang. One suspects that nothing short of a gun at his head, and perhaps not even that, could thereafter have persuaded Mr. Truman to throw his Secretary of State from the sleigh to the Republican wolves.

Finally, I need hardly do more than point with awe to the

three great negative powers of the Senate, two of which it draws from the Constitution, the third of which it has bestowed upon its own grateful self: 1) the power of a majority to withhold consent from the President's nominations; 2) the power of one-third (plus one) "of the Senators present" to withhold consent from the treaties he submits to it; and 3) the power of a "little group of willful men, representing no opinion but their own," to hamstring the desire of a majority of both houses to give the President a grant of authority or money for which he may have desperate need. Some of the most celebrated filibusters in the Senate's history have been directed against the policies and even the person of a President.

The real power of Congress to check or persuade a President lies in none of the positive weapons I have just reviewed, for the real power of Congress over him is essentially negative in character. Two points are worth remembering in this connection: first, that no great policy, domestic or foreign, can be maintained effectively by a President without the approval of Congress in the form of laws and money; and second, that there is no way under our Constitution for a President to force Congress to pass a law or spend money against its will. In the course of this book I have several times pointed with pride and awe to the unique independence of our executive, but I could also have pointed, with no less pride and perhaps more awe, to the unique independence of our legislature. If the members of Congress cannot force the President to resign by a vote of no confidence, neither can he dissolve Congress. If his term is rigidly fixed, so, too, is theirs. Ours is just about the only legislature in the world over whose decisions the executive has no final power of persuasion, either in political fact or constitutional theory. He has *influence,* and the influence may be great, as Franklin Roosevelt proved in March 1933, but he has no *power.* Nor is the indissolubility of Congress the only bulwark of its independence. It, too, draws its authority directly from the Constitution; it, too, arises out of a constituency essentially its own.

Let me illustrate this point with the aid of a passage from Beard's *Republic*. The Glaucon of the piece, Dr. Smyth, has just made a sweeping assertion of presidential power in foreign affairs—something like the one I made in the first chapter—and Socrates, Professor Beard, is not the man to let him get away with it:

Now let me put some yes or no questions to you, the kind you like to put to me. Can the President alone regulate intercourse with other countries at his pleasure—that is, tariffs, tonnage duties, financial exchanges, and travel?

No. Congress has that power.

Can the President at his pleasure regulate immigration and emigration?

No. Congress passes immigration acts.

Can the President determine the conditions of naturalization and the rights of aliens in the United States?

No.

Can the President fix the size and nature of our army, navy, and other armed forces?

No.

Can the President alone set up ministries and consulates in other countries and pick his own ministers and consuls?

No. Since Congress must provide the money for them, it could control this branch of foreign business, if it wanted to do so. Besides, the Senate must approve the persons named by the President as ministers or ambassadors.

Can the President make treaties with other countries?

No. A treaty must have the approval of two-thirds of the Senate. But the President can make minor agreements without asking the consent of the Senate.

Can the President declare war?

No. That power is supposed to be in the hands of Congress.

Can the President make peace?

If it takes a treaty, the Senate must approve.

Can the President declare the foreign policy of the United States and impose it on the country by his own will?

There are two questions. Certainly the President can declare the foreign policy of the United States. But he cannot impose it upon the country by mere declaration.

There is more of this kind of talk, but the passage will suffice to remind us of the President's reliance on Congress for support of even his most splendid prerogatives.

I could proceed indefinitely discussing this most crucial relationship in our system of government, yet I trust I have made my point with sufficient vigor: the most reliable single limitation on the American Presidency is the independent existence of a proud, jealous, watchful co-ordinate branch. No President ever lived who would not have agreed, reverently or ruefully, with this statement.

The restricting powers of the third independent branch are a delusive shadow compared with the sweep of authority just reviewed. For most practical purposes, the President may act as if the Supreme Court did not exist. It takes a raw action by an imprudent President to invite judicial condemnation, and most exertions of executive power, however raw, are directed to questions over which no court would presume to exercise the slightest measure of supervision or even judgment.

This is especially true of the President's activities in time of war, as one may read for himself in the *United States Reports* published during and after our three great conflicts. At the very moment when the President, whether Lincoln or Wilson or Roosevelt, was drawing most audaciously on the Commander in Chief clause for authority to regulate the lives and property of the people, the Court was drawing most sheepishly on its bag of tricks to avoid a showdown with him and his military subordinates. The reason for excessive judicial self-restraint in time of war is, of course, obvious and compelling. A challenge in court to an evacuation order or a plant seizure or a suspension of the writ of habeas corpus raises a question so politically explosive, perhaps so vital to national survival, that the very notion of "government by lawsuit" becomes unthinkable. Whatever we allow this process to settle in time of peace, we cannot submit to its vagaries in time of war—a truth that the Court itself has been the first to acknowledge by avoiding unfavorable judgments on the President's orders as Commander in Chief. Like Congress's power of the purse, the Court's power of judicial review is least useful when most needed.

Yet the Court does own a few spectacular victories over the President. Several of these, like *Humphrey's Executor* v. *U.S.* (1935), came too late to be of much use or warning to anyone involved. The most famous and confidently quoted of all limiting decisions, *Ex parte Milligan* (1866), was announced a full year after the assassination of the President who was being censured, in this instance for authorizing the trial of civilians by military commission in an area far removed from the theater of war. Cases like *Schecter Bros.* v. *U.S.* (1934) and *Youngstown Sheet and Tube Co.* v. *Sawyer* (1952), however, shot down high-flying Presidents at the top of their trajectories. Whatever else may be said of the Schecter case, which cut the legal ground from under the National Recovery Administration, it was a healthy exhibition of constitutional government in action, and it was the President, not the Court, who took the crucial step by ordering the N.R.A. to fold its tents without delay. The Steel Seizure case was an equally dramatic vindication of constitutional practice, and again it was the President who bowed deeply, if hardly reverently, to constituted authority by ordering the Secretary of Commerce to relinquish possession of the steel mills. To bring the story up to date, President Eisenhower was handed two irritating rebuffs by the Supreme Court in 1958: *Kent* v. *Dulles,* in which the Secretary of State's practice of using his own power to deny passports as an instrument of foreign policy was limited if hardly eliminated, and *Cole* v. *Young,* in which the Court chopped down the area to which the

President's statutory power of removal had been extended "in the interest of the national security of the United States"—or, in other words, put a crimp in his loyalty program.

In none of these cases was the President himself before the Court. Jefferson's rejection of Marshall's *subpoena duces tecum* in the Burr trial and Chase's opinion in *Mississippi* v. *Johnson* (1867), which spared Andrew Johnson the necessity of answering a writ of injunction, make clear that the judiciary has no power to enjoin or mandamus or even question the President. His subordinates, however, do not share his immunity from the judicial process. Whenever a claim or justification is based on the authority of a presidential order, the order itself may come under challenge in the form of a suit against those seeking to enforce it. The interesting old case of *Little* v. *Barreme* (1804) presents one clear-cut instance in which the Court held a presidential order to be without legal warrant; *Panama Refining Co.* v. *Ryan* (1934) presents another.

I do not wish to sound too harsh or hopeless in my final estimate of the Court as a restraint on presidential activity. No one can doubt the high moral standing of a case like *Humphrey's Executor* v. *U.S.*, least of all some future President who decides to stir up the hornets by removing a commissioner from one of the independent agencies. Even as he chooses a course of action that permits him to ignore Justice Sutherland's opinion in that case, he will have to explain carefully to Congress and people, and in time to the Court, just what distinguishes this removal from that effected by Franklin Roosevelt in 1934. Yet as the Humphrey case demonstrated and *Wiener* v. *U.S.* (1958) confirmed, the President can remove just about any official if he wants to badly enough, and the Court will not be able to give the removed man anything more than sympathy and some back salary. We delude ourselves cruelly if we count on the Court at all hopefully to save us from the consequences of most abuses of presidential power. The fact is that the Court has done more over the years to expand than to contract the authority of the

Presidency—as witness the *Prize Cases* (1863), in which it supported Lincoln's blockade of the South; *In re Debs* (1895), in which it approved Cleveland's strong line of action in the Pullman strike; *Myers* v. *U.S.* (1926), in which a President-turned-Chief Justice cut through every restriction ever thrown about the removal power; *United States* v. *Curtiss-Wright Export Corp.* (1936), in which the Court spoke glowingly of the President's power in foreign relations; and the long series of cases in which it purified and strengthened the powers to pardon offenses and veto bills. In the nature of things judicial and political, the Court can be expected to go on rationalizing most pretensions of most Presidents. It is clearly one of the least reliable restraints on presidential activity.

A more reliable restraint is to be found in the federal administration: in the persons and politics and prejudices of, let us say, the top 20,000 civil and military officials of the government of the United States. Were the Presidents of the last fifty years to be polled on this question, all but one or two, I am sure, would agree that the "natural obstinacy" of the average bureau chief or commissioner or colonel was second only to the "ingrained suspicions" of the average Congressman as a check on the President's ability to do either good or evil. Several would doubtless go further to insist that the President's hardest job is, not to persuade Congress to support a policy dear to his political heart, but to persuade the pertinent bureau or agency or mission, even when headed by men of his own choosing, to follow his direction faithfully and transform the shadow of the policy into the substance of a program. No President, they would tell us sadly, can accomplish anything lasting in influence without the energetic assistance of a whole train of civil servants, most of whom were on the job long before he arrived and will be there long after he has departed, and without the loyal support of a motley array of political executives, most of whom he had never heard of until the day he sent in their names to the Senate. In seeking to win this kind of assistance, in trying to "get on top and stay on top" of his administration or even a part of it, a President can easily dissipate all his time, energy, and capacity for leadership.

This is not to say that the federal administration is led and staffed by men whose one purpose in life is to ignore, emasculate, or otherwise frustrate the legitimate wishes of the President. Quite the contrary, our public servants are no less anxious than he to get on with the business of good and democratic government. But his idea and their idea of what is "good" or "democratic" must often be at stiff odds with one another, especially when he is pushing some untried and unconventional policy, even more especially when they have the support of strong men and groups in Congress. It is too much to expect, short of the kind of drastic therapy or surgery that may well leave an agency in no condition to act at all, that such a policy can be the same in execution as it was in conception. I think, in this instance, of all the written and spoken directives of our last three Presidents aimed at eliminating racial discrimination in the civil service and the armed forces, and I wonder how many thousands of times some stubborn or fainthearted official has made a mockery of the President's good intentions. I think, too, of the trials undergone by Truman and Eisenhower in persuading certain chiefs of staff, whose official lives depend entirely on the President's pleasure, to shape their acts and speeches to the policies of the administration. And I top off these thoughts with a memorable observation by a man who knew firsthand about the severe limits on the President's power to influence administrators, Franklin D. Roosevelt:

The Treasury is so large and far-flung and ingrained in its practices that I find it is almost impossible to get the action and results I want—even with Henry [Morgenthau] there. But the Treasury is not to be compared with the State Department. You should go through the experience of trying to get any changes in the thinking, policy and action of the career diplomats and then you'd know what a real problem was. But the Treasury and the State Department put together are nothing compared with the Na-a-vy. The admirals are really something to cope with—and I should know. To change anything in the Na-a-vy is like punching a feather bed. You punch it with your right and you punch it with your left until you are finally exhausted, and then you find the damn bed just as it was before you started punching.

I shall have more to say about the President's difficulties as an administrator in later chapters. Here I need only call attention to certain broad features of the administrative branch that can be counted on to hobble a crusading President, even when the crusade is obviously launched against the forces of darkness. The first of these is the mere size of the federal administration, which now makes it impossible for a President to know or see or influence personally more than a handful of those men whose day-to-day activities will determine whether some cherished policy is to succeed or fail. What Burke said of the old British Empire, we may say of the new American government: "In large bodies, the circulation of power must be less vigorous at the extremities. Nature has said it." At many extremities of the federal administration the circulation of presidential power cannot be felt at all.

The second feature is pluralism in law, and a close corollary is pluralism in fact. Many agencies are rendered independent of the President's immediate supervision by statute; many more are exempt from his influence because of political and personal circumstances. The most unusual circumstance, one that can frustrate any President, is that of an upright agency headed by a case-hardened chief who numbers more real friends among the leaders of Congress than any President who ever lived, not even excluding William McKinley. The Federal Bureau of Investigation under J. Edgar Hoover, the Passport Office under Mrs. Ruth Shipley and Miss Frances Knight, and the Corps of Engineers under almost anyone are examples of what I mean by "pluralism in fact." Although a President may count on these agencies to execute the laws faithfully according to their own lights, he would invite disaster, both administrative and political, if he tried to alter the course that each has been following for these many years. Mr. Hoover has a kind of tenure that even the most carefully sheltered administrator should have reason to envy; his time-tested ability to outlast the President of the moment must always give that President pause. I cannot help wondering how often President Truman thought of relieving Mr. Hoover—and then thought a second time, sighed, and went about his business.

Finally, I need only mention such qualities of any administration as tradition, pride, inertia, and professional knowledge to show that the President, be his intentions good or bad, is checked sharply by the mere existence of all those thousands of top-grade public servants over whom he simply cannot expect to have the control in fact that he does in law, and of those hundreds over whom he has no effective control at all. Nor does it afford him much comfort to know that he hires and fires the men on top of the executive departments, for few of these are his unquestioning supporters and all must suffer the existence of bureau and division heads who make their own deals with congressional committees for power, funds, and prestige. There are more programs under way in the federal administration than any one President has ever dreamed of initiating, terminating, or bending to his will.

Another series of restraints upon the President arises out of our political system, by which I mean the two major parties. We all know well the many ways in which the leaders of the opposition party can make hash of his plans and a misery of his existence. They can badger his assistants, investigate his methods, vote down his requests, question his motives, keep a record of the times he plays golf, and, as in the congressional elections of 1918 and 1946 and perhaps even in 1958, beat him in the process of beating his party at the polls. If the President is the grand sachem of his own party and thus the symbol of its hopes and instrument of its principles, the party that fought him tooth and nail at his election must continue to fight him, with perhaps a little more restraint now that he is President, all through his four years in office. His record is essentially the record of his party, and the party in opposition, which wants desperately to put its own man in the White House, cannot be expected to let him have his own way except in matters that touch upon our survival as a nation. Even as he struggles with these matters he will be harassed by the enemy's irregulars. Not the least effective check in our system of checks and balances is one the framers themselves tried to save us from with all their skill: the party in opposition, which now means the party that lost the Presidency in the last election. No party can think of itself as the governing party in this country unless it can claim the authority and prestige of the White House. Indeed, ours is just about the only country in the world in which a party can dominate the national legislature for years on end and still be described correctly as "the party out of power"—a commentary on the unique character and authority of the American Presidency that must be worth at least ten thousand words.

If the opposing party is a roadblock in the path of the President, his own party is at best a drag. He draws great power from his position as Chief of Party, but with it comes the obligation to work and live with the men who elected him to office —an obligation of which Representative Simpson of Pennsylvania reminded Mr. Eisenhower with a fervor just short of anger in January 1959. Not only must he be careful not to plunge too far ahead or lag too far to the rear of his allies in Congress; he must pay homage to the traditions of his party, select his chief lieutenants from its ranks, act as "honest broker" among its squabbling wings, and endure silently attacks upon his integrity by men who roam the outer reaches of party loyalty. In doing all these things for the sake of harmony, and for the sake of victory in the next election, he cannot help losing some of his zest for bold experiment. In most instances that

matter he must work with the party or not at all. The party, as
we well know from the history of a dozen administrations, is
more likely to tame him than he is to reshape it. Franklin Roosevelt, supposedly the most dominant of political leaders, felt the
drag of his own party through most of his years in office. The
Democrats on the House Rules Committee and Senate Judiciary
Committee, not the Republicans huddled together in the Cave
of Adullam, were the impenetrable barrier between him and
some of his most ardently sought goals. Dwight D. Eisenhower,
a man with little taste for adventure, was certainly hampered
rather than invigorated by his leadership of the Republican
party. The party that makes him also brakes him: this is the
lot, not entirely unhappy, of the modern President.

When we look beyond the national government and the parties
that are its lifeblood, we note at least three other centers or
dispersions of power that stand in the President's way and often
force him to take troublesome detours. The first of these is the
federal system—an involved network of fifty separate and independent governments and their countless subdivisions, all of
which possess powers whose use or disuse can seriously embar-
rass the President and his policies. Although the states no longer
have the restraining influence of the days when they defied Jefferson, ignored Madison, and heckled Lincoln, they remain an
obstacle to the determined President, especially to one who is
eager to push ahead boldly with experiments in education and
racial justice. In conducting foreign relations, too, the President
may discover that the states and even the cities still hold some
power to irritate if not to persuade him. Theodore Roosevelt's
Japanese policy nearly foundered on the anti-Oriental obstinacy
of the San Francisco Board of Education; the Board gave way
to the President only after he had promised to see what he
could do to reduce the flow of Japanese immigrants into California. The Republican-dominated legislature of California
made even more trouble for President Wilson by passing an

alien land law aimed primarily at the Japanese, despite the earnest pleas of the President, which Secretary of State Bryan delivered personally in Sacramento, that the nation be spared the consequences of this insult to proud Japan. Our policy in the Middle East, which has never been celebrated for its clarity of purpose, was thrown into even more of a state of frustrated confusion in 1957 by Mayor Wagner's childish behavior on the occasion of King Ibn Saud's visit to New York City. While I am on the subject of the Middle East, an area in which oil is the beginning and end of our foreign policy, I might call attention to the existence of the Texas Railroad Commission. One of these days we may need to export unusual quantities of oil to Western Europe—as we did for a short time in the Suez crisis of 1957—and just how much persuasion will our President be able to visit upon this powerful agency which, as few Americans seem to realize, has effective authority over the rate of production in most of the oil fields in the United States? I suppose we can always count on Texas to remind us that the states still exist.

Far stronger than the states as a check on the Presidency is the American system of free enterprise—that fabulous galaxy of corporations, small businesses, partnerships, individual enterprises, trade associations, co-operatives, unions, consumer groups, and foundations through which the power of economic decision is splintered and diffused in the interest of freedom and progress. The President must enlist a great deal of private support among both management and labor if he is to make his authority as Manager of Prosperity felt in the face of impending economic disaster. His bid for support may often be spurned by some group of men in the economy who just do not want to be managed into prosperity, at least prosperity as the President defines it.

And he can be spurned—no doubt of that. There have been several occasions in recent years when free enterprise, or even a single free enterpriser, has defied a President with impunity and even brought him to terms. John L. Lewis, the last of the robber barons, has driven at least three Presidents to consider either homicide or suicide, and Clarence Randall, a man who has served this country well, may be remembered most vividly for his televised attack on President Truman's order to seize the steel industry in April 1952. Mr. Randall's opening and closing words on that occasion are well worth recording, for they give a candid picture of an American mind wrestling with the prickly truth that the politician in the White House is also a king, and vice versa:

I have a deep sense of responsibility as I face this vast audience of the air. I am here to make answer on behalf of the steel industry to charges flung over these microphones last night by the man who then stood where I stand now. I am a plain citizen. He was the President of the United States.

Happily we still live in a country where a private citizen may look the President in the eye and tell him that he was wrong, but actually it is not the President of the United States to whom I make answer.

It is Harry S. Truman, the man, who last night so far transgressed his oath of office, so far abused the power which is temporarily his, that he must now stand and take it.

I shall not let my deep respect for the office which he holds stop me from denouncing his shocking distortions of fact. Nor shall I permit the honor of his title to blind the American people from the enormity of what he has done.

He has seized the steel plants of the nation, the private property of one million people, most of whom now hear the sound of my voice. This he has done without the slightest shadow of legal right. . . .

For whom has he done this? Let no American be misled. This evil deed, without precedent in American history, discharges a political debt to the C.I.O. Phil Murray now gives Harry S. Truman a receipt marked "paid in full." I present this forthright reply to the President only because I believe deeply in the truth of what I have said. I should feel derelict in my own duty as a citizen if I did not tonight call upon Americans everywhere to take up the challenge the President threw down last night.

Whereupon Mr. Randall and his associates took up the challenge themselves and, eight weeks later, drove the President and Secretary of Commerce Sawyer headlong from their mills. Their troubles were far from over, but they had defeated a President in a battle of his choosing.

I have already referred to the President's obligations to his colleagues and constituents overseas. No obligation that goes with this new dimension of leadership is more certain and pressing than his duty to listen carefully, and to pay heed when he can, to the suggestions of our friends, real or simply wished for, throughout the world; for on these terms alone can we maintain the alliances upon which we depend for survival as a self-governing people. This means, of course, that in shaping a military or foreign policy the President must give careful thought to how persons outside as well as inside the country will respond. He must henceforth sense a reduction in his freedom to conduct the delicate business of diplomacy and the nasty business of war because of pressures flowing from London and Paris and Tokyo, as well as from New Delhi and the United Nations building in New York. Dozens of times since World War II our Presidents have acted as they have because Sir Winston Churchill or Sir Anthony Eden or General de Gaulle or, let us not forget, Syngman Rhee has persuaded them to act that way. Would Mr. Eisenhower have gone to the Summit in 1955 if he had not been entreated by Eden and Premier Faure? And would Sir Anthony have entreated quite so persuasively had he not been faced with a general election, one that Mr. Eisenhower had a strong desire to see him win? Would not the way to the Summit in 1959-1960 have been a great deal easier if it had not been littered with the suspicions of Adenauer and de Gaulle? And would they have been so suspicious had they not been persuaded of the reluctance of millions of Germans and Frenchmen to face the Russians at the bargaining table? It would seem that the people as well as the political leaders of other nations can occasionally speed a President up or slow him down.

This brings me to the last and, over the long run, most effective check upon the President: the opinions of the people of the United States, which our pressure groups can be counted on to express with zeal. Lincoln is supposed to have said that he could do anything with "public sentiment" but nothing without it or against it; and if he did not say it, we can say it for him. The President draws immense authority from the support of the American people, but only if he uses it in ways they understand and approve, which generally means ways that are fair, dignified, traditional, and familiar. He can lead public opinion, but only so far as public opinion is willing to go, and it is splendidly inert on dozens of great issues. Indeed, there are times when it will not rouse to any appeal, when it wearies, as Franklin Roosevelt once confessed to a friend, of being "attuned . . . to a constant repetition of the highest note in the scale," which is another way of saying that the President must be careful not to become a bore.

The President can steer public opinion a bit, too, and occasionally redirect its course, but he cannot make it take a direction that goes against what I have called our "grand and durable pattern of private liberty and public morality." For if he flouts either the considered judgments or ill-considered prejudices of any vocal segment of the people, if he chances to roam too far outside the accepted limits of presidential behavior, he will find himself exposed to all those enemies who multiply like mosquitoes in a Jersey August whenever a President plays the game too hard. No President, certainly no peacetime President, ever wielded more power with less need to worry about the political consequences than did Franklin Roosevelt in 1933, yet even then the assumption was abroad that there were some steps he could not take, some measures he could not recommend to Congress, in his effort to rescue "a stricken Nation in the midst of a stricken world." Let me drive this point home with a few words from a devoted admirer of the President, Professor Harold Laski, who wanted a new deck more than a New Deal:

Vast innovations for which the public is unprepared are almost bound to fail, because they are almost certain to shock. There can be experiment in the tactics of policy; there can hardly, without great danger, be experiment in fundamental ideas. Those observers who say that Mr. Roosevelt missed a great opportunity in 1933 when he did not nationalize the banking system seem to me wholly to misconceive the nature of the presidential office. While it was possible that, at that grave moment, the president might have carried through such a scheme, it was so widely outside the range of common expectation that it would have destroyed his authority for the rest of his term in office. Nothing in previous discussion had prepared the public for such a measure. Nothing in the electoral conception of Mr. Roosevelt had prepared the public to associate him with such a strategy. He might have won the battle; he would have lost the campaign.

Thinking of Mr. Roosevelt's defeat in his fight to enlarge the Supreme Court in 1937, I would go a step beyond Laski and assert that he would not even have won the battle. Public opinion in this country in 1933, or at least the opinion of a large and dogged segment of it, would never have made peace with the idea of nationalizing the banking system, and it would surely have found a dozen ways to harry the President into surrender. These ways still exist and have, if anything, grown stronger in the past several decades. And by "ways" I do not mean simply such outlets for American opinion as radio, television, Gallup and Roper polls, letters to the White House, or even elections, useful as all these may be as storm warnings to a President. The real force of public opinion as a limit on the Presidency is felt through the other restraints I have described in this chapter. Public opinion, that is to say, works most effectively on a President when it encourages Congress to override a veto, persuades an investigating committee to put a White House intimate on the grill, stiffens the resolve of a band of

Senators to talk until Christmas, convinces an ousted commissioner that his ouster is worth fighting in the courts, and puts backbone in a Supreme Court asked to nullify a presidential order. The various institutions and centers of power that check the President are inept and often useless without public opinion —and with it wondrously armed.

All this is especially true of Congress, which never feels that life is so worth living as when it condemns the President or refuses to grant his request for power because it senses that for once it, not he, has "rightly interpreted the national thought." If he tries to persuade Congress improperly or pushes ahead in defiance of all the rules, he invites the one disaster from which Presidents rarely recover: the loss of genuine popular support.

In the end, of course, the checks that hold the President in line are internal rather than external. His conscience and training, his sense of history and desire to be judged well by it, his awareness of the need to pace himself lest he collapse under the burden—all join to halt him far short of the kind of deed that destroys a President's "fame and power." He, like the rest of us, has been raised in the American tradition; he, perhaps better than the rest of us, senses what the tradition permits and what it forbids in the conduct of high office. If he knows anything of history or politics or administration, he knows that he can do great things only within "the common range of expectation," that is to say, in ways that honor or at least do not outrage the accepted dictates of constitutionalism, democracy, personal liberty, and Christian morality.

And so we return to the point from which we set forth on this journey around the perimeter of presidential power, and again I beg the question of dictatorship by saying that the American system would not permit it. This republic has had its share of "God's angry men," and some of them have climbed up to high places and set off damaging explosions. But none has even got a good start on the climb to the highest place of all. Our political rules demand categorically that a candidate for the Presidency be, first, a politician able to unite a party in whose house there are a hundred mansions and, second, a statesman able to bid confidently for the votes of a majority of the American constituency. It has unfailing ways of singling out and rejecting the man who cannot do these things because he is too angry or anxious or unprincipled. Men like Thaddeus Stevens and Huey Long and Senator McCarthy may wield vast powers of provocation and intimidation in their time, but no party with the faintest hope of winning the big election will ever nominate such a man to lead it. I think a good test of a man's understanding of the American system was his recognition, even in 1952 and 1953, that Senator McCarthy might help to make or break a President but could never be one himself. At least one of Hamilton's confident observations in *The Federalist* still rings true:

The process of election affords a moral certainty, that the office of President will never fall to the lot of any man who is not in an eminent degree endowed with the requisite qualifications. Talents for low intrigue, and the little arts of popularity, may alone suffice to elevate a man to the first honors in a single state; but it will require other talents, and a different kind of merit, to establish him in the esteem and confidence of the whole Union, or of so considerable a portion of it as would be necessary to make him a successful candidate for the distinguished office of President of the United States. It will not be too strong to say, that there will be a constant probability of seeing the station filled by characters preeminent for ability and virtue.

Or at least by characters with enough ability to lead an American-style party and enough virtue to appeal to a majority of one of the world's most enlightened electorates.

Let me refix attention upon the President who is already in office, upon the one, indeed, in office at the moment of writing. Like all our Presidents, he is quite unlikely to hazard a dictatorship; but, again like all of them, he is quite likely to indulge in occasional misuses of power. My concern has been to describe the network of restraints that keeps him from indulging too often and too perniciously in such misuses, and I think it essential to round off this description with two observations. First, no one of these mighty centers of power—Congress, Court, administration, parties, states, economy, people—operates alone in restraining him. They form, as I have said, a network, and the strength of the network arises from the interlocking of all its parts. One fortifies the other and is in turn fortified by it. A genuinely indecent performance by the President will arouse fierce opposition in every part of our system, and even a questionable course of action, such as Eisenhower's series of blunders in the Dixon-Yates affair, will move Congressmen, administrators, lobbyists, and politicians to unite in opposition. Several observers were moved to remark in the midst of that controversy that the President seemed never to have heard of John C. Calhoun's doctrine of the "concurrent majority," or surely he would have realized that no important program can be brought off in this country without the concurrence of a clear majority of the social and economic interests with a stake in the outcome. One always had the feeling that Eisenhower would lose in the end—if not the battle, certainly the campaign. And when he did lose the battle, he lost not only to the city of Memphis but to a whole host of other interests that had fought him implacably on a dozen fronts. There are those, to be sure, who think of the Dixon-Yates contract as a proper agreement properly made, which is as useful a thought as any to illustrate the truth that the system can prevent a President from doing good as well as evil. In the end, however, we must hold fast to the faith, which is surely borne out by history, that the network of restraints on the President works about as well as we have a right to expect our institutions to work. Much, after all, is left to chance among free men. As we cannot expect power to be used only to do good, so we cannot expect limitations to be used only to block evil.

My second point is that the President is not a Gulliver immobilized by ten thousand tiny cords, nor even a Prometheus chained to a rock of frustration. He is, rather, a kind of magnificent lion who can roam widely and do great deeds so long as he does not try to break loose from his broad reservation. Our pluralistic system of restraints is designed to keep him from going out of bounds, not to paralyze him in the field that has been reserved for his use. He will feel few checks upon his power if he uses that power as he should. This may well be the final definition of the strong and successful President: the one who knows just how far he can go in the direction he wants to go. If he cannot judge the limits of his power, he cannot call upon its strength. If he cannot sense the possible, he will exhaust himself attempting the impossible. The power of the Presidency moves as a mighty host only *with* the grain of liberty and morality.

CHAPTER **3**

THE PRESIDENCY IN HISTORY

The roots of the American Presidency run deep into history. In a world in which model constitutions with their model executives have come and gone in profusion over the past 150 years, this office stands forth as a truly venerable institution. We cannot take its full measure unless we know something of its history, and its history, in any case, is worth studying for its own exciting sake. With no further ado I plunge headlong into it.

The point of origin to which I would first direct attention is the Constitutional Convention of 1787, although like all such points it had origins of its own, in this instance far back in English constitutional history. To understand the kind of executive created in Article II of the Constitution, we must know something of the men who wrote it, the purposes they had in mind, the materials with which they worked, and the experience that was their "final guide."

The men most influential in shaping the Presidency were James Wilson, who campaigned tirelessly for an executive that could operate with "energy, dispatch, and responsibility"; James Madison, who swung around slowly, but in the end decisively, to Wilson's advanced yet sensible views; and Gouverneur Morris (the one-legged man of page 47), who led the battle for an energetic executive on the floor of the Convention and then sealed the victory by writing the final draft of the Constitution.

74

Hamilton and Washington, too, each in his own way, deserve some credit for the original Presidency.

The purposes of all these men were the purposes of the whole Convention: to rescue the new republic from the turbulent aftermath of revolution by establishing a government with sufficient energy to insure domestic tranquillity, secure the blessings of ordered liberty, protect private property, create conditions favorable to commercial prosperity, gain respect for itself and fair treatment for its citizens abroad, unite the states in pursuit of common ends, and return the reins of power to the "enlightened gentry." Men like Wilson and Morris understood more clearly than men like Roger Sherman and Edmund Randolph that a strong and independent executive was an essential element of any such government.

The materials with which they worked were the colonial governorships and thus, more remotely, the British monarchy, the various solutions to the problem of executive power in the first state constitutions, the administrative departments that had developed under the Articles of Confederation, and the writings of such exponents of balanced government as Locke and Montesquieu. The experience, both happy and unhappy, of the leaders of the Convention finally dictated the choice of the New York Constitution of 1777 and the Massachusetts Constitution of 1780 as the chief materials. The contrast between these two states, where independent executives served the cause of stability and order, and states like North Carolina and Rhode Island, where unchecked legislatures engaged in all sorts of unseemly activities, did not escape the attention of the delegates at Philadelphia. They had had their fill of governments, both state and national, in which "everything has been drawn within the legislative vortex." Between 1776 and 1787 there had been a noticeable shift in the constitutional theory of the moderate Whigs, from whose ranks came the framers of the Constitution —a shift away from innate confidence in popular assemblies and toward the suspicion that, as Jefferson wrote in his *Notes on Virginia,* "173 despots would surely be as oppressive as one." The sharp decline in the prestige of Congress and the state assemblies among conservatives throughout the new republic was a major factor in the decision to adopt a form of government in which the legislature would be balanced by a strong executive, not mismatched with a "mere Cipher." Even George Mason went on record as opposing "decidedly the making the executive the mere creature of the legislature as a violation of the fundamental principle of good government."

The progress of the Convention toward this decision was labored and uncertain, however, and it often seemed that the hard lessons of the previous decade would be wasted on a majority of the delegates. Persistent voices were raised against almost every arrangement that eventually appeared in Article II, and Wilson and his colleagues were able to score their final success only after a series of debates, decisions, reconsiderations, references to committees, and private maneuvers that still leave the historian befuddled. I have followed the tortuous progress of the incipient Presidency through Madison's *Notes* several times, and I am still not sure how the champions of the strong executive won their smashing victory. It can be said for certain, however, that at least eight decisions on the structure and powers of the executive were taken at different stages of the proceedings, and that out of these arose the Presidency. Every one of these decisions, with one partial exception that history was shortly to remedy, was taken in favor of a strong executive. The consequences for the Presidency, indeed for our whole system of government, would have been enormous had any one of them been taken differently—as it could easily have been. Let me list these decisions briefly, first giving notice that this list lends a deceptive appearance of order to a highly disordered train of events:

1) An executive would be established separate from the legislature. Although this was surely the easiest of all eight deci-

sions to adopt, there were those like Sherman who continued to wonder aloud if it would not be wiser to leave the legislature free to create and appoint such executives "as experience might dictate." To most delegates it was clear from the outset that the executive should be created in the Constitution itself. This had not been done in the first American constitution, and most hardheaded patriots considered this one of the serious defects in the Articles of Confederation.

2) The executive would consist of one man, a President of the United States. This fateful decision was taken only after considerable debate, and only after Wilson had used his position as chairman of the Committee on Detail to spike the plans of those like Randolph who feared the one-man executive as a "foetus of monarchy." Had Randolph and his friends had their way, the Presidency, or whatever it might have been called, would probably have been shared among three men.

3) The President would have a source of election outside the legislature. To no problem of the executive did the framers devote more time, talk, and votes. Most of the delegates originally shared Sherman's view that the executive "ought to be appointed by and accountable to the legislature only, whicn was the depository of the supreme will of the Society." Both the Virginia and the New Jersey plans provided for election of the executive by the legislature, and five times in the course of the Convention the delegates voted for this method. Not until the very end were enough of them swayed by the eloquence and diplomacy of Morris to adopt the electoral system outlined in Article II, Section 1, which was borrowed from the method for electing state senators in the Maryland Constitution of 1776. Morris and Wilson, an ill-assorted pair of prophets, were the only delegates to raise their voices clearly for election by the people. Another forty to fifty years would pass before the onward sweep of American democracy would carry the election of the President the rest of the way to the people, but the key

decision in behalf of his independence was taken at Philadelphia: the removal of the regular machinery for choosing him to a location outside the legislature and beyond its control.

4) The President would have a fixed term of office, which could be terminated only by the extraordinary method of conviction on impeachment for a high crime or misdemeanor. Hamilton devoted an entire number of *The Federalist* to arguing the vast merits of this decision, which, he insisted, would guarantee the "personal firmness" of the President and the "stability" of his administration. Yet neither he nor any of his associates recognized the real implication of the fixed term: that it would render impossible the rise of a parliamentary form of government. They can hardly be blamed for not recognizing it, since the sharpest minds in England had not yet noticed how far their constitution had moved in the direction of responsible cabinet government.

5) The President would be eligible for re-election to an indefinite number of terms. Had this decision been taken differently, had no President been permitted even to seek a second term, the office would surely be a less splendid and powerful one than it is today. The second terms of Washington, Jackson, Wilson, the two Roosevelts, and Truman, landmarks in the evolution of the Presidency, would never have taken place at all; and their first terms, no mean landmarks themselves, would have been severely hampered had not friend and foe alike expected them to go for a second. And as Hamilton wrote in *The Federalist:*

> Would it promote the peace of the community, or the stability of the government to have half a dozen men who had had credit enough to be raised to the seat of the supreme magistracy, wandering among the people like discontented ghosts, and sighing for a place which they were destined never more to possess?

6) The President would be granted his own powers by the Constitution. It is a matter of great moment that he has prerogatives of his own, that all his authority does not come to him in

the form of grants from Congress. What would he be without the constitutional right to command, nominate, pardon, negotiate treaties, supervise the execution of the laws, convene Congress, and, above all, defend himself with the qualified veto? How could Hamilton, writing as *Pacificus,* have vindicated Washington's proclamation of neutrality in 1793, how could the first Roosevelt have spun out his "Stewardship Theory," how could Chief Justice Taft have written the breath-taking opinion in *Myers* v. *U.S.*—if the opening words of Article II were not so inclusive in their simplicity? "The executive power shall be vested in a President of the United States of America": could an apologist for the strong Presidency ask for anything more?

7) The President would not be encumbered with a council to which he would have to go for approval of his nominations or vetoes or other acts. In every state government of the time the executive was restrained in the use of one or more of his powers by a "council of revision," and the disappointed advocates of a plural executive insisted strenuously that the unity of the Presidency be qualified at least to this extent. "The Grand Signor himself," Mason grumbled, "had his Divan," but he grumbled in vain. The last of a persistent series of efforts to saddle the President with a council was beaten off at the end of the Convention. The unity of the executive had been preserved against all assaults.

8) A clause was inserted in Article I that would forbid any "person holding any office under the United States" to be a "member of either house during his continuance in office." The concern of the delegates over "corruption and the low arts of intrigue" was responsible for this copy of the ill-fated Place Bill of 1692; its real significance, which naturally escaped their notice, lay in the roadblock it still throws up against the evolution of any system of cabinet responsibility to Congress. A motion to strike this clause from the Constitution in preparation was frustrated by a tie vote. There is no telling what a President like

James Monroe or Franklin Pierce, or even Thomas Jefferson, might have made of the absence of this prohibition against a backstairs union of executive and legislature.

It is not hard to think of decisions the Convention might have taken to strengthen the Presidency even further. It could have fixed a longer term, granted the President an item veto over appropriations, named four or five departments and made them clearly responsible to him, and required only a majority of the Senate to confirm treaties. But we can well be satisfied with Article II. When we realize that just two weeks from the end of the Convention the proposed Senate held exclusive authority to make treaties and appoint ambassadors and justices, we must marvel at the way in which the story came to a happy ending for Wilson and Morris.

The framers were fully aware, as they read over their finished work, that the Presidency would come under severe attack from those who had opposed the whole idea of the Convention from the beginning and were now about to learn that some of their worst fears had been realized. The case against the Presidency was well summed up in Patrick Henry's warning that this new executive office was an "awful squint toward monarchy." Hamilton, to be sure, proved equal to the task of refuting the charge. One can almost hear him sigh under the burden as he begins the eleven numbers of *The Federalist* devoted to the Presidency with the remark:

> There is hardly any part of the system which could have been attended with greater difficulty in the arrangement of it than this; and there is, perhaps, none which has been inveighed against with less candor or criticized with less judgment.

The big if silent gun in the arsenal of those who insisted upon the essential republicanism of the proposed Presidency was the universal assumption that George Washington, the Cincinnatus of the West, would be chosen as first occupant of the office, and chosen and chosen again until claimed by the grave. This assumption surely had something to do with the fact that all arguments over the executive at Philadelphia were resolved in favor of power and independence. As Pierce Butler wrote to a relative in England about the powers of the executive, "Entre nous, I do [not] believe they would have been so great, had not many of the members cast their eyes toward General Washington as President; and shaped their ideas of the Powers to be given a President, by their opinions of his Virtue." And it made things a good deal easier for those who carried the brunt of the debate in 1788.

Let me now review briefly the outlines of the Presidency as it left the hands of the framers. Considering the temper of the times, it was an office of remarkable vigor and independence. Hamilton pointed out in *The Federalist* that it combined energy, unity, duration, competent powers, and "an adequate provision for its support" with "a due dependence on the people" and "a due responsibility." The President had a source of election divorced from the legislature, a fixed term, indefinite re-eligibility, immunity from conciliar advice that he had not sought, and broad constitutional powers of his own. It was his first task to run the government: to be its administrative chief, to appoint and supervise the bureaucrats, and to "take care that the laws be faithfully executed." He was to be ceremonial head of the nation, a republican king with the prerogative of mercy, and he was to lead the government in its foreign relations, whether peaceful or hostile. Despite the principle of the separation of powers, he was not to be completely isolated from the houses of Congress. To them he could tender occasional advice, and over their labors he held a qualified but effective veto. The President was to be a strong, dignified, nonpolitical chief of state and government. In two words, he was to be George Washington.

The Presidency today has much the same general outlines as it had in 1789, but the whole picture is a hundred times magnified. The President is all the things he was intended to be, and he is several other things as well. If we compare the Presidency under Washington with the Presidency under Eisenhower, we can see several remarkable changes in its character.

First, it is distinctly more powerful. It cuts deeply into the powers of Congress; in fact, it has quite reversed the expectations of the framers by becoming itself a vortex into which these powers have been drawn in massive amounts. It cuts deeply into the lives of the people; in fact, it commands authority over their comings and goings that Hamilton himself might tremble to behold.

Next, the President is more heavily involved in making national policy. It was, to be sure, the nineteenth-century Whigs who insisted most arrogantly that his sole task was to carry out the policies determined by an all-wise Congress, but even Washington cannot be said to have taken much of a hand in making policy except in the fields of foreign and military relations. Although Hamilton, his Secretary of the Treasury, exercised imaginative leadership and independent judgment in the areas he occupied by right or had invaded by stealth, his was considered a virtuoso performance that would probably not be repeated. Yet it has been repeated and much improved upon by every President worth his salt. Whether as legislator, opinion-maker, commander, or administrator, the President molds lasting policy in every sector of American life.

To a large extent this is true because he is now so highly political a figure, and over this development the framers would have shaken their heads in wonder and sorrow. The plunge of the Presidency into party politics, which Jefferson took for himself and all his successors, may seem to have been unavoidable. The framers, however, would not have seen it that way. They believed sincerely in the idea of a patriot President, one who would rise coolly above the "heats of faction"; they would have considered it a mockery of all their pains to create a republican king if the king, like George III, were to turn his energies to party intrigue.

Another development would probably have shocked the framers, although one or two of them seem to have suspected that it was in the offing: the conversion of the Presidency into a democratic office. The extent to which he has become the "tribune of the people" is never so apparent as in an election year. When we contrast the decentralized, nonpolitical, dignified election of Washington with the "heats and ferments" of the presidential canvass as it has existed at least since 1840, we begin to sense how far the American people have gone to make the Presidency their peculiar possession.

Finally, the office has a kind of prestige that it did not know under Washington and lacked as late as the turn of this century. Washington, after all, lent his prestige to the Presidency, but today quite the reverse process takes place when a man becomes President. He becomes the great figure in our system because the office is the great institution. We forget too easily that Congress—with sometimes the House on top and at other times the Senate—was the focus of the people's interest in their government through most of the first century under the Constitution. The Presidency carried with it very little of the magic that is now so notable an element in its strength.

All this evidence leads me to assert that the outstanding feature of American constitutional development has been the growth of the power and prestige of the Presidency. This growth has not been steady, but subject to sharp ebbs as well as massive flows. Strong Presidents have been followed by weak ones; in the aftermath of every "dictator," Congress has exulted in the "restoration of the balance wisely ordained by the fathers." Yet the ebbs have been more apparent than real, and each new strong President has picked up where the last strong one left off. Lincoln took off from Jackson and Polk, not from Pierce and Buchanan. Franklin Roosevelt looked back to Wilson over the barely visible heads of the three Presidents who came between them. As to the fate of the Presidency under the assaults of Thaddeus Stevens, Ben Wade, Schuyler Colfax, and their friends and heirs, I call Henry Jones Ford to witness: "Although once executive power, in the hands of an accidental President, was bent and held down by the weight of a huge congressional majority, its springs were unbroken, and it sprang up unhurt when the abnormal pressure was removed." In the face of history, it seems hard to deny the inevitability of the upward course of the Presidency—discontinuous, to be sure, but also irreversible.

Why should the Presidency have proved so resilient and resolute? Why has it outstripped both Congress and Court in the long race for power and prestige? The answer lies in the whole history of the United States. Let me dwell for a few pages on the major forces in our history that have hastened the ascent of the Presidency.

The first of these is the rise of the "positive state," the big government that regulates, stimulates, and operates in every part of the American economy and society and, further, strikes "a respectable posture of defense" in a shrinking world. The growth of our industrial civilization has brought in its train a thousand problems of huge concern to the American people, and the people have turned again and again to beg their national government for help in solving them. Congress has responded, too eagerly for some Americans and too timidly for others, by passing laws that reach deeply into our lives and even more deeply into our pockets. To execute these laws, Congress has created more than two million federal jobs. The positive state, that is to say, is the administrative state, and although much of the administration operates by design or default outside the President's range of supervision, much operates in his name and under his final direction. Moreover, as I have noted before, no law of Congress, no tricky technique aimed at insuring independence for some new arm of the positive state, can ever rob him of the exclusive constitutional power to "take care that the laws be faithfully executed." The historic shift in the nature of our Constitution away from a catalogue of limitations and toward a grant of powers has singled out the President as its chief beneficiary. Our progress as an industrial people has elevated him to a position of administrative authority without precedent in all history. Indeed, his authority is so vast that he cannot begin to exert it.

No book on an American subject is thought complete these days without a few insightful words from Alexis de Tocqueville, so I call upon that prince of cultural anthropologists to point out the second development that has raised the Presidency so high. Seeking for those "accidental causes which may increase the influence of executive government," Tocqueville commented:

It is chiefly in its foreign relations that the executive power of a nation finds occasion to exert its skill and its strength. If the existence of the Union were perpetually threatened, if its chief interests were in daily connection with those of other powerful nations, the executive government would assume an increased importance in proportion to the measures expected of it and to those which it would execute.

So long as America held relatively aloof from the world, Congress could pose as the dominant branch of our government. Our self-elevation to the status of a major power, however, upset the old balance of the nineteenth century completely and finally. Woodrow Wilson wrote in Theodore Roosevelt's last year in office:

The President can never again be the mere domestic figure he has been throughout so large a part of our history. The nation has risen to the first rank in power and resources. The other nations of the world look askance upon her, half in envy, half in fear, and wonder with a deep anxiety what she will do with her vast strength. . . . Our President must always, henceforth, be one of the great powers of the world, whether he act greatly or wisely or not. . . . We can never hide our President again as a mere domestic officer. We can never again see him the mere executive he was in the thirties and forties. He must stand always at the front of our affairs, and the office will be as big and as influential as the man who occupies it.

Even more influential and bigger, one may say with assurance, for even a Harding or Pierce or a succession of Fillmores could not remove America from the top of the world and turn the Presidency back into a cipher, and even an army of Radical Republicans in Congress led by a healthy Thad Stevens would not be equal to the tasks of negotiation and force. Congress continues to take a major part in shaping foreign policy and overseeing foreign affairs, but it can no longer seriously challenge the leadership of the President. We may take it as an axiom of political science that the more deeply a nation becomes involved in the affairs of other nations, the more powerful becomes its executive branch. The authority of the President has been permanently inflated by our entrance into world politics and our decision to be armed against threats of aggression, and as the world grows smaller, he will grow bigger.

An associated cause of the growth of the Presidency is the shattering series of emergencies, both foreign and domestic, that have been our lot during the past century—especially the emergency of all-out war. Another axiom of political science would seem to be this: great emergencies in the life of a constitutional state bring an increase in executive power and prestige, always at least temporarily, more often than not permanently. As proof of this point, we need only think of the sudden expansion in power that the Presidency experienced under Lincoln as he faced the rebellion, under Wilson as he led us into a world war, or under Franklin Roosevelt as he called upon Congress to extend him "broad Executive power to wage a war" against depression. Each of these men left the Presidency a visibly stronger instrument than it had been before the crisis. Nor should we forget lesser Presidents in lesser crises, for these men, too, left their mark on the office. When Hayes dispatched troops to restore peace in the railroad strike of 1877, when McKinley sent 5,000 soldiers and marines to China during the Boxer uprising, and when Harry Truman acted on a dozen occasions to save entire states from the ravages of storm or fire or flood, the

Presidency moved to a higher level of authority and prestige, principally because the people had now been taught to expect more of it.

The long decline of Congress has contributed greatly to the rise of the Presidency. The framers, as I have explained, expected Congress to be the focus of our system of government. The President was granted several of his powers not so much for the sake of efficiency as to keep him from being drawn out of his orbit into that of the legislature, there to tag along weakly in the wake of this sovereign force. What the framers did not reckon with was the astounding growth of the republic, which has turned Congress into a cumbersome pair of assemblies that speak in a confusion of tongues. Congress is a mighty instrument of constitutional democracy, one of which Americans may well be proud. Yet it is an instrument that cannot, by reason of its structure, constituency, and mission, do some things very well and other things at all. It cannot operate in the grand style without external leadership, which the President alone is in a position to offer. When Congress finally gave up primary responsibility for preparing the budget in 1921, it had no choice but to call on the President to come to the rescue. By abdicating an ancient function it could no longer perform, it gave a tremendous boost to the power of the President, not only to control his administration, but to influence the legislative process.

The knife of reality cuts even deeper: Congress generally cannot exercise its own authority without, in turn, increasing that of the President. There are obvious limits to what it can accomplish effectively by setting up independent commissions to execute new laws, and he must therefore be the chief beneficiary of most expeditions into unexplored territory. A delicious example of the way in which Congress is forced to expand his power while expanding its own is Title II of the Taft-Hartley Act of 1947. Few Congresses have ever distrusted presidential power more earnestly than that led by Joseph W. Martin and Robert A. Taft. Yet in enacting the long-awaited law "to bring the unions into line," it had to grant the President new statutory authority to act in major strikes. To make the whole episode even more delicious, it will be recalled that Mr. Truman spurned the gift, had it forced upon him by two-thirds of each house, and then used it spectacularly on ten separate occasions. Whether because of its exertions or insufficiencies, Congress has done its part to make the President what he is today.

Henry Jones Ford, in his perceptive *Rise and Growth of American Politics* (1898), was the first to call attention pointedly to the one giant force that has done most to elevate the Presidency to power and glory: the rise of American democracy. Most men who feared the proposed Presidency in 1787 were prisoners of the inherited Whig assumption that legislative power was essentially popular and executive power essentially monarchial in nature. The notion that a democratic President might be pitted against an oligarchical legislature occurred to few at the time, most notably to Gouverneur Morris, who spoke of the executive, with his tongue somewhere in his cheek, as "the guardian of the people" against the tyranny of the "great and wealthy who in the course of things will necessarily compose the legislative body." As a matter of history, it took only about forty years to make Morris's masked prophecy come true. Since the days of Andrew Jackson the Presidency has been generally recognized as a highly democratic office. It depends directly on the people for much of its power and prestige; it shrinks to a rather mean thing when it loses their support. It is not, I feel sure, an accident of history that the upsurge of democracy and Jackson's resurrection of the Presidency went hand in hand, nor that he gave his name to the mighty movement that swept him into office and bade him act boldly in the name of the people. Our Presidents could never have challenged Congress so often and successfully were they, too, not popularly elected and popularly sustained. American democracy finds in the President its single most useful instrument. Small wonder, then, that he stands as high as he does in the mythology and expectations of the American people. There is virtually no limit to what the President can do if he does it for democratic ends and by democratic means.

It is all very well to write about the forces that have made the Presidency what it is today, but I think it high time that I also wrote about men. None of these mighty events—the upbuilding of the positive state, our plunge into the world, the crises of war and depression, the hard times of Congress, or the triumph of democracy—would have had such influence on the Presidency if strong, alert, capable men had not come to this high office and shaped the event to their ends. The President acts every day, consciously or unconsciously, in the image of the Presidents who have gone before him. There are a hundred things he could not do, certainly not without raising a deafening outcry, if his predecessors had not done them already. The Presidents, too, helped build the Presidency, and I would therefore think it proper to devote the rest of this chapter to a review of the major contributions of the major Presidents. Just who those Presidents were—I count eight—will shortly become clear. At the same time, I shall not neglect entirely those other Presidents—I count six—who also gave strength to the Presidency, if only by defending it valiantly in a period of congressional ascendancy. Let it be clear that I am judging these men as Presidents and weighing their contributions to the Presidency. Herbert Hoover is a much abler man than he was a President; James Madison's total impact on history should not be judged by his bumbling activities between 1809 and 1817.

George Washington enjoyed a long head start toward being a great President simply because he was the first man to fill the office. This, however, is far from the whole story of George Washington. The most meaningful judgment one can make of his eight years is that he fulfilled the hopes of the friends of

the Constitution and spiked the fears of its critics, and that in
turning both these tricks with vigor and dignity he proved himself the best of all possible first Presidents.

The hopes of its friends were that the creation of an energetic
executive, independent of the legislature yet integrated into the
constitutional structure, would introduce the one factor most
sorrowfully missing from the equation of government under the
Articles of Confederation: authority to execute the laws of the
United States with force and dispatch. The government of the
new republic was in desperate need of power—power to make
policy and power to carry it through. Article I of the Constitution as interpreted by Madison, Ellsworth, and the other
gentlemen of Congress proved to be the answer to the first
half of this need. Article II as interpreted by Washington
proved to be the answer to the second half.

He was certainly not a President in the image of the Roosevelts or Harry S Truman. When faced with a situation that
called for decisive action, he took a painfully long time to
make up his mind. For example, he sought the advice of both
Hamilton and Jefferson even when he knew that they would
only confuse and delay him with their antithetical counsels.
He recognized that his decisions would quite possibly set
precedents for men who would still be unborn when he was two
centuries in his grave, and this recognition gave an extra measure of gravity to his conduct of office. When Washington was
ready to act, however, he acted with confidence and courage.
The remarkable thing is how consistently he chose to act
strongly rather than to abstain huffily, to advance rather than to
retreat in his skirmishes with Congress over the uncharted territory left between them by the Constitution. In the field of
foreign relations alone he set a dozen precedents that no later
period of congressional ascendancy could ever erase—for example, the recognition of republican France, the proclamation
of neutrality, the reception and dismissal of the French Minister
Genêt, the negotiation of Jay's Treaty, the use of executive

agents, and the refusal to lay diplomatic correspondence before the House. Thanks to Hamilton he was an influential leader of legislation, thanks to his experience he was an excellent administrator, and thanks to himself he was a head of state who made every king alive seem like a silly goose.

The fears of the critics of the Constitution were that the executive outlined in Article II would prove too rich a blend of strength and independence, and that the government of the United States would go the way of most other popular governments in history: straight into tyranny. That it did not go this way was the result of many factors: the political maturity of the people, the widespread spirit of liberty, the vigilance of the opposition, the excellence of the Constitution, and, not least important, the single-minded devotion of Washington to the principles of republican government. It was no easy trick to be the first occupant of a mistrusted office under a dubious Constitution. Two or three missteps might have touched off a popular demand for an amendment designed to cut the Presidency down to size—the size, for example, of the governorship of North Carolina. But Washington, who had a nice feeling for the delicacy of his task, never did commit a serious misstep. His conduct was always eminently constitutional, and he repeatedly proved the point that Hamilton had labored in *The Federalist:* that executive power was wholly "consistent with the genius of republican government" and even essential to the steady conduct of such government. "For he was no monarchist from preference of his judgment," Jefferson wrote some years after Washington's death. "The soundness of that gave him correct views of the rights of man, and his severe justice devoted him to them." Washington's Presidency was nothing if not painfully constitutional.

It is not easy or indeed pleasant to imagine the fate of this great gamble in constitutional government if Washington had refused to accept his election to the Presidency. If he had stayed at Mount Vernon, as he wanted desperately to do, another

man—probably John Adams or John Rutledge or John Jay
or George Clinton—would have been the first President of the
United States, and that could easily have meant the undoing
of the Constitution. We can go right down the list of all those
who ever held high office in the United States and not discover a man so perfectly suited for the delicate task of finding
the right balance of authority and restraint in the executive
branch. Washington did the new republic a mighty service by
proving that power can ennoble as well as corrupt and by
fitting the Presidency carefully into the emerging pattern of
American constitutionalism.

He did a great deal more than this, of course, for he lent his
vast prestige to the new Constitution and thus rendered it acceptable to the American people. Men like Senator Maclay
of Pennsylvania poked fun at the pomp and circumstance of
"the Washington court," but they did not understand as clearly
as he that magic may be reduced but never eliminated entirely
from the processes by which free men are governed. John
Adams did, however, and he explained it all to Benjamin
Rush many years after Washington's death:

> Washington understood this Art very well, and we may say of
> him, if he was not the greatest President he was the best Actor of
> the Presidency we have ever had. His address to The States when he
> left the Army: His solemn Leave taken of Congress when he re-
> signed his Commission: his Farewell Address to the People when
> he resigned his Presidency. These were all in a strain of Shake-
> spearean and Garrickal excellence in Dramatic Exhibitions.

Even the Republicans could not deny that Washington's grand
tours through the states—for example, through New England
in 1789 and the South in 1791—strengthened the people's
trust in the Constitution and excited their interest in the Presidency. On the first of these trips he fought a polite but dogged
battle with Governor John Hancock of Massachusetts over
one of the most ancient questions of applied political science:
who should call first on whom? The battle was fierce, and con-

sumed most of his first two days in Boston; but a stubborn Washington, who insisted icily that Hancock make the first call, finally won a victory of profound symbolic importance for the authority of the new national government and, more to the point, for the prestige of its Chief of State. The humbling of vain John Hancock in 1789 and the enforcement of the laws in the Whiskey Rebellion of 1793 are two precedents that stood Dwight D. Eisenhower in good stead in the Little Rock crisis of 1957.

Washington's great gifts to the Presidency and to the republic were dignity, authority, and constitutionalism, and the greatest of these, surely, was constitutionalism. It has been said of him that he could have been a king but chose to be something more exalted: the first elected head of the first truly free government. In his inaugural address he made clear the solemnity of his mandate:

The preservation of the sacred fire of liberty and the destiny of the republican model of government are justly considered, perhaps, as *deeply,* as *finally,* staked on the experiment entrusted to the hands of the American people.

It was Washington's glory as President that he never broke faith with this solemn vision of the American Mission. Well could Jefferson write in gratitude that he had conducted the councils of the new nation "through the birth of a government, new in its form and principles, until it had settled down into a quiet and orderly train," chiefly by "scrupulously obeying the laws through the whole of his career, civil and military, of which the history of the world furnishes no other example." And lest we forget that Washington was also a human being, I end with this passage from Senator William Maclay's delightful *Journal,* which describes a scene in which members of Congress waited upon the President:

The President took his reply out of his coat pocket. He had his spectacles in his jacket pocket, having his hat in his left hand and his paper in his right. He had too many objects for his hands. He shifted his hat between his forearm and the left side of his breast. But taking his spectacles from the case embarrassed him. He got rid of this small distress by laying the spectacle case on the chimney piece. . . . Having adjusted his spectacles, which was not very easy considering the engagements of his hands, he read the reply with tolerable exactness and without much emotion.

The Presidency of Thomas Jefferson presents a slippery problem to the judgment of history. That he was a great man there can be no doubt, but that he was a great President there is considerable doubt. To his lasting credit are the injection of large doses of republicanism into an office that was coming to look just a shade too kingly, the breath-taking assertion of power (which took even his own breath away) in the purchase of Louisiana, and the flat declaration of presidential independence in his rejection of Marshall's subpoena in the Burr trial.

His most important contributions, of course, were his conversion of the Presidency to a political office and his leadership of Congress, and it is exactly at these two points that we run into trouble with Jefferson's reputation as a strong President. His successes in molding and leading a party and then in using it to influence Congress leave us no choice but to judge him an effective leader. As Professor Binkley has written: "No president has ever exceeded Jefferson's feat of putting the extraordinarily drastic Embargo Act through Congress in one day, December 22, 1807." Yet the very methods through which he brought strength to his own Presidency were calculated to weaken the office grievously once he had turned it over to lesser men, to men who were not and could never be the kind of party chieftain and ideological arbiter that he had proved to be. John Marshall made a remarkable prediction about Jefferson's methods and influence in a letter written to Hamilton while the election of 1800 hung in the balance.

Mr. Jefferson appears to me to be a man, who will embody himself with the House of Representatives. By weakening the office of President he will increase his personal power. He will diminish his responsibility, sap the fundamental principles of the government, and become the leader of that party which is about to constitute the majority of the legislature.

We need not subscribe to the full bitterness of this statement to recognize that Marshall was a shrewd observer and an even shrewder prophet. Jefferson did embody himself in the House of Representatives, thereby increasing his power ten times over. The power, however, was personal and not presidential; it flowed from him and not from his office. The leaders of Congress were his trusty lieutenants, the party caucus was his instrument to use pretty much as he pleased—so long as he did not wander from Republican principles. (And who, after all, had first defined these principles?) Timothy Pickering, another bitter foe, wrote that Jefferson tried to "screen himself from all responsibility by calling on Congress for advice and direction. . . . Yet with affected modesty and deference he secretly dictates every measure which is seriously proposed." This, I think, was the essence of Jefferson's Presidency, and this is why our final judgment of his influence must always be ambiguous. If we concentrate our gaze on his eight years, then shift it swiftly down to the middle of either the nineteenth or twentieth centuries, we can say that it was a strong and great Presidency. If we let our gaze halt at any year between 1809 and 1829, we must conclude that Jefferson damaged the office severely by compromising its independence. Since we are dealing with one of the greatest Americans, perhaps we should take the long-range view and hail him as a President whom it would be unthinkable to exclude from the inner circle of greatness.

Andrew Jackson plucked Jefferson's chestnuts from the fire by putting on a show of authority that still commands our fascinated respect. Coming as it did after twenty years of con-

gressional supremacy and government by committee, his resolute Presidency was, in Professor Corwin's words, "no mere
revival of the office—it was a remaking of it."

Jackson regained control over his own house by putting
each department head in his place and cutting the Cabinet
down to size, distributed the spoils of victory in such a way as
to build a team almost fanatical in its loyalty to him, revived
the veto and purified it of the niceties that had grown up
around it, acted simultaneously as an imposing Chief of State
and a hard-driving Chief of Party, and made clear to South
Carolina that his power to execute the laws would be fully
equal to the task of preserving the Union. He never missed
an opportunity, by word or deed, to reassert the independence
of an office that had become much more dependent on Congress
than the framers could possibly have intended. His veto of
the Bank Bill, his proclamation against the Nullifiers, and his
"solemn protest" against the Senate's resolution of censure are
assertions of presidential independence and authority that make
exciting reading even today.

Small wonder that Jackson's enemies, who remembered the
deferential years of Madison and Monroe, should judge his
performance to be subversive of the republic. "I look upon
Jackson," Chancellor Kent wrote to Justice Story, "as a de-
testable, ignorant, reckless, vain and malignant tyrant." "The
President carries on the government," Webster cried in the
Senate; "all the rest are subcontractors." And Clay spoke for
all the Whigs:

We are in the midst of a revolution, hitherto bloodless, but tend-
ing rapidly toward a total change of the pure republican character
of the Government, and to the concentration of all power in the
hands of one man.

Clay was right: he and his friends were caught up in a
revolution, but he was incapable of noting its origin or character. The revolution was abroad among the people, shifting the

basis of our government from aristocracy to democracy without destroying its essential republicanism. Jackson was more a beneficiary than a leader of this revolution. He rode into office on a wave of protest that he never directed and whose character he barely understood himself. Yet he was exactly the kind of President—truculent, charismatic, and more than a little bit demagogic—the revolution needed to bring it full circle. The Presidency would surely have become a democratic office had Jackson never held it, but he was the one who presided imperiously over the radical reversal in the roles of President and Congress as instruments of popular power and targets of popular feeling. And it is here, of course, that Clay and his friends went astray, for they could not rid their minds of the assumption, the very marrow of Whiggery, that executive power is inherently antipopular. Jackson's insistence that he, too, represented the people, at least as well as the House and better than the Senate, seemed to them the babbling of a fool or the bluster of a tyrant. No small part of his success may be traced directly to the fact that he was the first President of the United States elected by the people, and to the added fact that he knew it:

The President is the direct representative of the American people; he possesses original executive powers, and absorbs in himself all executive functions and responsibilities; and it is his especial duty to protect the liberties and rights of the people and the integrity of the Constitution against the Senate, or the House of Representatives, or both together.

Jackson's mistakes were many, his legacies not all bright; more than one such President a century would be hard to take. Yet he was a giant in his influence on our system of government, and the influence, on balance, seems to have been wholesome. Well might he write in defense of his conduct: "I shall anticipate with pleasure the place to be assigned me in the history of my country." I would place him fifth in the list of

Presidents in terms of performance and impact on history, and second only to Washington in terms of influence on the Presidency.

The reaction to Jackson's Presidency was pronounced and prolonged; it was still in progress when Lincoln entered the White House. Yet the reaction, even though aided immeasurably by the depressing influence of the slavery issue on the Presidency, could never undo the work the old hero had done. The Jacksonian theory of the office prevailed, and Lincoln, untutored as an administrator but richly experienced in the arts of purposeful politics, drew upon it resolutely in his hour of need.

Lincoln came to the Presidency with very few advance thoughts about the authority it embodied. He had never put himself publicly in either the Whig or Jacksonian camps (I am speaking, of course, of theories of the Presidency and not of party politics), and many of his critics were certain that his administration would prove too feeble for the awesome task at hand. Lincoln soon proved them grossly wrong in their judgments of his character and in their fears for the Presidency. He had sworn "an oath registered in Heaven" to defend the Constitution, and in his inaugural address he promised his fellow citizens to save the Union without which the Constitution would be nothing but a scrap of paper. In sharp contrast to the vacillating Buchanan, who had denied his own authority to coerce a state to remain in the Union, he turned to military force as the final answer to secession. He was never greatly concerned about the forms his actions might take. It was enough for him to act—as commander in chief, as supervisor of the faithful execution of the laws, as sole legatee of the shapeless grant of power we can read for ourselves in the opening words of Article II of the Constitution.

It became necessary for me to choose whether, using only the existing means, agencies, and processes which Congress had provided, I should let the Government fall at once into ruin or whether, availing myself of the broader powers conferred by the Constitution in cases of insurrection, I would make an effort to save it, with all its blessings, for the present age and for posterity.

In his effort to save the government and the Union, Lincoln pushed the powers of the Presidency to a new plateau high above any conception of executive authority hitherto imagined in this country. During the course of his famed eleven-week "dictatorship" he called out the militia, clamped a blockade on the South, enlarged the regular army and navy beyond their statutory limits, advanced public moneys to persons unauthorized to receive them, pledged the credit of the United States for a sizable loan, closed the mails to "treasonable correspondence," authorized the arrest of potential traitors, and, in defiance of all precedent, suspended the writ of habeas corpus along the line of communication between Washington and New York. In a message to Congress of July 4, 1861, the date he had selected for convening the houses in special session, he described most of the actions he had taken, rationalized the more doubtful of these by referring to "the war power of the government" (his phrase and evidently his idea), and invited congressional ratification. Lincoln himself apparently entertained no doubts about the legality of his calling out the militia and establishing the blockade, nor did he find it necessary to explain why he had chosen to postpone the emergency meeting of Congress to July 4. For his actions of a more legislative and therefore constitutionally more doubtful character, he advanced a different justification:

These measures, whether strictly legal or not, were ventured upon under what appeared to be a popular demand and a public necessity, trusting then, as now, that Congress would readily ratify them. It is believed that nothing has been done beyond the constitutional competency of Congress.

He asserted that the power to suspend the writ of habeas corpus could belong to him as well as to Congress, but he tactfully left the subsequent disposal of this matter to the legislators. The whole tenor of his message implied that the government of the United States, like all governments, possessed a final power of self-preservation, a power to be wielded primarily by the President of the United States. And this power extended even to the breaking of fundamental laws of the nation —if such a step were unavoidable.

Are all the laws but *one* to go unexecuted, and the Government itself go to pieces lest that one be violated? Even in such a case, would not the official oath be broken if the Government should be overthrown when it was believed that disregarding the single law would tend to preserve it?

In other words, in an instance of urgent necessity, an official of a constitutional state may act more faithfully to his oath of office if he breaks one law in order that the rest may endure. This was a powerful and unique plea for the doctrine of paramount necessity. It established no definite rule for the use of emergency power in this country, but it does stand as a fateful example of how a true democrat in power is likely to act if there is no other way for him to preserve the constitutional system he has sworn to defend.

Once Congress had reassembled in answer to the President's call, it did what it could to cut him down from an Andrew Jackson to, at the very most, a James K. Polk. Lincoln, however, although always respectful of Congress, went forward resolutely on his power-directed course, taking one extraordinary action after another on the basis of the "war power." In all this activity he had the help, if never the full respect, of what many historians consider the most effective Cabinet ever assembled. Having brought the office of the Presidency to new heights of prestige, he kept it there to the end. His interpretation of his powers was stabilized at an exalted level, and it appears that he considered himself constitutionally empowered to do just about anything that the military situation demanded. "As

Commander-in-Chief in time of war," he told some visitors from Chicago, "I suppose I have a right to take any measure which may best subdue the enemy." We need not look beyond the Emancipation Proclamation and the declaration of martial law in Indiana to learn what he meant by "any measure."

There is a good deal more than this to tell about Lincoln's Presidency: the shabby performance as administrator, the creditable performance as diplomat, and the astounding performance as politician and leader of public opinion, not to mention the refusal of Congress to acquiesce in either the sweep or exclusiveness of his assertion of the war power. Enough has been said, I trust, to make this point clear: through the boldness of his initiative, through an unprecedented plea of necessity, and through a unique interpretation of executive power, Lincoln raised the Presidency to a position of constitutional and moral ascendancy that left no doubt where the burden of crisis government in this country would thereafter rest. When Eisenhower's lieutenants spoke in 1955 of the "inherent powers of the Presidency" as our chief crutch in the wake of atomic disaster, they were reaching out to the mighty figure of Abraham Lincoln. And as they did, I trust that they pondered the truth that Lincoln was a democrat as well as a "dictator," that he went to the well of power in behalf of humanity and rededicated the Presidency to the cause of liberty.

Lincoln, like Jefferson, left the Presidency temporarily enfeebled. The reaction was savage, and poor Andrew Johnson, a far braver President than Madison, was left to reap the wild wind that Lincoln had sowed unconcernedly when he permitted the War Department and Congress's Committee on the Conduct of the War to strike up an intimate relationship. There were times in the next thirty years—especially under Grant and Harrison—when the Presidency seemed to have declined permanently in relation to Congress. But our rise to industrial might and our grand entrance upon the stage of world politics turned the course of the Presidency once more upward, and Colonel Roosevelt galloped into the White House as our first modern President.

It is hard to come to grips with Theodore Roosevelt, just as it is with any boy of six. There are times when he has the look of a genuinely great man, and times when he has the look, as Mark Hanna said, of a "damned cowboy." He was, beyond a doubt, a strong President, and no small part of his strength lay in the fact that he always was a kind of cowboy. Roosevelt gave the Presidency the absorbing drama of a Western movie, and he never left the audience in doubt that he was the "good guy" and the other fellows—Democrats, Senators, monopolists, Socialists, diplomats, "nature fakers," muckrakers—the "bad guys." With the help of an attractive and active family, he put the Presidency on the front page of every newspaper in America, and there it has remained ever since with huge consequences for its status and authority. Teddy lived the dreams of every red-blooded American boy of his time: he punched cattle, led a cavalry charge, became President, argued with the Pope, and, when it was all over, went off to shoot lions and elephants in Africa.

Roosevelt himself described a significant milestone in the evolution of the Presidency:

When the dinner was announced, the mayor led me in—or to speak more accurately, tucked me under one arm and lifted me partially off the ground, so that I felt as if I looked like one of those limp dolls with dangling legs carried around by small children. . . . As soon as we got in the banquet hall and sat at the head of the table the mayor hammered lustily with the handle of his knife and announced, "Waiter, bring on the feed!" Then, in a spirit of pure kindliness he added, "Waiter, pull up the curtains and let the people see the President eat."

T. R. contributed a great deal more to the office than a cheerful willingness to let the people see him eat. He was a

brilliant molder and interpreter of public opinion, who confessed happily that the White House was a "bully pulpit." He
scored several genuine triumphs as leader of Congress and
thus gave substance to his theory that "a good executive under
present conditions of American life must take a very active
interest in getting the right kind of legislation." He conducted
our diplomacy with unusual vigor, although his stick was not
so big nor his voice so soft as he liked to boast. Still, the
Panama Canal and the Treaty of Portsmouth were rather substantial achievements for those days, and who can say that
he did not act grandly when he started the fleet off around
the world and left it up to Congress to buy enough coal to
bring it back?

Unfortunately for the Colonel, but probably fortunately for
the country, there was no real crisis in all his seven years that
would permit him to prove conclusively that he was, as he
insisted, a "Jackson-Lincoln" as opposed to a "Buchanan"
President. The nearest thing to such a crisis was the anthracite
coal strike of 1902, which he managed to settle before being
pushed into executing his plans, first revealed fully in his *Autobiography* (1913), to have the army seize and operate the
mines. This event, his land withdrawals, and several other
minor exertions of authority led him to state the famed "Stewardship Theory," which is still the most adroit literary justification of the strenuous Presidency:

The most important factor in getting the right spirit in my Administration, next to the insistence upon courage, honesty, and a
genuine democracy of desire to serve the plain people, was my insistence upon the theory that the executive power was limited only
by specific restrictions and prohibitions appearing in the Constitution or imposed by the Congress under its Constitutional powers.
My view was that every executive officer, and above all every executive officer in high position, was a steward of the people bound actively and affirmatively to do all he could for the people, and not
to content himself with the negative merit of keeping his talents un-
damaged in a napkin. I declined to adopt the view that what was

imperatively necessary for the Nation could not be done by the President unless he could find some specific authorization to do it. My belief was that it was not only his right but his duty to do anything that the needs of the Nation demanded unless such action was forbidden by the Constitution or the laws.

William Howard Taft, speaking also as a former President, derided the notion that the "executive . . . is to play the part of a universal providence and set all things right," and the strict theory of the Constitution is certainly on his side. Whatever the theory, the facts have always been with Roosevelt in moments of extreme national emergency.

Woodrow Wilson was the best prepared President, intellectually and morally, ever to come to the White House. I have quoted several times from the chapter on the Presidency in his *Constitutional Government* (1908), and I think it fair to sum up the first four years of his Presidency by saying that he went as far as any man could go in converting those elegant, somewhat exaggerated words into reality. He was an able administrator, a shrewd leader of his party, a sensitive "spokesman for the real purpose and sentiment of the country," an impressive head of state, and, thanks to his academic theory of the President as a prime minister in relation to Congress, a genuinely effective leader of legislation. A devoted traditionalist, he was nevertheless unafraid of innovation. I would give a considerable sum to have seen Theodore Roosevelt's face when he picked up his evening paper April 8, 1913, and read that Wilson, honoring tradition and working innovation in the same act, had brought off successfully the first personal appearance of a President before Congress since the days of John Adams. Many historians think that the American Presidency, and with it our whole system of government, reached its highest peak of democracy, efficiency, and morality in the first four years of Woodrow Wilson.

In his second term, to be sure, he came to grief in more ways than one, although his record as a wartime President is every bit as admirable as the records of both Lincoln and the second Roosevelt. The most striking feature of this record is the way in which he acquired his vast authority over the American economy. Most of his emergency powers were delegated to him by laws of Congress. Confronted by the problem of raising and equipping an army to fight overseas rather than by a sudden threat to the Republic, Wilson chose to demand express legislative authority for almost every unusual step. Lincoln had shown what the office was equal to in crises calling for solitary executive action. Now Wilson showed what it could do by working with the legislature. The source of Lincoln's power was the Constitution, and he operated in spite of Congress. The source of Wilson's power, except in the area of command and a few related matters, was a batch of statutes, and he co-operated with Congress.

In the end, sad to relate, he lost his hold on Congress, the country, and even himself. His haughty appeal for a Democratic Congress in 1918 was a serious blunder; his whole course of action in behalf of the League of Nations foundered on his own obstinacy. Yet his journey to Europe in December 1918 was a herald of things to come, a rehearsal of the grand role the President would fill in the aftermath of World War II. Wilson carried the Presidency to new moral and political heights, and the strength of his days can be measured in the weakness of those that followed.

My seventh and eighth candidates for presidential greatness are Franklin D. Roosevelt and Harry S Truman, but I am going to put off the pleasure of dealing with them until Chapter 5. In the meantime, what of those men who, if not worthy to be ranked with Washington and Lincoln at the top, with Wilson and Jackson at the next level down, or with T. R. and Jefferson just below them, were none the less Presidents who turned in

creditable or at least unusual performances? Let me call off
these six names in order, several of which, I am aware, are
not on every historian's roll of notable Presidents:

Grover Cleveland, whose persistent display of integrity and
independence (symbolized by the 414 vetoes of his first term)
brought him very close to greatness in the Presidency.

James K. Polk, the one bright spot in the dull void between
Jackson and Lincoln, of whom the historian George Bancroft
could write a half-century later:

> His administration, viewed from the standpoint of results, was
> perhaps the greatest in our history, certainly one of the greatest.
> He succeeded because he insisted on being its center and in over-
> ruling and guiding all his secretaries to act so as to produce unity
> and harmony.

Dwight D. Eisenhower, of whom more hereafter.

Rutherford B. Hayes, a vastly underrated President, whose
successful struggle to name his own Cabinet, dogged devotion
to civil-service reform, seven stout vetoes of legislative riders,
and dispatch of troops in the railroad strike of 1877 were all
long steps forward from the Waste Land of Grant.

John Adams, who had the misfortune to follow Washington,
but whose grand theory of the President as a "patriot king"
was applied with rare stoutness of heart in the move for peace
with France in 1799.

Andrew Johnson, a man of few talents but much courage,
whose protests against the ravages of the Radicals in Congress
were a high rather than a low point in the progress of the
Presidency.

This is not, be it noted, a list based exclusively on intelligence
or even competence. There have been at least seven men—John
Quincy Adams, Van Buren, Tyler, Arthur, McKinley, Taft,
and Hoover—who were far better Presidents than Johnson
from a technical point of view. None of them, however, was
so important to the history of the Presidency as the despised
man from Tennessee.

To round out the presidential list, an irresponsible sort of exercise when done so abruptly, let me place Madison, Monroe, Fillmore, Benjamin Harrison, and Coolidge in the next slot down; W. H. Harrison, Taylor, and Garfield in a category that reads "insufficient data for ranking"; and Pierce, Buchanan, Grant, and Harding at the bottom. Buchanan was a man of rich experience, Grant a genuinely great general, and Harding a gentle man, but each in his own way was a near disaster for the Presidency. As for Pierce, let us nod to Nathaniel Hawthorne's reaction to the news of his election—"Frank, I pity you—indeed I do, from the bottom of my heart"—and then let the gentle poet from New Hampshire have the last word:

> She had one President (pronounce him Purse,
> And make the most of it for better or worse.
> He's your one chance to score against the state).

It would be a near disaster for me to end this chapter on so low a note, and I therefore call attention once again to the six—I am still avoiding Roosevelt and Truman—who contributed most handsomely to the Presidency as it stands today. These men were more than eminent characters and strong Presidents. They were and are luminous symbols in our history. We, too, the enlightened Americans, feel the need of myth and mystery in national life—of magic parchments like the Declaration of Independence, of shrines like Plymouth and the Alamo, of slogans like "Fifty-Four Forty or Fight!," of hymns like "America," of heroics like Pickett's charge, of heroes like John Paul Jones. No one can have lived through Davy Crockett and deny the force of the American myth; no one can stand at Gettysburg and deny its meaning. And who fashioned the myth? Who are the most satisfying of our folk heroes? With whom is associated a wonderful web of slogans and shrines and heroics? The answer, plainly, is the six Presidents I have pointed to most proudly. Each is an authentic folk hero, each a symbol of some virtue or dream especially dear to Americans.

Together they make up almost half of the company of American giants, for who except Christopher Columbus, Benjamin Franklin, Daniel Boone, Robert E. Lee, and Thomas A. Edison in real life, Deerslayer and Ragged Dick in fiction, and Paul Bunyan and the Lonesome Cowboy in myth can challenge them for immortality? Washington the spotless patriot, Jefferson the democrat, Jackson the man of the frontier, Lincoln the emancipator and preserver of the Union, Theodore Roosevelt the All-American Boy, Wilson the peacemaker—these men are symbols of huge interest and value to the American people.

Lincoln is the supreme myth, the richest symbol in the American experience. He is, as someone has remarked neither irreverently nor sacrilegiously, the martyred Christ of democracy's passion play. And who, then, can measure the strength that is given to the President because he holds Lincoln's office, lives in Lincoln's house, and walks in Lincoln's way? The final greatness of the Presidency lies in the truth that it is not just an office of incredible power but a breeding ground of indestructible myth.

CHAPTER 4

THE MODERN PRESIDENCY

★

The Presidency to which Dwight D. Eisenhower came on January 20, 1953, was a visibly different office from the Presidency that Herbert Hoover had surrendered on March 4, 1933. In the course of these twenty years it had been laden with all kinds of new duties by a people unwilling to submit patiently to the disorders of an industrial civilization or to withdraw sullenly from the turmoils of a mad world. It had taken on all kinds of new help, both personal and institutional, to save it from collapse under the mounting burdens of war and peace. And it had moved even higher, if that were possible, in the esteem of the American people, most of whom counted it a mighty weapon in the struggle for liberty at home and security abroad. The Presidency had been modernized, conspicuously if not completely.

My purpose in this chapter is to examine the new dimensions added to the office by Presidents Roosevelt and Truman. Lest it be thought that this is a partisan review, I hasten to point out that Dwight D. Eisenhower moved ahead, steadily if not quite so theatrically, with the work of modernization begun by the Democrats who preceded him. If he was not as strong a President as Roosevelt or Truman, he occupied an equally strong Presidency. He was, in any case, the first beneficiary of two decades of unusual executive activity. The Presidency, like any vital institution, is always in transition, but this has been an especially propitious period for experiment and growth, and we must now take account of the significant changes in the authority and structure of the Presidency during the past quarter-century.

The first change is in the working relations of President and Congress. I have already made some comments on the President's part in the lawmaking process, the sum of which was that he has now become a sort of prime minister or "third House of Congress." He is no longer restricted in his legislative activities to the points of input and output on the congressional transmission belt, that is, to recommending measures in general terms at one end and then, after sitting quietly for a decent or indecent interval, to stamping the mangled results "OK" or "Reject." Rather, he is now expected to make detailed recommendations in the form of messages and proposed bills, to watch them closely in their tortuous progress on the floor and in committee in each house, and to use every honorable means within his power to persuade the gentlemen of Congress to give him what he wanted in the first place. One of the chief concerns of the modern President is to push politely but relentlessly for enactment of his own or his party's legislative program. If he lacks a program of the most detailed nature, he is considered a sluggard; if he cannot persuade Congress to enact at least a few of the details, he is considered a failure. In judging the performance of the modern President, we rely heavily on the "box score" of his hits and outs and errors in the game of persuasion he is always playing with Congress.

It was not always thus. The role of the President as active participant in every stage of the legislative process is almost wholly the creation of three twentieth-century incumbents: Theodore Roosevelt, Woodrow Wilson, and Franklin D. Roosevelt. Each of these men came to the Presidency from a successful tenure as governor of a progressive state, and the extent of his success had been measured in terms of his leadership of the legislature. Each came at a time when the state of the Union demanded that new laws be placed on the books; none was strangled by wearing the "old school tie" of either house of Congress. The meeting of their forceful personalities with the crises of the age produced a revolution in the relations of the President to Congress and in the standards with which the American people rate his total performance.

This revolution, it should be noted, was still unfinished in the last days of Franklin Roosevelt, for Congress, the party of the second part, remained unconvinced of the President's right to interest himself so strenuously in its independent activities. The members of Congress could hardly be blamed for believing that the times were out of joint, that Roosevelt had exerted a kind of leadership that would not outlast his incumbency or the end of the emergency, and that there would be a retreat to Hoover (if never again to Harding) under the next President. But the next President, despite the perky pride with which he himself wore the old school tie, refused to play dead. Mr. Truman kept the pressure turned on throughout his eight years, even when his hopes of accomplishing anything constructive must have been entirely empty, and by the end of his second term even the Republicans in Congress professed an eagerness to have his thoughts on such red-hot issues as labor, taxes, inflation, and education. What is still more revealing of the change of climate, they considered it a wholly natural thing to be invited to the White House to hear from the President directly what he had in mind. Things had moved a long way from the days when Senator George F. Hoar had testified:

The most eminent senators would have received as a personal affront a private message from the White House expressing a desire that they should adopt any course in the discharge of their legislative duties that they did not approve. If they visited the White House, it was to give, not to receive, advice. Any little company or coterie who had undertaken to arrange public policies with the president and to report to their associates what the president

thought would have rapidly come to grief. . . . Each of these stars
kept his own orbit and shone in his sphere, within which he toler-
ated no intrusion from the president or from anybody else.

This development has been carried the rest of the way
(beyond the point of no return, I would judge) by President
Eisenhower. That point was reached and passed in a press
conference on January 13, 1954. During the first session of the
Eighty-third Congress Mr. Eisenhower had submitted few proposals to Congress and had exerted little continuous pressure
in their behalf. Observers were wondering aloud whether he
was aware of the change that had come over the Presidency or
of Congress's need for prudent guidance. But as the second
session approached, the President began to gather steam, and
within a few days of the opening of Congress in 1954 he was
sending over detailed messages outlining his wishes on farm
policy, social security, foreign policy, labor, and finance. And
now at the press conference this exchange took place:

Q. Mr. President, could you say what percentage of your recommended proposals you would expect to be passed at this session?
A. The President said, Look, he wanted to make this clear. He
was not making recommendations to pass the time away or to look
good. . . . He was going to work for their enactment. Make no
mistake about that. That was exactly what he was in the White
House for and what he intended to do.

Fifty years ago this remark, especially as and to whom
delivered, would have brought most members of Congress
spluttering to their feet and set the President's few remaining
friends to shaking their disbelieving heads. Even as late as
twenty years ago it would have been considered a gratuitous
insult by the die-hards and a show of bad taste by the moderates
in Congress. In 1954 it passed unchallenged and even unnoticed except by those whose reaction was "Well, it's about
time."

From that moment of awakening on, President Eisenhower
did his best, within the obvious limits of his tastes and politics,

to make good his pledge. He used arts of persuasion that were once controversial but are now considered altogether regular, and that is the essence of this first ingredient of the modern Presidency: the irregular has become the regular, the unexpected the expected, in the area of executive-legislative relations. The President has no weapons that were not available to Harding or, for that matter, to McKinley. The appeal to the people is more easily brought off in the age of electronics; on the other hand, the dangled patronage has lost much of its influence, thanks to the success of civil-service reform. The White House conference, the appeal to party loyalty, the threat of a veto—these weapons, too, are no keener than they were a half-century ago. The President's own machinery for drafting legislative proposals and for maintaining good relations with Congressmen is vastly enlarged and improved; Congress itself calls ever more insistently upon the President for reports and recommendations. Yet the two houses, despite the pleas of Senators Kefauver and Monroney, have made no important institutional changes in recognition of his increased responsibility for providing them with leadership. And the Constitution, needless to say, reads exactly as it did in 1789 in those passages that govern the relations of executive and legislature. The remarkable change in these relations has been neither institutional nor constitutional but, rather, meteorological, a change in the climate of politics and custom. The country now expects the President to have a program and to work hard for its enactment. He is more likely to be criticized in today's press for timidity and inertia than for resolution and activity. What the country expects, Congress also expects. Henceforth it will react with mild irritation rather than wild indignation to presidential attempts to goad it into action.

The President's right, even duty, to propose detailed legislation to Congress touching every problem of American society, and then to speed its passage down the legislative transmission belt, is now an accepted usage of our constitutional system. So far has this revolution gone that the thought occurs: we need new standards with which to judge the "strength" of a President. We need new techniques of executive-legislative co-operation, too, and I shall return to this persistent problem in my final chapter.

The emergence of the President as active leader of Congress has been accompanied by a second change: the opening of new channels of communication through which he can mold and measure public opinion. Who can say how much power and drama have flowed toward the President and away from the houses of Congress because he can chat with the nation easily over radio and television and they cannot? Programs like "Capitol Cloakroom" and "Face the Nation" have never been in the same class as a fifteen-minute broadcast and telecast from the White House. Nor can the "spectaculars" staged by Senators McCarthy and Kefauver for the housewives of America be said to have raised our interest in or respect for Congress as an institution. Let us acknowledge that the President has been the chief gainer from the miracles of electronics, and let us pray that Congress never succumbs to the urge to compete with him by putting its regular proceedings on the air. What Stephen Potter would call the "natural one-upness" of the President is a hard fact of life with which Congress must learn to live, just as he has had to learn to live with the hard fact that, thanks to his uniquely exposed position, privacy is a right to which he has practically no claim at all so long as he is President.

The most influential channel of public opinion to and from the President that has been opened up in recent years is the press conference. The President's regular meeting with the press is now a completely accepted institution, and it therefore comes as a surprise to recall that its unbroken existence in present form dates only from the first year of Franklin Roosevelt. The Presidents have been in close touch with the press from the beginning, but not until the administration of Woodrow Wilson was the regularly scheduled conference, open to newspaper-men as a matter of right and not of personal privilege, established on a fixed footing. When America entered World War I, Wilson abandoned the conference to avoid embarrassment to his administration, and the three Republican Presidents who followed him were unable or unwilling to match his able performance between 1913 and 1917. Harding made such a mess of several hot grounders hit in his direction that he changed the rules and required questions to be written out and submitted in advance; Coolidge continued this practice and generally kept the press at arm's length; and Hoover, who also insisted on written questions, held fewer and fewer conferences until finally, as the darkness of impending defeat gathered over his head, he abandoned them altogether.

Franklin Roosevelt, who would have been lost without the press, revived the conference and brought it to new heights of influence and public interest. Any journalist certified by the correspondents' own association was admitted to the conference, and questions were asked and answered "from horseback." Roosevelt maintained the wise rule first laid down by Wilson that he was not to be quoted directly without specific permission, but otherwise the conference became a wonderful game of give-and-take—with the President, a genius at sarcasm, doing most of the giving. Mr. Truman, despite some occasional lapses in his first term, carried forward the precedents set by President Roosevelt. He gets the credit and blame, which have been dished out in roughly equal amounts, for shifting the conference from the President's office to the "treaty room" in the old State building, an auditorium with seats for several hundred persons, and thus for establishing it on a much more formal basis.

Mr. Eisenhower, too, did his manful best to meet the press once a week when he happened to be in Washington, and he went on record repeatedly and "emphatically" in praise of the press conference as "a very fine latter-day American institution." On January 19, 1955, a day to remember, he presided over the first press conference ever to be filmed by television and newsreel camera; millions of Americans sat at home that evening and watched their President go through his paces. He went through them, let it be recorded, with an air of dignity, sincerity, and competence, and even the most hardened observers fell all over themselves praising this "marvelous example of democracy at work." There were some complaints, largely political in inspiration, over the decision of the White House to review the footage before releasing it to the telecasters and movie companies, but this was a perfectly proper extension of the well-understood prohibition against quoting the President directly without permission. The experiment having succeeded, the televised press conference has become a regular weekly feature. As might be expected, it is losing its appeal to many people, and the networks now present only the juiciest excerpts from the conferences. The moral is an old one, familiar to all the able Presidents: when you find a bright new tool, don't dull it with too much use. So long as the televised press conference is not overdone, it bids well to remain an important, not to say informative and entertaining, technique of American democracy. More than that, the taped films of the press conference will provide a kind of documentation for future historians that should make the writing of presidential biographies a happier if less creative experience.

Televised or not, the presidential press conference is now a fixed custom in our system of government. It is conceivable that a President with no taste for this kind of half-circus, half-inquisition could cut the growth of custom short, but the next President would be certain—in fact, he would pledge himself bravely while still a candidate—to start it up again. In part this is true because the people have come to expect it and dislike being disappointed in their expectations, in part because it is, on balance, so useful a platform for the man who stands on it. No President can afford to be without it, certainly no sociable, outgoing President of the kind we are likely to elect from now on.

There has been considerable talk in the press and in textbooks about the kinship of the President's press conference and the question-and-answer period in the British House of Commons. The press conference does serve us in some ways as a method for interrogating the government of the day, but several sharp differences are to be noted. The President controls the questions (if only by retreating into the shell of "no comment") as the Prime Minister does not. The questioners are in no sense his peers, even though they like to think of themselves as representatives of the American people, a fourth estate with a grave responsibility. To the best of my knowledge, no gentleman of the press has ever risen to scold the President for an unsatisfactory answer and to push him for a better one. Indeed, the first gentleman to do it will probably be the last. And the questions must generally be of a kind that, far from nailing the President to the wall on a specific point, permit him to take off on a free flight in any direction he chooses. The fact is that the President could not ask for a tool of leadership more perfectly designed to his ends, for a pulpit more artfully constructed from which to preach sermons to us and to the world, for a listening device more finely tuned to hear the opinions and fears and complaints of the American people. As Mr. Eisenhower himself testified:

> As a matter of fact, I think this is a wonderful institution. I have seen all kinds of statements that Presidents have considered it a bore and a chore, but it does a lot of things for me personally.
>
> Moreover, I rather like to get the questions because frequently I think they represent the kind of thinking that is going on.

The press conference is not a restraining but an enabling device, as our last three Presidents have demonstrated repeatedly; and that, I would guess, is why it will never again be abandoned outright nor even reduced to the cold, gray event it was under Herbert Hoover. An unbriefed, irritable, shoot-from-the-hip sort of President may do himself serious damage in the give-and-take of the press conference, but so may he in reaching out along any of his channels to the people. I conclude with a comment from Louis Brownlow, certainly the wisest head among those who watched the press conference grow to its present stature.

> It would be almost impossible, in my opinion, for any President now to change this pattern or to interfere in any material way with this institution, set up without authority of the law, required by no Constitutional mandate, embodying no rights enforceable in a court of law, but nevertheless an institution of prime importance in the political life of the American people.

It would be almost impossible and altogether imbecile. No President in his right mind would surrender gladly the power he draws from this unique institution, which puts him, in a light that he selects for himself, on the front page of every newspaper in the land and, as often as not, in the world.

The role of the President that has undergone perhaps the most rapid growth in the past quarter-century is that of Protector of the Peace. Thanks to the eagerness with which Roosevelt and Truman responded to calls for help from the people, we now look upon the President as a one-man riot squad ready to rush anywhere in the country to restore peace and order. While state and local authorities usually deal with fire, drought, flood, pestilence, or violence, disasters that spread over several states or touch upon federal interests or are simply too hot for a locality to handle can be sure of attention and action from the White House.

This is especially true of labor disputes that disturb the peace of the United States. The sudden expansion of government interest in labor-management relations under the New and Fair Deals has worked visible influence upon the office and powers of the President. He has little to do with the normal processes of government participation in such relations, but in labor disputes that are national emergencies he has now become, even when he refuses to act, a dominant third party. The Taft-Hartley Act of 1947 speaks wistfully of "sound and stable industrial peace." The prime responsibility of the President to preserve and protect the peace is now universally assumed. His powers in this area fall under three headings:

1) The power literally to "keep the peace of the United States" by instituting military action in strikes attended by violence and public disorder.

In most cases the policing of disorderly strikes is the duty of state and local authorities. The President will intervene in industrial warfare in two situations only: when he has been requested to act by the proper authorities, who thereby acknowledge their own inability to preserve order; or when federal laws and rights are being openly flouted and the national interest in a restoration of order is clear. The President may refuse to intervene when asked; he may also, as Cleveland proved in the Pullman strike of 1894, intervene unbidden and even unwanted. In recent years this power has rested on the shelf. We seem to have less violence in our labor disputes, and local officials seem better qualified to handle them in the severe yet neutral fashion the public interest demands. Yet the power remains in the President's possession, stretching all the way from the mere threat of force to outright martial law, and I suspect we will live to see it used again.

2) The power to remove obstructions to the flow of industrial production in time of war, or just before or after war.

The President must display unusual interest in wartime labor disputes. As Commander in Chief he is concerned before all others that production and delivery of weapons and supplies continue without interruption. Under conditions of total war he becomes the dominant figure in industrial relations. His power is exerted along two related lines. First, he makes it his immediate business to see that peaceful relations are maintained between labor and management. To this end he institutes special agencies to aid them in resolving their differences. Second, he enforces the rulings and orders of these agencies by applying "indirect sanctions"—for example, by focusing publicity on a recalcitrant union or employer, by threatening to reclassify workers in the draft, or by cutting off a plant's supply of scarce raw materials—and he prevents critical work stoppages by the final sanction of presidential seizure. Presidents Roosevelt and Truman both wielded this vast authority with vigor and considerable success. Between them they ordered more than sixty seizures in the years 1941-1946. The most notable of these was the "Battle of Montgomery Ward" in 1944, in which the enemy was finally defeated by the simple maneuver of having its commander, Mr. Sewell Avery, carried from his office by two bewildered enlisted men of the United States Army whose mothers had certainly not raised them to be this kind of soldier. This power received a salutary if hardly crippling check in the Steel Seizure case of June 1952.

3) The power to intervene in disputes that constitute economic national emergencies.

Quite apart from the open threat to our national well-being presented by large-scale violence or a halt in war production is the continuing problem of strikes in the basic industries and transportation system. The American people know from experience how injurious a widespread stoppage of work in the telephone system or steel mills can be, and long before Judge T. Alan Goldsborough began his famous lecture course for John L. Lewis (which the student failed miserably), we were aware that a strike of long duration in the railroads or coal mines might cause "society itself" to "disintegrate." It is therefore not surprising that the wave of strikes in 1946 and 1947 should have persuaded the authors of the Taft-Hartley Act to insert broad provisions authorizing the President to act in disputes "imperilling the national health and safety." He already had some power in this area: his prestige as President, which allowed him to intervene informally in the manner of Theodore

Roosevelt in the anthracite coal strike of 1902, and a grant of limited authority, which had been enfeebled by overwork, in the Railway Labor Act of 1926. Now Congress was prepared to go further and empower the President to seek an injunction in the federal courts that would delay a crippling strike for eighty days. Although Mr. Truman, in vetoing the Taft-Hartley Act, expressed particular disapproval of its emergency provisions, he made use of them on seven occasions in 1948 and on three in his second term, for the most part with circumspection and at least modest success. Mr. Eisenhower, who presided in less turbulent times and was more reluctant than Mr. Truman to brandish this kind of power, nevertheless used this power himself seven times in his first seven years. The dock and steel strikes of 1959 revealed all too painfully the limited reach of Title II of the Taft-Hartley Act, and a stronger set of emergency provisions would seem to be on the agenda of the future.

Whatever techniques we may create to prevent the crippling of the nation by widespread strikes, it should be plain to see that from this time forward the most important single factor in labor disputes of this character will be the heart, mind, and politics of the President of the United States. His position in such disputes is, to be sure, extremely delicate. As the final guardian of the public interest he must stand clear of partisanship and wield his weapons with discretion. In particular, he must avoid using them in such a manner that one of the parties to a dispute will go out of its way to invite intervention. He must recognize that his powers in this field are emergency powers only, that the regular processes of collective bargaining and of government mediation and conciliation are not to be disturbed. He must draw upon his matchless capacity to mobilize and express public opinion with shrewd frugality. He must resist the temptation to interpose his prestige in disputes that are being threshed out, however slowly, by regular statutory and administrative machinery, or he may pull down the whole structure of government intervention about his ears. "Equality for both and vigilance for the public welfare" must be the President's high resolve.

Limited though his powers are, we are better off with them than without them. It is reassuring to know that in an economic system that invites and rewards the struggle for self-interest there is a boundary beyond which the contestants will push at some peril, and that we have a high sheriff to patrol it.

It might be well to close this discussion by recalling my comments in Chapter 1 on a role that is still very much in its infancy, that of Manager of Prosperity. The President is now expected to act before and not just after an economic crisis develops, and he is steadily amassing powers with which to do it. It is still too early to measure the full dimensions of this role, but not too early to recognize that they are genuinely impressive. When we come face to face with the next grave threat of depression, the President, whoever he may be, will be a "spectacle unto the world."

If there is any one point I have hammered on in this book, it is that the Presidency is an essentially democratic office. The people have done much to make it what it is today; the man who holds it reaches out to them for support and repays them with guidance and protection. There is no more impressive evidence of this truth than a fourth development in the modern Presidency: the elevation of this office to a commanding position in the ongoing struggle for civil liberties and civil rights. We have become increasingly conscious of our shortcomings and wrongdoings in these related fields in recent years. Even as we sin against one another in the area of freedom of expression, even as we drag our feet in the march toward justice for our minorities, we feel the gaze of the whole world upon our necks and are uncomfortable. And as we have become more conscious, the President, who has a sizable part of this world for a constituency, seems to have grown in stature as a friend of liberty.

Here as everywhere he operates under severe limitations. A

wing of his party may have a stake in discrimination; public opinion may be riding a wave of intolerance; Congress may refuse him even the most watered-down authority to protect minorities against intimidation. Yet there are many things he can do if he is resolute and perceptive, if he steers a middle course between serene abstention and demagogic meddling in events and areas critical for American liberty. Here are some of his powers, all but one or two of them the creations of our last three Presidents:

He can recommend legislation to Congress—in the grand style of Harry S Truman's message of February 2, 1948, which made ten controversial proposals ranging from the establishment of a fair employment practices commission to home rule for the District of Columbia, or in the more modest manner of Dwight D. Eisenhower's request for legislation to permit federal prosecution of private persons, as well as state and local officials, for intimidating voters in presidential or congressional elections. And he can summon all his authority as Chief Legislator to push his proposals past the recalcitrants in Congress.

He can veto illiberal legislation, as Presidents Cleveland, Taft, and Wilson all vetoed bills that set up a literacy test for immigrants. (For the record, such a bill was finally passed into law over Wilson's veto in 1917.) So long as the Supreme Court stays "on the hot spot" in the continuing struggles over freedom of expression and desegregation, it will need all the protection it can get against an irate Congress; and I can think of no protection quite so comforting as the President's power to veto genuinely ill-willed and ill-considered attempts to limit the Court's jurisdiction.

He can make broad use of his authority as Commander in Chief. Like Roosevelt he can establish an F.E.P.C. by executive order as a means of speeding up production in time of war, like Truman he can establish a President's Committee on Equality of Treatment and Opportunity in the Armed Forces, and like Eisenhower he can push ahead with the work begun by his two predecessors aimed at putting an end to segregated units in all branches of the service. Few Americans seem to realize how far we have gone, thanks largely to the President's authority as Commander in Chief, toward eliminating segregation as a way of life on military bases throughout the United States.

He can issue similar orders and push for similar practices in his capacity as Chief Executive. Examples of this use of presidential authority are Truman's regulations of 1948 prohibiting discrimination in personnel practices "throughout the federal establishment" and Eisenhower's Committee on Government Contracts, which was set up to secure compliance with fair employment practices by companies with government contracts.

He can use his power of appointment to strengthen the Supreme Court as a bulwark of freedom, or to bring acknowledged friends of civil liberty and representatives of minority groups into the top levels of the administration; he can use his power of removal, if he doesn't mind the storm he will surely raise, to dismiss officials who insist on ignoring or even sabotaging his antidiscrimination orders.

He can prod his chief assistant for law enforcement, the Attorney General, to push steadily for relief and assistance to minority groups in the federal courts. Like Eisenhower, he can order him to file a brief as "friend of the court" in private suits against segregation in education; like Truman, he can order him to institute actions under Title 18, chapter 13, sections 241-242 of the *United States Code*. These provisions, which date from 1870, make it a federal offense to engage in various activities that "injure, oppress, threaten, or intimidate any citizen in the free exercise or enjoyment of any right or privilege secured to him by the Constitution or laws of the United States." They are not easy to use, but an occasional conviction has been obtained under them. The President can also prod the Federal Bureau of Investigation to be on the alert for offenses in this category. Another string was added to the President's bow in the Civil Rights Act of 1957, which authorizes the Department of Justice to seek injunctions in the federal courts against state or local officials who discriminate against Negro voters.

He can establish commissions of distinguished citizens to survey and report on the state of freedom in this country, or co-operate wholeheartedly with one established by Congress. The leading example of such a commission was Mr. Truman's own Committee on Civil Rights, whose memorable report of 1947 pointed out the way for many of our advances in recent years.

He can use a number of his ancient and honorable powers to advance the cause of justice and humanity: for example, the pardoning power to correct a sentence made heavier because of the criminal's race, the treaty-making power to pledge his own faith (if not the Senate's) to wiping genocide from the face of the earth, and his power as chieftain of his party to bring leaders of minorities into its high councils.

He can take special pains to eliminate the disgraceful vestiges of discrimination in the District of Columbia. Although Truman was doubtless correct in denying that he had the power to end racial segregation outright in the District by executive order, there is much the President can do with a quiet order here and a good example there. For example, Attorney General Brownell's vigorous intervention in a case in 1953 resulted in the Supreme Court's upholding legislation prohibiting discrimination in Washington restaurants, after which a commissioner of the District government appointed by the President gave restaurant owners forty-eight hours to comply with the law.

I doubt that any one in the world who has heard the words "Little Rock" needs to be reminded of the existence of still another of the President's powers in this controversial area, but let me at least set down the fateful truth that his broad authority to keep the peace of the United States with armed might extends forcefully to situations like that faced by Mr. Eisenhower in September 1957. Whether the President mixed force and prudence to the proper degree in that great constitutional and social crisis is a question we will be arguing for years to come, but the argument over his power to use the United States Army to enforce the desegregation orders of a federal court came to an end the very day it began. If he cannot use bayonets to pave the road to a more just and decent America, he can certainly use them to hold the road open.

Finally, and most important, he can draw upon his authority as spokesman for the nation in such a way as to inspire those who are working for a more democratic America and to rebuff those who would drag us backward into the swamps of primitivism and oppression—or, better still, to educate all of us in the ways of brotherhood. The moral force of this great office is never so apparent as when he lashes out at the vigilantes who spoil the vines of the First Amendment, its prestige never so imposing as when he sets out quietly to persuade the leaders of Southern opinion that a new day has dawned. One thing is certain about our attempt to solve the crisis of desegregation in the schools: a key factor in the equation of success will be a succession of Presidents determined to use all the resources of this great office.

I am aware that I have given only one side of the picture in this review. The President also has it in his power to dampen the struggle for civil rights by his indifference and to invade the field of civil liberties in force. Franklin Roosevelt's order authorizing the evacuation of all persons of Japanese ancestry from the Pacific Coast in early 1942 and the combined Truman-Eisenhower record in the area of loyalty and security are proof that even the most conscientious President may blunder or be pressured into dubious acts. I am aware, too, as I noted at the outset of this discussion, that he must use his powers shrewdly and with an eye out for the limits of possibility. He cannot, for example, comment critically on every patent violation of liberty and justice throughout the land, especially when the violence is done by judges and juries; he cannot declare rhetorical war on an entire section or interest or school of opinion in this country, not if he expects to get on with his other tasks. Yet he is now in a position to be one of the most potent forces behind our progress in civil rights and our defense of civil liberties. From this time forward the President will have no choice but to serve as the conscience and strong right arm of American democracy.

The most notable development in the Presidency in recent years is a change in structure rather than a growth in power, although the latter is certainly the first cause of the change. As the burdens of the President have mounted steadily, he has taken on auxiliary machinery to help him bear them. Inseparable from the modern Presidency, indeed essential to its effective operation, is a whole train of officers and offices that serve him as eyes, ears, arms, mouth, and brain. The encompassing title of this machinery is the Executive Office of the President, and it numbers roughly a thousand persons whose sole purpose in public life is to aid the President in the execution of his own duties. The Executive Office exists for him, and he could not exist without it.

The Executive Office was established in 1939 through the associated, if not entirely harmonious, endeavors of Franklin D. Roosevelt and the Seventy-sixth Congress. The immediate impulse for organizing it was Roosevelt's own candid recognition that an otherwise professional performance during his first term in the Presidency had been hampered by the lack of a staff to help him stay on top of his ever-growing duties. He was not the first person to make this discovery. Long before the New Deal began to pile new burdens on the Presidency, students of the national government, the most vocal of them the Presidents themselves, had been calling the attention of Congress and the nation to the hapless plight of the "final object of the public wishes."

Mr. Roosevelt's solution was thoroughly in character. Never one to let an important problem lie around unstudied by a special commission, he set the wheels turning in early 1936 with the appointment of the President's Committee on Administrative Management. Under the adroit guidance of Louis Brownlow (Chairman), Charles E. Merriam, and Luther Gulick, a corps of noted scholars probed every part of the federal administration. Particular attention was devoted to the heart of the system, the Presidency itself. The Committee reported to Mr. Roosevelt in January 1937, and in the shortest scholarly sentence on record told him what he had known ever since his first day in the White House: "The President needs help." In forwarding the Committee's reports to Congress, Mr. Roosevelt summed up the parlous state of the Presidency in these words:

> The Committee has not spared me; they say, what has been common knowledge for twenty years, that the President cannot adequately handle his responsibilities; that he is overworked; that it is humanly impossible, under the system which we have, for him fully to carry out his constitutional duty as Chief Executive, because he is overwhelmed with minor details and needless contacts arising directly from the bad organization and equipment of the Government. I can testify to this. With my predecessors who have said the same thing over and over again, I plead guilty.

The controversial recommendations of the President's Committee ranged the whole field of executive management. Central to its purposes, however, was the immediate problem of the presidential burden, which it proposed to lighten by creating a team of six executive assistants and an administrative staff of experts who would handle the President's managerial functions in budgeting, planning, and personnel management. These proposals ran afoul of the epic battle over the "Court-packing" scheme and the efforts of numerous members of the Seventy-fifth Congress to pin the label of "dictator" on the President. Not until two years later did Congress grudgingly bestow on Mr. Roosevelt a limited power of executive reorganization. The sweeping proposal of the Committee on Administrative Management that "the whole Executive Branch of the Government should be overhauled and the present 100 agencies reorganized under a few large departments in which every executive authority would find its place" was frustrated by those sections of the Reorganization Act that forbade the President to lay profane hands upon a full nineteen agencies, including the Civil Service Commission. With the latter exception, however, he was able to deal pretty much as he saw fit with his own problems.

This he did in Executive Order 8248, dated September 8, 1939, and described correctly by Mr. Gulick as a "nearly unnoticed but none the less epoch-making event in the history of American institutions." The effect of the order was to create the Executive Office, designate six components within it, and authorize the President to appoint the personal assistants for whom the Committee on Administrative Management had called. The logic of this order can be most clearly grasped by quoting a passage from Professor Leonard D. White, in which he succeeded admirably in expressing the "basic objectives" underlying the "proper organization of any large-scale executive office in government." These, it would seem, were the purposes for which the Executive Office was created:

1. To insure that the chief executive is adequately and currently informed.
2. To assist him in foreseeing problems and planning future programs.
3. To ensure that matters for his decision reach his desk promptly, in condition to be settled intelligently and without delay; and to protect him against hasty and ill-considered judgments.
4. To exclude every matter that can be settled elsewhere in the system.
5. To protect his time.
6. To secure means of ensuring compliance by subordinates with established policy and executive direction.

There was a more profound purpose, too, for this was a President, not just a department head, who was to be rescued from overwork—but more of that presently.

Through all the years of crisis since 1939 the Executive Office has functioned at a high level of proficiency and morale. By no means a faultless instrument of public administration, it has nevertheless served President and nation with distinction and has given an entirely new cast to the question of executive management in the national government, as well as to the Presidency itself. For some years now, it has been popular, even among his friends, to write off Mr. Roosevelt as a "second-rate administrator." In the light of Executive Order 8248, an accomplishment in public administration superior to that of any other President, this familiar judgment seems a trifle musty.

Rather than wander wearily through the many changes in the Executive Office under each of the last three Presidents, let me describe the major components that exist today. This is the President's "general staff":

The White House Office, which serves him directly and intimately, numbers about two dozen top-flight personal aides, two dozen aides to these aides, and roughly 350 clerks, stenographers, messengers, and secretaries who are needed to handle the documents and correspondence and appeals for help that descend upon the White House in torrents. Although each President can be expected to divide his personal load in whatever way seems to suit him best, some positions in the White House have already taken on an air of permanence, notably those of the Assistant to the President, Press Secretary, Staff Secretary, Special Counsel, Secretary to the Cabinet, secretary for appointments, liaison man with Congress, and chief speech writer. Associated with these men are a whole crew of Assistants, some labeled "Special" and others "Administrative," who cover a wide range of presidential responsibilities—economic problems, science, minority relations, government personnel, liaison with the states, foreign affairs, patronage, and any other problem, such as disarmament or farm surpluses or air safety, that calls loudly for the attention the President wishes he could give it himself. The President may often designate officials with jobs

of their own to serve him personally, as Mr. Eisenhower designated Chairman Lewis L. Strauss of the Atomic Energy Commission and Chairman Philip Young of the Civil Service Commission, and he may quietly borrow officials with special skills
from any part of the administration for just about any length
of time. Finally, he has one aide for each of the armed services.

The National Security Council was established in 1947 "to
advise the President with respect to the integration of domestic,
foreign, and military policies relating to the national security."
The current membership of the Council includes the President,
the Vice-President, the Secretaries of State and Defense, and
the Director of the Office of Civil and Defense Mobilization.
The core of this interdepartmental committee is a permanent
staff headed by an executive secretary. Suspended from the
National Security Council, although not an integral part of the
Executive Office, is the Central Intelligence Agency. The Council, which usually invites other officials like the Joint Chiefs of
Staff and the Secretary of the Treasury to sit with it, is actually
a specialized cabinet to advise the President in the whole field
of foreign and military affairs. In 1957 the Operations Coordinating Board was placed within its structure as a kind of expe-
diting agency for the Council's policies—that is to say, the
President's policies—in this critical area. The total personnel
of N.S.C. and O.C.B. is about sixty.

The Council of Economic Advisers, a team of three econo-
mists aided by thirty staff and clerical aides, joined the presidential camp under the terms of the Employment Act of 1946,
which directed it to assist and advise the President in the preparation of an annual economic report on the state of the Union;
"gather timely and authoritative information concerning economic developments and economic trends" and submit studies
based on this information to the President; "develop and recommend to the President national economic policies" designed
to "promote maximum employment, production, and purchasing power"; and "make and furnish such studies, reports

thereon, and recommendations with respect to matters of federal economic policy and legislation as the President may request." The breadth of this mandate affords the Council full opportunity to serve the President as a formalized "brain trust" in all matters that touch upon the economic state of the Union. Without it he could hardly be expected to be our Manager of Prosperity.

The Office of Civil and Defense Mobilization is the result of a merger in 1958 of the Federal Civil Defense Administration and the Office of Defense Mobilization. It is charged "with the responsibility of directing, planning, and coordinating the mobilization and non-military defense functions of the nation," and as such it very obviously helps the President to discharge several of his major duties as Commander in Chief. Despite this fact, and despite the technical location of O.C.D.M. in the Executive Office, it hardly seems sensible to class this 1,600-man agency as an integral part of the presidential machinery. Perhaps we can compromise with the cold logic of the *Government Organization Manual* by agreeing that the top three or four officials in O.C.D.M. are servants primarily of the President, but why not then go on to include the Civil Service Commission in the Executive Office?

Last but far from least in importance is what Richard Neustadt salutes as "the oldest, toughest organism in the presidential orbit," the Bureau of the Budget, which serves the President as an "administrative general staff." The Bureau is one of the two original components of the Executive Office, having been transferred in 1939 from the Treasury Department, and is sure to be functioning in much the same way when most other components have passed into history. Without it the President could not begin to do his job as Chief Executive or Chief Legislator. In addition to taking the burden of the budget almost completely off his back, it engages in a broad range of activities designed to achieve "more efficient and economical conduct of the Government service," assists in preparing the President's executive orders and proclamations, and acts as his clearinghouse for proposed legislation and enrolled bills. To cite only one instance of the importance of the Bureau in the pattern of presidential responsibility, its Office of Legislative Reference shoulders every part of the burden of the veto power except the final decision to say "yes" or "no." The Bureau counts 420 employees, and no one in his right mind has ever suggested that it could get along with any fewer.

In and around the four key agencies, especially the White House Office, swirls a whole galaxy of persons—Secretaries, Under Secretaries, study groups, presidential commissions—who give some, most, or all of their time and best thoughts directly to the President. One of the features of the White House Office is its unusual plasticity. The President is, as he should be, entirely free to parcel out his immediate burden among his assistants, to establish or disestablish interdepartmental committees or secretariats, to call on persons anywhere in the executive branch to perform special tasks, and, like all who preceded him, to take counsel with private citizens. If Mr. Eisenhower chose to use Sherman Adams as a chief of staff or to put special trust in his Vice-President or to revive the Cabinet as a co-ordinating agency, if he chose to take his television cues from Robert Montgomery or to ask Willie Mays about juvenile delinquency or to hold a White House Conference on Education, that was entirely his business. He ran his team in one way, each of the men he succeeded ran his in another, the men who succeed him will run theirs in ways yet unimagined.

At the same time, we must understand that the hard core of this machinery, especially the Bureau of the Budget, is now a permanent fixture in the national government. Many persons in it can look forward confidently to a long life of service for a long line of Presidents. Although those immediately around him are his personal choices, most of the men and women who serve them have tenure in their jobs. Although his personal touch is necessary to give the whole Executive Office its sense of direction, it could run for some time entirely on its own. The fact is that the Presidency has become "institutionalized," and if it is a fact to cause us concern—as I shall point out in my final chapter—it is also one that is here to stay. The President is still one man, but he is also, like any man with a thousand helpers, an institution. Most of the wheels go around steadily whether he watches them or not, as we learned so well during Eisenhower's illnesses. Many orders and suggestions and leaks emerge from "the White House" about which the President knows nothing. One must be especially careful today in reading newspapers to distinguish among what he says for himself, what his aides say for him, and what his aides say for themselves. If the distinction is not easy to make (and Washington is full of people who wish they could make it unerringly), that should remind us of the unity into which President, White House, and Executive Office finally merge.

I have already pointed out, with the help of Professor White, the momentous administrative significance of this development in the modern Presidency. Its constitutional significance, it seems to me, is even more momentous. It converts the Presidency into an instrument of twentieth-century government; it gives the incumbent a sporting chance to stand the strain and fulfill his constitutional mandate as a one-man branch of our three-part government; it deflates even the most forceful arguments, which are still raised occasionally, for a plural executive; it assures us that the Presidency will survive the advent of the positive state. Executive Order 8248 may yet be judged to have saved the Presidency from paralysis and the Constitution from radical amendment. At $8,000,000 (the annual appropriation for the four key agencies), the Executive Office of the President is almost the best bargain we get in the federal budget.

I trust it will be thought proper in a book of nearly three hundred pages on the Presidency to devote seven to the Vice-Presidency, although even this ratio of forty to one is no measure of the vast gap between them in power and prestige. The Presidency is the greatest constitutional office the world has known, a splendid chieftainship sought eagerly by just about every first-rate political figure in the nation, not to mention a horde of second-raters. The Vice-Presidency is a hollow shell of an office, an uncomfortable heir apparency sought by practically no one we should like to see as President. It has perked up noticeably in the years since 1948, but fundamentally it remains a disappointment in the American constitutional system.

The Vice-Presidency is one of our oldest problems. Some of the more astute members of the Convention of 1787 doubted that there was any need for a Vice-President, and Hamilton was forced to refute numerous criticisms of the office in *The Federalist*. There were apparently three reasons for creating the Vice-Presidency: to establish a constitutional heir for the President, to facilitate the selection of "continental characters" under the original electoral system (of which more hereafter), and to provide a presiding officer for the Senate not immediately devoted to the interests of any particular state. The framers also recognized the advantage of a moderator for this body with a deciding vote in the event of a tie. In general, they expected the office to be filled by the nation's number-two political figure, the man who had polled the second highest number of votes in the presidential election.

However cogent the reasons of the framers, and however high their expectations, the Vice-Presidency was a failure, and was recognized as such, almost from the outset. John Adams, the first to hold it, lamented that "my country has in its wisdom contrived for me the most insignificant office that ever the invention of man contrived or his imagination conceived." Thomas Jefferson, his successor, said something more meaningful than he realized when he described the "second office of government" as "honorable and easy," "the first" as "but a splendid misery." And several early statesmen referred to the Vice-President as "His Superfluous Excellency." The rise of the Federalist and Republican parties, the near disaster of the Jefferson-Burr election of 1800-1801, the consequent adoption of the Twelfth Amendment, and the establishment of the "Virginia Succession" (under which the Secretaryship of State became the "bullpen" of the Presidency) all contributed to the decline of the office. The first two Vice-Presidents may have been Adams and Jefferson, but the fifth and sixth were Elbridge Gerry and Daniel D. Tompkins; the seventh, John C. Calhoun, resigned to enter the Senate. And somewhere along the line there was a Vice-President named Throttlebottom—and a good one, too. Public men then, like public men today, apparently preferred misery with power to ease without it.

For the record, let me set down the powers of the Vice-President as they exist today. He draws two clear duties from the Constitution—to preside over the Senate and exercise a tie-breaking vote—and, as I count them, six from the laws: 1) to appoint five midshipmen to the Naval Academy; 2) to appoint four Senators to its Board of Visitors; 3) to recommend two candidates to the President for appointment to the Military Academy; 4) to sign enrolled bills and joint resolutions before they are sent to the President; 5) to be a member of the Smithsonian Institution and its Board of Regents; and 6), the one grant of any consequence, to sit as a statutory member of the National Security Council. Occasionally he is designated to appoint several members to a special commission. He also draws his pay: $35,000 a year plus $10,000 for expenses.

These, plainly, are dimensions of impotence, and impotence is the mark of a second-class office. Suspended in a constitutional limbo between executive and legislature, and in a political limbo between obscurity and glory, the Vice-Presidency has lost most of its significance as an instrument of government. Woodrow Wilson summed up the problem of the Vice-Presidency neatly when he wrote in exasperation: "The chief embarrassment in discussing his office is, that in explaining how little there is to be said about it one has evidently said all there is to say." I would sum it up myself by taking note of the fact that there have been fifteen occasions in the history of the republic, a total of more than thirty-six years, when we had no Vice-President and never knew the difference.

The fact that the Vice-President has little to do is not in itself a danger spot in our constitutional system. In considering what he is, however, we must remember what he may be: President of the United States. John Adams, discerning as ever, remarked in the very first days: "I am possessed of two separate powers, the one *in esse* and the other *in posse*. I am Vice President. In this I am nothing, but I may be everything." The reality of vice-presidential impotence has generally loomed far more prominently in the nation's political consciousness than the possibility of a succession to the Presidency; the *esse* of the office has too often blotted out the *posse*. The real danger of the powerless Vice-Presidency is therefore this: that it is rarely occupied by a man for whom a majority of the people would have voted as a candidate for the Presidency. The potential importance of the Vice-President as heir apparent to the President, pointed up by seven successions in 170-odd years, has not been sufficient to attract leading political figures to seek it as a matter of course. Most men of ability and ambition would still rather be a leading Senator or Secretary of State than Vice-President, even after all the good and exciting times enjoyed by Richard Nixon. While the office is not quite the political county farm that some of its critics have portrayed, few men of presidential stature have occupied it since Adams and Jefferson, and they usually had to be dragooned into accepting their party's nomination. We have had distinguished Vice-Presidents, but who since Van Buren has been second only to the President as a political figure, even of his own party? Mr. Dooley's creator echoed our opinion of most Vice-Presidents when, alarmed at the prospect of Charles W. Fairbanks as President, he pleaded with Theodore Roosevelt not to go down in a submarine, and ended on the note, "Well, you really shouldn't do it—unless you take the

Vice-President with you." Roosevelt had already added his bit to the lore of the Vice-Presidency by stating, "I would a great deal rather be anybody, say a professor of history, than Vice-President." The man who served under Wilson and longed for a good five-cent cigar, Thomas R. Marshall, went Roosevelt one better by describing himself as "a man in a cataleptic fit," who "is conscious of all that goes on but has no part in it," and then topped that by noting the propriety of his membership in the Smithsonian Institution, where he had "opportunity to compare his fossilized life with the fossils of all ages."

Like the Vice-Presidency itself, the danger of a second-rater as Vice-President is everything *in posse* and little *in esse*. Many a party hack has served his four years presiding over the Senate and passed into oblivion. On the other hand, several party hacks have succeeded to the Presidency with rather painful results. Only one of the original reasons for this office is valid today—the necessity of a constitutional heir for the President—and it is exactly here that the Vice-Presidency has failed most conspicuously. The only ways to erase the danger spot are to eliminate the office or to make it a highly attractive place of honor and power. If the history of the Vice-Presidency means anything, the former course is inconceivable and the latter unlikely.

To the credit of both Presidents Truman and Eisenhower, the Vice-Presidency has experienced something of a renaissance in recent years. Alben Barkley was probably the most distinguished man nominated for the office since John C. Calhoun, and he proved extremely useful to Mr. Truman as a link to Congress. Richard Nixon, however—and I do not mean this disrespectfully—was hauled up to the second rung from far down the ladder for reasons that had nothing to do with his qualifications for the Presidency. Mr. Nixon, thanks to the President's mind and the President's heart, was easily the busiest and most useful Vice-President within memory. Yet he was still inferior to Secretary of State Dulles or Speaker Rayburn or a dozen Senators in influence and prestige, and the Vice-Presidency is still very far from being in fact the "second office of the land." One of the few lessons we should have learned clearly from the anxious weeks following Mr. Eisenhower's heart attack was that the Vice-President, even when favored openly by the President, is unsuited to serve in emergencies as an "acting President"—unless, of course, the President's disability is clearly established. Sherman Adams, George Humphrey, John Foster Dulles, James Hagerty—all these men were more important and influential than Mr. Nixon in the conduct of the Presidency during those troubled weeks. The weaknesses of the Vice-Presidency were never more dramatically exposed than at the moment when a bewildered nation turned to it for strength and guidance. Neither in law, custom, nor political circumstance was it prepared to assume the burden that many well-meaning citizens tried to thrust upon it, and tried again after each of the next two illnesses.

Mr. Nixon, to be sure, made as much of a success of this frustrating office as any man could be expected to make. He sat by invitation in the Cabinet and presided over it in the President's absence, sat by right in the National Security Council and took part in decisions of great moment, made important statements of policy that might have been impolitic for the President to make, relieved the President of any number of trips to the airport to greet distinguished visitors, served as chairman of both the Committee on Government Contracts and the Cabinet Committee on Price Stability for Economic Growth, visited several dozen countries (not all of them exactly friendly) as special envoy of the President, served as chief campaigner in 1958, and acted as both trouble-shooter and pacifier in executive-legislative relations. Most important of all, on two occasions he stood for a few days—and stood with reserve and dignity—on the brink of the Presidency; and he was surely the first Vice-President in history to state publicly that he had stopped off at the White House on the way home from work "to see if there are any loose ends I can take care of." Yet even on the brink he was a thousand times bigger *in posse* than he was *in esse*.

Within the inherent limitations of the office, which have never been more apparent, the Vice-Presidency is generally what the President chooses to make it. President Eisenhower chose to make it something much more than it usually is, and Vice-President Nixon, unlike many of his predecessors, was delighted to go along. It must be recognized, however, that no permanent solution to the problem has been worked out, and I doubt very much that it can be. From time to time it is suggested that the Vice-President be converted into the President's top executive assistant—I once made such a proposal myself, which I hereby recant—but the road to this revolution would, I feel sure, prove rocky and dangerous. If an officer not subject to the power of removal should be authorized to execute the laws in the President's name, it would violate one of the soundest principles of our system of government. The Vice-Presidency would be a dagger aimed constantly at the precious unity of the executive power, and that would be a condition we could not tolerate. The leading men in the State Department seem to have had some such thought in their minds when they successfully thwarted Nixon's appointment to the chairmanship of the Operations Coordinating Board, and we can hardly blame them for their concern lest a barrier of unpredictable obduracy be placed between them and the President.

The most we can now hope for, I think, is that Congress will increase the Vice-President's emoluments, establish an official residency, and give him an even larger staff of his own; that a series of Presidents will follow Mr. Eisenhower's lead and fix some of these recent departures in constitutional custom; and that the parties will seek consciously to nominate men who are qualified by experience, character, and prestige to succeed to the Presidency. It would be reassuring to know that from this time forward neither party would nominate a man to the second office who had not been considered seriously for the first. There is evidence that the people think a great deal more of it than do the politicians, and the latter should face up to the blunt fact that every time they select a candidate for the Vice-Presidency they are selecting one for the Presidency. It might be of interest to hear Eisenhower's testimony on this subject, delivered at a press conference in 1955:

Q. (by Mr. Reston of the New York *Times*) Mr. President . . . what I was trying to get at was what is your philosophy about the role of the nominee in the selection of the Vice-President? Is it your view that the convention is sovereign, it can pick anybody it likes, or should it, in your judgment, follow the recommendation of the Presidential nominee?

A. Well, I would say this, Mr. Reston: It seems obvious to me that unless the man were acceptable to the Presidential nominee, the Presidential nominee should immediately step aside. . . . If there isn't some kind of general closeness of feeling between these two, it is an impossible situation, at least the way I believe it should be run.

I personally believe the Vice-President of the United States should never be a nonentity. I believe he should be used. I believe he should have a very useful job.

Plainly, then, it is up to each future President—first as nominee, then as incumbent—to make whatever can be made of this disappointing office.

To return in conclusion to the Presidency, I have tried to indicate some of the major developments that lead many observers to believe that the office is in a period of pronounced transition. There were other developments to which I might have called attention—for example, the blending of the President's roles as Chief Diplomat and Commander in Chief (to the advantage of each) and the addition of new statutory emergency powers to his already large stock—but the five discussed in detail are evidence enough of this transition. His strong posture of legislative leadership, his new channels of opinion, his increased concern for domestic peace and prosperity, his emergence as a leader in the struggle for personal liberty and racial equality, and above all his conversion into an institution—these are the fresh ingredients of the Presidency. If I may mix the metaphor, the foundations of the office remain as firm as ever, but there are some interesting changes going on in the superstructure.

CHAPTER **5**

THE MODERN PRESIDENTS

It has not been easy to suppress the giddy urge to liven up this portrait of the Presidency with comments about the men who have been in and around it during the past quarter-century, and now I am about to give way all at once. I do not give way merely to gratify a weakness for gossip about "the man in the White House." We cannot come to close grips with the modern Presidency as an institution or as a force in history unless we talk in highly personal terms about the men who have held it. Woodrow Wilson once remarked that "governments are what politicians make them, and it is easier to write of the President than of the Presidency." With his blessing I turn to the delicate but delightful task of judging the performances of Franklin D. Roosevelt, who created the modern Presidency, of Harry S Truman, who defended it, and of Dwight D. Eisenhower, who inherited it and made it acceptable to the American people. Let us place ourselves, if we can, on the throne of posterity, and from that serene point of vantage let us look back objectively, as we expect our great-grandchildren to look back, at the achievements of each of these men.

"Ranking the Presidents" has always been a Favorite Indoor Sport of history-minded Americans, and I see no reason why we should not play it with Roosevelt, Truman, and Eisenhower as happily as we play it with Jackson, Cleveland, and Harding.

I am especially concerned to anticipate the opinions of our descendants about the "greatness" of our last three Presidents. Will Roosevelt be ranked with Lincoln or Wilson? Will Truman be compared with Johnson or Theodore Roosevelt? Will the old soldier named Eisenhower be placed just below the old soldier named Washington or just above the old soldier named Grant? The answers to these questions lie in still other questions which historians like to ask about Presidents long dead. I have made a rough content analysis of more than one hundred serious presidential biographies, and I have found the same standards applied again and again. These are the questions, the accepted standards of presidential achievement, against which I propose to measure Roosevelt, Truman, and Eisenhower and thus attempt to predict the judgments of our posterity on the Presidents of our time:

In what sort of times did he live? A man cannot possibly be judged a great President unless he holds office in great times. Washington's eminence arose from the founding of the republic, Jackson's from the upsurge of democracy, Lincoln's from the Civil War, and Wilson's from World War I. We have no right even to consider a man for membership in this exclusive club unless he, too, presides over the nation in challenging years. This standard may work unfairly on Presidents who live under sunny skies, but that is the way that history is written.

If the times were great, how bravely and imaginatively did he bear the burden of extraordinary responsibility? A successful President must do a great deal more than stand quiet watch over the lottery of history: he must be a forceful leader—of Congress, the administration, and the American people; he must make the hard decisions that have to be made, and make most of them correctly; he must work hard at being President and see that these decisions are carried out.

What was his philosophy of presidential power? To be a great President a man must think like a great President; he must follow Theodore Roosevelt and choose to be a "Jackson-Lincoln," a man of strength and independence, rather than a "Buchanan," a deferential Whig. Indeed, if he is not widely and persistently accused in his own time of "subverting the Constitution," he may as well forget about being judged a truly eminent man by future generations.

What sort of technician was he? How efficiently did he organize his energies, direct his lieutenants, and thus exercise his powers? Lincoln could be an indifferent administrator and yet a great President, but the rise of the modern state has made it impossible for an inefficient President to discharge even a fraction of his duties with much hope of success.

What men did he call on for help? Did he, like Washington, have his Jefferson and Hamilton? Did he, like Lincoln, have his Seward and Chase? Did he have his great lieutenants, and his efficient sergeants, too? If the modern Presidency, as I have insisted, is irrevocably institutionalized, the modern President must do even better than Washington and Lincoln on this score, for he can no longer expect to accomplish much of anything unless he surrounds himself with able technicians as well as wise statesmen and shrewd politicians.

What manner of man was he beneath the trappings of office? We remember a President as much for his quirks and quips as for his deeds and decisions. If he is not the sort of man around whose person legends will arise in profusion, he will surely not meet the final test of presidential greatness: to be enshrined as a folk hero in the American consciousness.

What was his influence on the Presidency? We are not likely to rate a President highly if he weakens the office through cowardice or neglect. A place at the top of the ladder is reserved only for those Presidents who have added to the office by setting precedents for other Presidents to follow.

Finally, what was his influence on history? In particular, did he inspire or represent, and find words to explain, some earth-shaking readjustment in the pattern of American society? More than one President has been granted a high place in history because he sensed the direction of American democracy in his times and bent or hastened its onward course—or even, as in the case of Theodore Roosevelt, confined himself largely to pointing out the way that his successors would have to travel.

Before I hazard this informed guess about the future status of Roosevelt, Truman, and Eisenhower, let me remind my readers of one cardinal fact: American history is written, if not always made, by men of moderate views, broad interests, and merciful judgments. Time works for, rather than against, most Presidents. The men who write texts for our great-grandchildren, like the men who wrote them for us, will be concerned with broad accomplishments and failures, not with petty tales of corruption, ill temper, and intrigue, and I would hope that some of their spirit would rub off on this effort to anticipate them.

Franklin D. Roosevelt's times may well be judged to have been the most exciting and demanding in the history of the republic, as uncertain as the first fluid years under Washington, as hazardous as the first dark years under Lincoln. We bestow the accolade of greatness on a President like Wilson for having led the nation safely through one major crisis. Franklin Roosevelt, who led us through two, must therefore enjoy a long head start toward the eminence he surely wished for in his heart. It would have been sufficient unto posterity for him to have weathered the Hundred Days and launched the New Deal. What can posterity do but think grandly of a President who also led us into, through, and very nearly out of the greatest war in history, and in the midst of this travail launched the United Nations? The willingness of the American people to give Roosevelt a third term and then a fourth is the most eloquent of all witnesses to the glory of his times.

The essence of Roosevelt's Presidency was his airy eagerness to meet the age head on. Thanks to his flair for drama, he acted as if never in all history had there been times like our own. Thanks to his sense of history, he exulted in the vast responsibilities that were thrust upon him even as he sought them. In the first Hundred Days he gave Congress a kind of leadership it had not known before and still does not care to have repeated. In the golden days of the New Deal he initiated a dozen programs designed to save a society from the defects of its virtues. In the hard days before Pearl Harbor he led us step by step to a war we always knew we would have to fight, and in the harder but somehow happier days thereafter he was a Commander in Chief no less awesome than Lincoln himself.

His blunders and trimmings are all on record: the casual manipulation of the dollar in 1933, the ill-conceived assault upon the Court in 1937, the ill-starred interference in the primaries in 1938, the shabby hesitation in the Spanish Civil War, the offhand acquiescence in the evacuation of the Japanese-Americans from the Pacific Coast in 1942, the misplaced confidence in his own ability to "handle Stalin," the shocking unconcern over the education of his Vice-President in 1945, and above all the failure of the New Deal to achieve genuine economic recovery. Yet I have an idea that most of these black marks will be expunged from the memories of our posterity by his undoubted successes in launching the Tennessee Valley Authority and social security, swinging the Lend-Lease Program and the "Destroyer Deal," setting the grand strategy of the war, initiating the atom-bomb project, and converting America into a bountiful arsenal for fifty countries in addition to his own. Nor are these memorable events the whole story of his capacity for decision and leadership. When many of his acts as Commander in Chief are long forgotten, grateful men will remember that he was as devoted a conservationist as Theodore Roosevelt, as warm a friend of culture as Jefferson, and as ardent a free trader as any President who ever lived. We may never hear the end of arguments over the direction in which he led us, but few are left to argue that he preferred drifting to leading. "He demonstrated the ultimate capacity to dominate and control a supreme emergency," Sumner Welles has written, "which is the rarest and most valuable characteristic of any statesman."

No sane observer has ever placed Franklin Roosevelt in the Buchanan line of Presidents. He was, to be sure, a constitution- alist, but his Constitution was that of Jackson, Theodore Roose- velt, Lincoln, and Wilson. Like the first of these he considered the independence of the office to be its most precious asset, like the second he thought of himself as a steward of the people, like the third he made himself a "constitutional dictator" in time or severe national emergency. The gamy flavor of his theory of presidential power may be tasted in some remarkable words delivered to Congress on September 7, 1942. In demanding the repeal of an inflationary provision in the Price Control Act of 1942 he stated flatly:

I ask the Congress to take this action by the first of October. Inaction on your part by that date will leave me with an inescapable responsibility to the people of this country to see to it that the war effort is no longer imperiled by threat of economic chaos.

In the event that the Congress should fail to act, and act ade- quately, I shall assume the responsibility and I will act. . . .

The President has the power, under the Constitution and Con- gressional acts, to take measures necessary to avert a disaster which would interfere with the winning of the war. . . .

The American people can be sure that I will use my powers with a full sense of my responsibility to the Constitution and to my country. The American people can also be sure that I shall not hesitate to use every power vested in me to accomplish the defeat of our enemies in any part of the world where our own safety de- mands such defeat.

When the war is won, the powers under which I act automati- cally revert to the people—to whom they belong.

Finally, like Wilson he considered himself a lay preacher to the American people. Just a few days after his first election he remarked:

The Presidency is not merely an administrative office. That is the least of it. It is pre-eminently a place of moral leadership.

All of our great Presidents were leaders of thought at times when certain historic ideas in the life of the nation had to be clarified. Washington personified the idea of Federal Union. Jefferson practically originated the party system as we know it by opposing the democratic theory to the republicanism of Hamilton. This theory was reaffirmed by Jackson.

Two great principles of our government were forever put beyond question by Lincoln. Cleveland, coming into office following an era of great political corruption, typified rugged honesty. Theodore Roosevelt and Wilson were both moral leaders, each in his own way and for his own time, who used the Presidency as a pulpit.

That is what the office is—a superb opportunity for reapplying, applying to new conditions, the simple rules of human conduct to which we always go back. Without leadership alert and sensitive to change, we are bogged up or lose our way.

Not more than two or three Presidents, it seems safe to say, ever took so broad a view of their constitutional and moral authority as did Franklin D. Roosevelt.

Even his stoutest friends admit that Roosevelt was not much of an administrator. His working habits were casual, personal, and opportunistic; he permitted the inevitable feuds of an active administration to flare too hotly and run too long; he was unbelievably reluctant to discipline the feckless and fire the useless; he was an improviser who lacked the improviser's most essential quality—the candid courage to admit a failure and begin all over again. Yet it is possible that his friends give away too much to his enemies on this particular count. Governments bent on social reform are bound to be wasteful of time and money; Presidents who lead such governments have bigger things to think about than petty details of administration. Roosevelt was aware of his own shortcomings and took a bold step to correct the most glaring of them in Executive Order 8248, which I described in Chapter 4. Beyond that he did not care to go, for he chose to save his energies for his larger responsibilities as leader of the American people. A successful President is something more than a skilled administrator; it almost seems as if Roosevelt set out consciously to reverse the record of Hoover by being a second-rate administrator and a first-rate President. In the end, his deficiencies as an administrator were nearly swallowed up in his genius for bringing politics to the support of policy. A master politician, he rarely lost sight of a truth that most politicians have yet to perceive: that politics is only a game, and a shabby game at that, if it is not directed to larger and nobler ends. His generally masterful leadership of Congress was the most significant application of this principle.

In the course of two major crises and twelve strenuous years, Roosevelt called on hundreds of able men to help him in his tasks. He called on some odd and disreputable characters, too, four or five of whom had no business being within fifty miles of the White House, but for the most part he displayed a remarkable talent for putting the right man in the right job. Harold Ickes as Secretary of the Interior, James A. Farley as chairman of the Democratic National Committee, David Lilienthal as head of T.V.A., Robert H. Jackson as Attorney General, Harold D. Smith as Director of the Budget, Sumner Welles as Under Secretary of State, Robert E. Sherwood and Samuel Rosenman as speech writers, and Stephen Early as Press Secretary are a few examples of what I mean by "the right man in the right job."

In time of war, when it was no longer necessary for the President to confine his search for help to men of his own political stripe, this talent broadened into genius. It is easy to forget that Leahy, Marshall, King, Arnold, Eisenhower, Stimson, Vinson, Patterson, Land, McCloy, Knudsen, Forrestal, Winant, Nelson, Byrnes, Harriman, Donovan, and all the others were, in almost every instance, his personal choices to fill their critical positions. It is just as easy to forget that several of his appointments to the Supreme Court were extremely distinguished or that his elevation of Harlan Fiske Stone to the Chief Justiceship was, in the context of the times, an act of statesmanship. In the end, what impresses me most vividly about the men around Roosevelt is

the number of flinty "no-sayers" who served him, loyally but
not obsequiously, and the way in which he always remained "the
boss." I think, in this regard, of Nathaniel Hawthorne's musing
on Andrew Jackson, a President who was also thought to be
inferior in intellect to the clever men surrounding him:

> Surely he was a great man, and his native strength, as well of
> intellect as of character, compelled every man to be his tool that
> came within his reach; and the more cunning the individual might
> be, it served only to make him the sharper tool.

Roosevelt is already well on his way to enshrinement as folk
hero, although, to be sure, he will have to double as folk devil
for at least another generation. Those millions who still hate him
lavishly may as well face the hard fact bravely that *Sunrise at
Campobello* will be in the repertory of every amateur company,
and that their great-grandchildren's children will read with affec-
tionate interest of the bird walks on the Hudson, the manly
training under Dr. Peabody, and the dogged triumph over crippling pain. Roosevelt's virtues and faults are either too well
known or too bitterly contested for me to review in this short
space, but I would like to point to several qualities that made
him a man for posterity to remember: his buoyancy, which
made it possible for him to love the job as no other President
except the first Roosevelt had loved it; his breadth of vision,
which in time of war gave him a clearer grasp of America's
productive potential than the leaders of industry seemed to have
themselves; his delight in danger, which made him a natural
leader for a generation whose lot was, as a critic remarked, "one
damned crisis after another—and with F.D.R. the damnedest
crisis of all"; his sense of history, which invited him even before his inauguration to join the company of Presidents to whom
monuments are raised long after their death; and his personal
conservatism, which provided a solid base for his political lib-
eralism and kept it from running beyond the aspirations of the
American people. (To those who doubt the existence or influence of this last quality, I recommend a trip through the old

house at Hyde Park.) Roosevelt will never, I am sure, be ranked with Washington and Lincoln, for there were touches of softness and mummery about him that will keep him from sainthood. If he was as busy as Rabbit and as bouncy as Tigger, he was too often, I fear, as big a bluffer as Owl.

Roosevelt's influence on the Presidency was tremendous. Only Washington, who made the office, and Jackson, who remade it, did more than he to raise it to its present condition of strength, dignity, and independence. I often wonder if Mr. Eisenhower ever paused during his period of apprenticeship to think how many of the powers and privileges he commanded, and how much of the respect and assistance he enjoyed, were a direct gift from Franklin Roosevelt. The press conference, the Executive Office, the right to reorganize the administration, and the powers to protect industrial and financial peace are all parts of Roosevelt's legacy to the modern President. Generals obey the President, Congress defers to him, and leaders of other nations honor him far more readily than they would if Roosevelt had not been so forceful a President. Like every such President, he left his successor in boiling water, and in at least one instance—the passage of the Twenty-second Amendment—the reaction to his high-riding incumbency was sufficiently angry to weaken the office permanently. Yet the verdict of history will surely be that he left the Presidency a more splendid instrument of democracy than he found it.

His influence on history is something for our descendants to assess. They will know firsthand, as we can only guess from afar, whether the two great "revolutions" he set in motion turned out to be blessings or curses for the American people. The first of these was the New Deal, which was essentially a decision to preserve American capitalism by invoking the positive power of the national government to support and stabilize the economy. Roosevelt, the master of public opinion, found the words to rationalize this vast readjustment in our ways of thinking and doing. He will long be remembered, fondly by some, contemptuously by others, for having read the word "security" into the American definition of "liberty."

The second great change took form in the coalition of warring powers and the plans for the United Nations, both of which involved a series of decisions aimed at plunging America permanently, for America's own sake, into world affairs. Roosevelt's skill with words was again equal to the high occasion, and men in every land will quote them for centuries to come. We must not forget that this record in war and diplomacy made him a giant figure in world as well as in American history. If we fail to honor him, other men will do it for us, as Winston Churchill honored him in the House of Commons:

> Of Roosevelt, however, it must be said that had he not acted when he did, in the way he did, had he not felt the generous surge of freedom in his heart, had he not resolved to give aid to Britain, and to Europe in the supreme crisis through which we have passed, a hideous fate might well have overwhelmed mankind and made its whole future for centuries sink into shame and ruin. It may well be that the man whom we honor today not only anticipated history, but altered its course, and altered it in a manner which has saved the freedom and earned the gratitude of the human race.

This has been much too simple a review of a complicated man and his turbulent times, but it would be capricious of me not to end by registering my opinion, to which I did not come easily, that Franklin Roosevelt is fixed firmly in the hierarchy of great Presidents a small step above Jackson and Wilson, a sizable step, which may grow smaller over the years, below Washington and Lincoln. He had his own rendezvous with history, and history will be kind to him.

Harry S Truman presents a much tougher case for objective evaluation than does Franklin D. Roosevelt. At times he had the look of greatness, at times he gave off the sound of meanness. But lest we prejudge him too easily and emotionally, let us subject him to our eight tests of presidential greatness. In so doing, I would recall my warning, which is especially pertinent to his amazing Presidency, that history is written, if not always made, by men of moderate views.

His times were not so laden with drama and hazard as those of Franklin Roosevelt, but they were at least as decisive for the American future as those of Jefferson and Wilson. He, too, has a head start for glory, a point that his most savage detractors must concede in his favor. In his two terms we passed through a whole series of nagging crises. We had decadence and destruction prophesied for us again and again. Yet on January 20, 1953, we stood before the world a free, prosperous, liberty-loving people with no more wounds and neuroses than we probably deserved. History may record that it was no mean achievement simply to have gone through the motions of being President in these eight years. This fact alone will surely elevate Mr. Truman above the Adamses and McKinley and quite probably above Polk and Cleveland.

The larger fact is that Harry Truman, once he had got the bearings that Roosevelt neglected to give him, did a great deal more than go through the motions of forwarding messages to Congress, greeting kings and Eagle Scouts, paying political debts, and saying "no comment" to the press. He studied, read, conferred, and dictated as long and hard as any President who ever lived, and he faced up to at least a dozen decisions that gave the world a hard shake. He, too, has a record of sins of commission and omission, especially in domestic affairs. In the former category, I would list his proposal to draft the railroad strikers in 1946 and his seizure of the steel industry in 1952, in the latter his offhand manner toward painful evidence of subversion, corruption, and shoddiness in high places. Yet these must certainly fade into obscurity before the dropping of the first atom bomb (and the second), the pursuit of nuclear research and production on a massive scale, the Truman Doctrine and the Berlin airlift, the Marshall Plan and the North Atlantic

Treaty Organization, and the decision to resist in Korea. Not one of his grave steps in foreign and military affairs, not even the fateful and controversial decision to use the atom bomb on live targets, has yet been proved wrong, stupid, or contrary to the best judgment and interests of the American people. He took all of them as the people expect their President to take such fateful steps: resolutely, solemnly, and hopefully. Truman rarely if ever had Roosevelt's sure touch of leadership, perhaps because he often appeared dizzy from the speed of his ride to the top, but there is small disposition among either his admirers or detractors to hold anyone but him responsible for his actions.

Truman came in time to an even more exalted view of the Presidency than did Roosevelt. His spacious understanding of its powers and obligations will surely impress posterity more than his disturbing lapses from decorum. Certainly no President ever spoke so grandly and yet humbly of his authority. Certainly no President ever gave a more imaginative and accurate description of his job:

And people talk about the powers of a President, all the powers that a Chief Executive has, and what he can do. Let me tell you something—from experience!

The President may have a great many powers given to him in the Constitution and may have certain powers under certain laws which are given to him by the Congress of the United States; but the principal power that the President has is to bring people in and try to persuade them to do what they ought to do without persuasion. That's what I spend most of my time doing. That's what the powers of the President amount to.

An entirely new theory of the Presidency can be spun out of that folksy statement, which Truman repeated with amusing variations on at least a dozen occasions.

If he did not always show himself sufficiently aware of the limitations of his office, it must be remembered that less impetuous men than he—Lincoln, Wilson, and Franklin D. Roosevelt—might also have considered themselves empowered to seize the steel mills in 1952. In any case, for all his alleged lack of learning and of disposition for pondering great truths, Mr. Truman demonstrated a more clear-cut philosophy of presidential power than any predecessor except Woodrow Wilson. The heaviest black mark against his reading of the Presidency, in my opinion, was his cavalier disregard of the sensibilities and prerogatives of Congress in the harsh debate of 1951 over the power to station troops in Europe. His failure to associate Congress more quickly and positively in the decision to fight the Korean war and his partisan seizure of the steel mills were hardly less censurable.

As a technician Truman had few equals in the long history of the Presidency. Most experienced students of public administration agree that he organized his time, which meant a seventy-hour week, and distributed his energies, which were legendary, with the sure touch of the professional. Yet he was not a professional at all, which is another way of saying that he learned his job on the job with astounding success. On several counts he is open to severe criticism: his methods of dealing with Congress were inexcusably irritating; he permitted raw politics to hold sway in areas to which it should have been rigidly denied entry; the moral tone of his administration unsettled even some of his most devoted admirers. Yet in the White House itself things were remarkably serene and efficient. The conjunction of cold war, which threw a hundred new burdens on an already overburdened office, and Mr. Truman, who learned to delegate his own authority as well as any President in this century, speeded and made secure the institutionalization of the American Presidency. To those around him he was the very model of a modern executive.

One final point might illustrate both his technical competence and his awareness of his responsibilities. At the very moment when his stature seemed at its lowest, when he seemed to many Americans to have surrendered all sense of dignity or authority, Mr. Truman did something that not a single President in history had cared to do: with efficient grace he transferred power and information to an incoming administration of the opposite political party. From this time forward, outgoing Presidents will be expected to assist incoming Presidents in the image of his high-minded co-operation with Dwight D. Eisenhower.

The roll call of those whom Truman enlisted in his staff and ranks runs the whole scale of virtue and talent from selfless greatness to dishonest incompetence. It has been suggested by some observers, and I am inclined to agree, that he made a more or less conscious deal with himself to insist upon non-partisan excellence in military and diplomatic affairs and to tolerate partisan mediocrity in domestic affairs. The names of Marshall, Lovett, Forrestal, Acheson, Bedell Smith, Hoffman, Bohlen, Symington, Foster, Bradley, Clay, Lewis Douglas, Kennan, Draper, Jessup, Harriman, Finletter, Patterson, McCloy—and of Eisenhower and Dulles—are proof enough that Truman mobilized even more talent than Roosevelt in the areas that touch upon survival. The names of McGrath, McGranery, Snyder, Caudle, and Sawyer should be enough to remind us that the rest of the nation's business was carried on with little distinction and much bumbling. To complete a group portrait that has General Marshall sitting on one side of the President and General Vaughan on the other, I think we may say with sorrowful conviction that Truman's appointments to the Supreme Court were about the least distinguished in history.

Harry S Truman is a man whom history will delight to remember. Those very lapses from dignity that made him an object of scorn to millions of Republicans—the angry letters, testy press conferences, whistle stops, impossible sport shirts, and early-morning seminars on the streets of dozens of American cities—open his door to immortality. It is a rare American, even a rare Republican, who can be scornful about a man one hundred years dead, and our descendants will be chuckling over his Missouri wit and wisdom long after the "five-per-centers" have been buried and forgotten. They will read with admiration of the upset he brought off in 1948, with awe of the firing of General MacArthur, and with a sense of kinship of the way he remained more genuinely "plain folks" than any other President. They will be moved by the simple dignity of his confession: "There are probably a million people in this country who could do the presidential job better than I, but I've got the job and I'm doing the very best I can." He was fascinating to watch, even when the sight hurt, and he will be fascinating to read about. The historians can be expected to do their share to fix him securely in history, for he provides a classic case study of one of their favorite themes: the President who grows in office.

Truman's influence on the Presidency can be summed up in the simple judgment that he was a highly successful Andrew Johnson. The Presidency had grown enough in Franklin Roosevelt's time to satisfy most Americans for at least another generation; it was his successor's high duty to see that the new tools of democratic leadership were not blunted or stolen by the forces of reaction. This duty Mr. Truman discharged with enthusiasm and success. He defended the integrity of the Presidency stoutly against the grand challenge of MacArthur and the sabotage of McCarthy, and even after his departure he defended it against the vulgar showmanship of Representative Velde, whose subpoena to appear before the House Committee on Un-American Activities in 1953 Truman thrust aside magisterially. Whatever damage he did to the office by intruding too one-sidedly into labor disputes or by insulting Congress gratuitously or by losing control of some of his subordinates was altogether temporary in effect. The office he handed over to Eisenhower was no less magnificent than the office he inherited from Roosevelt. Looked at in the light of what took place during the term of every other man who succeeded a great President

—John Adams, Madison, Van Buren, Johnson, Taft, and Harding—this may well appear as Truman's most remarkable achievement.

There appear to have been two great events in Truman's eight years for which he may be remembered as Madison or Grant or Taft or Hoover will never be remembered. One was domestic in character: the first real beginnings of a many-sided program toward eliminating discrimination and second-class citizenship in American life. The other was international: the irrevocable commitment of the American people to active co-operation with other nations in search of world peace and prosperity. Over neither of these vast beginnings did Mr. Truman exercise much control, yet to each he gave the full support of the Presidency. He will surely be remembered, and may yet be supremely honored, for the President's Committee on Civil Rights and the resulting message to Congress of February 2, 1948. He will as surely be remembered, and as possibly supremely honored, for his action in support of collective se-curity against Communist aggression. It was a grand accomplishment in the total sweep of American history to take this nation into its first peacetime military alliance (NATO), to commit us for the first time to defend an area in which we had no obvious national interest (the Greek-Turkish program), to meet Communist force with force of our own making (Korea, 1950), and to call for a long-range constructive program that could open the gate to world peace (Point Four). The Marshall Plan is also credited to his account.

Mr. Truman often remarked that equal opportunity for all Americans and lasting peace for all men were the two consuming goals of his administration. The achievement of these goals (if we are blessed enough to achieve them) must inevitably add luster to his name. His uncompromising opponents are certain that both courses, civil rights and internationalism, will lead us to disaster. As Truman himself often reminded us, we must all wait for history to judge between him and Governor

Byrnes in the struggle for equal opportunity, and between him and Senator Bricker in the search for peace with freedom. My feeling is that he may wait with confidence.

On the basis of this evidence I am ready to hazard an opinion, to which I came, I confess manfully, with dragging feet, that Harry S Truman will eventually win a place as President alongside Jefferson and Theodore Roosevelt. There will be at least a half-dozen Presidents strung out below him who were more able and large-minded, but he had the good fortune to preside in stirring times and will reap large credit for having survived them. I cannot, in good conscience, predict the greatness of Washington, Lincoln, Franklin Roosevelt, Wilson, and Jackson for his name. Certain deficiencies of intellect and perception must always bar him from the seats of the mighty. We must remember that his consuming hobby has always been political and military history. He knew that there was a game called "Ranking the Presidents"; he confessed repeatedly, and with a candor that embarrassed his listeners, that he was an accident of history who did not belong on the ladder at all. Despite or because of this harsh self-appraisal, he made a determined effort to climb the ladder by imitating the well-remembered Presidents of the past and by acting beyond his gifts. As he himself put it, "I may not have been one of the great Presidents, but I had a good time trying to be."

Harry S Truman will be a well-remembered President because he proved that an ordinary man could fill the world's most extraordinary office with devotion and high purpose. He may serve as a lasting symbol of the noble truth that gives strength and meaning to the American experiment: plain men *can* govern themselves; democracy *does* work. And his epitaph will read: He was distressingly petty in petty things; he was gallantly big in big things.

I feel bound to preface my prediction of Dwight D. Eisenhower's standing among all the Presidents by confessing to a

downward shift of opinion between the first and second editions
of this book.* I now foresee, not the least bit happily, a somewhat lower ranking for the third of our modern Presidents
than I had anticipated in 1956. At that time I wrote in conclusion to my assessment: "Eisenhower already stands above
Polk and Cleveland, and he has a reasonable chance to move
up to Jefferson and Theodore Roosevelt. To label this President another Grant is merely absurd. We shall all say a lot of
silly things for or against Eisenhower before this campaign is
over, but we really should let General Grant rest in peace."

General Grant, I think, may continue to rest in peace;
General Eisenhower will surely be placed well above him by
our descendants. Just how far above him is a guess I will hazard
only at the end of these remarks, limiting myself to the pre-
liminary observation that he fumbled away that "reasonable
chance" early in his second term, and that I now expect
him to be left outside the magic circle of presidential greatness. It is, of course, an act of temerity if not folly to attempt
the long view of a man with whom we have all lived, so to
speak, in daily intimacy. Still, this is a game that is fun to play
even on a muddy field and a murky day, and so let us ask our
eight questions about Dwight D. Eisenhower—the President, not
the General.

His times were certainly less exacting than those of Roosevelt
and Truman. They were difficult, to be sure, but they were
not perilous, and it is out of peril that men have risen
to glory in the American Presidency during the twentieth
century. I think it important to make a distinction, which I will
make at several points in this survey, between the first and

* Although this assessment was written at the end of Eisenhower's
seventh year, it is pitched in a style and tense more appropriate to a
final reckoning. I have done this for the sake of art, objectivity, and
convenience—and in full recognition of the fact that I have taken something of a gamble on the President's performance in his eighth year.
I have followed the same practice throughout the book, most noticeably
in my discussion of Vice-President Nixon on pages 137-140.

second terms of Eisenhower's Presidency. The first was, almost by definition, a time in which a President could win gratitude but not immortality. For all his bold talk as a candidate in 1952 about a "crusade," we knew (and if we did not know it in 1952, we knew it by 1953) that his mission was to bring us peace at home and abroad, even at the price of a future reckoning. We were weary of reform in the one area and of adventure in the other, and we elected a President who would give us a breathing spell from both without taking us back over the ground we had already covered. We got that spell, and we can be thankful that we did. Mr. Eisenhower would be the last man to complain of the price he paid in the coin of a diminished reputation in the annals of history. Not only was he elected in a time of conservatism; he elected to be a conservative President, and I doubt that he knew or cared that history finds it hard to rise in wild acclaim of such a President in such a time.

In his second term events began to move a little faster, but the crisis of our age is still more impending than real. Things at home and abroad are going to get a lot worse before they get a lot better, but it would be hard to convince most Americans, including President Eisenhower, that this is the true nature of our present discontents. We are still basking in the luxury of catching our breath. The most strong-minded and adventurous of Presidents would have had trouble stirring us to actions that do more than hold the line, and Mr. Eisenhower was certainly never that kind of President. In short, he was not cut off completely from greatness by the nature of his times and mission, but he, like Theodore Roosevelt, was asked to travel farther and faster in search of it. As a gradualist in a time of gradualism, an earth-smoother rather than an earth-shaker, he never really put his heart in the attempt. He had very little sense of history to begin with; and even if he had had it to the full measure of Harry S Truman, he was too modest to do an imitation of Jackson and Lincoln. I think it both cruel and crude to describe the Eisenhower years as a time in which "the bland led the bland," but I also think it absurd to acclaim them as a time in which a crusader led a crusade.

President Eisenhower's manner of meeting his responsibilities at home and abroad was that of the moderate conservative he repeatedly professed to be. To his credit are the measures against recession in 1954, the improved administration of the defense budget, the initiation of a major program of highway construction, the modest efforts in behalf of civil rights, and such sporadic displays of executive independence as the angry veto of the natural-gas bill in 1956 and the rejection of congressional attempts to remake his Cabinet. To his debit are the blunder of Dixon-Yates, the injustices and inanities of the loyalty-security program (more apparent in his first term than in his second), the miscalculation of the public interest in the broad fields of conservation and regulation, the untidy handling of the government's obligations in the polio vaccine fiasco, the unprecedented refusal to support his own budget in 1957, and all the starts and stops and wrong turns in pursuit of his promise to get the farm problem into manageable shape. In the unceasing campaign against corruption in high places, Eisenhower was largely content to govern by setting a tone for others to match as best they could, and by cutting a man loose when he had made too unpleasant a mess, something he rarely did with either grace or candor. The departures into limbo of Edmund F. Mansure, Harold E. Talbott, and above all Sherman Adams did nothing to enhance the President's reputation for either political finesse or administrative command. I must leave it to each reader to decide for himself whether Eisenhower handled the challenge of Senator McCarthy in a manner consistent with his position as President. I limit myself to the double-barreled observation that the Senator was a badly beaten man long before his death in 1957, and that Eisenhower may well have done all that he could do (within the limits of dignity he had imposed upon himself) to help administer the beating.

All these pluses and minuses are likely to fade into insignificance, however, in the harsh light of Mr. Eisenhower's two most apparent failures to focus his unique prestige upon domestic problems: his abdication of both moral and political leadership in the crisis of integration in the South, and his refusal to push steadily for solutions to the crisis of education throughout the Union. In each of these situations, which deteriorated visibly during his years in office, his pattern of action was one of long periods of drift punctuated by sharp bursts of anger, a pattern hardly calculated to persuade the recalcitrants in Little Rock or in the House of Representatives to take even the first step into a future that must surely come. The temper of the times, the folkways of the people, and the hostility of some of the nation's most vested interests were all ranged against him in his appeals for peaceful schools in the South and adequate schools everywhere, yet he fought back, when he fought at all, with only a fraction of his powers. Worse than that, he too often talked more boldly than he was prepared to act. As James Reston put it, "Both in golf and in politics, his backswing has always been better than his follow-through." Other Presidents have failed in such matters as these and been pardoned by history, but this President, I fear, may be dealt with much more harshly by a posterity that, God willing, will have made a reality of our present hopes. It was not so much that he failed to catch the right vision of the future, but that he was unwilling to draw steadily on his overflowing reservoir of popularity to get us moving in the direction of the vision. Historians will be reluctant to accord the judgment of greatness to a President who kept so much of his immense influence in reserve. To put the matter another way, no President in history was ever more powerfully armed to persuade the minds of men to face up to the inevitable—and then failed more poignantly to use his power.

In foreign affairs Mr. Eisenhower was, on his own terms, a successful President, thanks largely, we can agree, to a Secretary of State with no superior in history for courage and devotion to duty. For a man who had been around as long as he had in the hot spots of diplomacy, Eisenhower got off the mark like a lead-footed amateur. But he rallied quickly, especially after the armistice in Korea, and no one can deny that we have all come a long way back from the degrading days when Cohn and Schine roamed Europe and the image of a free America was tarnished in the eyes of even our most steadfast and forgiving friends. The President gave us as satisfactory a peace as we could possibly have expected in Korea; he kept us from being bogged down in the morass of French colonialism; and he took the lead—not a bold lead, but at least a prudent one—in bringing the atom to the service of all mankind. We went once to the Summit at Geneva and heard our President speak for peace with honor as only he could do; we went twice to the wall at Quemoy and roused to his refusal to give way meekly to the blackmail of force. Few will deny that he acted with prudent resolution in his successful effort to save the legitimate government of Lebanon from subversion in 1958. He had his failures, in Cairo and Caracas and Congress, but even the most alert and purposeful President will have his fair share of failures from now on. Success in diplomacy must be judged in the perspective of the long years, and it is altogether possible that Eisenhower —and the battle-scarred Secretary of State who gave him the best six years of his own life—may eventually be given credit for a successful performance. (I doubt, however, that any sizable part of his success will be attributed to the Grand Tours of 1959. Grand Tours of our Presidents are exciting to follow, to be sure; but, as Woodrow Wilson proved a full forty years ago, they are no substitute for tough diplomacy.)

Yet he was a success, I repeat, on his own terms, and they were never the terms of creative greatness. If he is remembered by history for his feats of diplomacy, it will be as the President who "kept the shop," faithfully but unimaginatively, which was set up before him by Harry S Truman in pursuit of the general directions of Franklin D. Roosevelt. I cannot think of a single major departure in the course of Eisenhower's stewardship from the new line of diplomacy that was first laid out in the Truman Doctrine, the Marshall Plan, the Reciprocal Trade Acts, the Point Four program, and our simultaneous commitment to NATO and the United Nations; and I take wry comfort in the knowledge that neither the Chicago *Tribune* nor the *Nation* can think of one either. If history finally decides that this was the line to take, the President will be remembered for having carried it forward dutifully. If history decides that it was a mistake from the beginning, he may suffer even more than the men who launched us upon it. By 1958 we knew far better than we did in 1948 the price we might have to pay for collective security against Soviet designs.

Taken all in all, Mr. Eisenhower's performance in the Presidency was not the kind that will bring posterity to its feet in waves of applause. Indeed, if we put his performance to the three tests of leadership I mentioned on page 143, we are bound to say that he never did measure up to the lofty expectations of the American people—expectations, alas for him, that no President could have satisfied. We called upon him to lead Congress, but he simply could not bring himself to dish out steadily those plums to the good boys and spanks to the bad that do more than a thousand speeches to influence the legislative process. The kind of decisive influence he exerted in behalf of labor-reform legislation in 1959 was only rarely brought to bear in the course of his presidential career. It may be said in his defense that he had to face a Democratic majority in Congress for fully three-fourths of his tenure, but this defense collapses before the notorious fact that his prerogatives as President were more carefully respected by Senators Johnson, Russell, George, and Green than they were by Senators Knowland, Taft, Bricker, and McCarthy, and before the related fact that most points in his programs were at least as appealing to the opposition as to his own party.

He was not much more determined a leader of the administration. If moral exhortation (at which Mr. Eisenhower was admittedly a genius) is not enough to goad Congress into action, it is even less effective as an ingredient of presidential leadership of the makers and executors of policy in the federal administration, and in this area, too, he was a disappointment to those who thought of him as another Jackson. No President could have had a more eager and devoted team (with a few glaring exceptions like Scott McLeod), and no team could have been more consistently befuddled about the coach's plans to move the ball. Mr. Dulles knew the President was all for peace, but he could never be sure what price the President was willing to pay for peace at each of the major trouble spots around the world. Mr. Rogers knew the President was all for brotherhood, but he never got the kind of support he had a right to expect in Little Rock and Atlanta and Montgomery. Mr. Brundage handed the President a "modern Republican" budget to lay before Congress in 1957, but he found out to his surprise (or was he surprised?) that Mr. Humphrey had another kind of budget in mind. The plain truth is that Mr. Eisenhower was not especially interested in either the purposes or mechanics of most parts of the federal administration, and the first requisite of a successful administrator at the top of the pyramid is, surely, an unforced interest in what goes on below.

Finally, history will very likely judge Mr. Eisenhower's leadership of the American people to have been most disappointing of all. No man ever got a more astounding show of support in the one popularity poll that counts—a margin of 6.5 million in 1952 and of 9.5 million in 1956—and no man since Harding (another big winner) had less success in exchanging this popularity for the hard currency of influence. By running more than seven million votes ahead of his party in 1956 he scored a personal triumph without parallel in American history, but this feat could also be looked at as a shocking default of political leadership. It was the first time in more than a hundred years that a President had gained re-election and his party had failed to capture control of Congress. Future historians may have trouble understanding how a President could persuade so many Americans to vote for him but not for his party. They are sure to have a field day accounting for his failure to live up to the popular image of an iron-willed leader, but they are all likely to agree on the first and greatest reason: that he could not lead because he would not lead.

A dozen factors militated against a steady display of Jacksonian leadership in these years, but the most important factor of all, we must acknowledge regretfully, was Mr. Eisenhower's inability or unwillingness (they are really the same thing) to "work hard at being President." I could drag up a score of examples of his refusal to apply himself eagerly and consistently to the job at hand, but one should suffice to make the point: his general inaccessibility to individual members of Congress. It is astounding to note that those Congressmen who seem to have had the hardest time getting in to see him were his most zealous supporters. If any Senator can beat Clifford Case's record for cooling his heels at the White House door, I have not heard of him. Not all Congressmen are as loyal and forgiving as Senator Case, and a good part of the blame for Mr. Eisenhower's indifferent leadership of Congress can be laid to his refusal to cultivate the garden personally. There are limits to the practice of personal leadership in this and the other areas in which the President must set men into creative motion, but Mr. Eisenhower, it now seems plain, never even approached these limits for more than a few short periods in his years in. the Presidency, notably the opening months of 1954 and 1959. The eagerness with which most Washington correspondents and Republican politicians seized upon and paraded each scrap of evidence of a "new Ike" (or, more exactly, of the "old Ike") is evidence itself that the President rarely operated under a full head of steam. By 1959 he was getting extravagant praise for sporadic displays of the sort of leadership that Wilson and the Roosevelts offered throughout their careers.

One clearly established reason for this refusal to play the strong leader day in and day out was Eisenhower's modest conception of the authority of the Presidency. He came to the office with practically no thoughts of his own about its powers and purposes. He came, moreover, as a Republican, and therefore committed to the Whig theory of a partnership between President and Congress in which the latter sets the nation's goals without much help from the former. He had swallowed a good deal of the propaganda directed at Roosevelt and Truman, and the result was a first year in office during which his view of his powers was not much different from that announced long ago by William Howard Taft. In the late fall of 1953 he began to broaden this view considerably. His matured theory of the Presidency should not be confused with that of Taft or even Hoover, for he proved himself on several occasions to be a staunch defender of the independence of the executive. But it also should not be confused with that of Lincoln or even Washington, the two Presidents he is said to have considered his favorites, for he never really saw himself, neither in his proudest moments nor in his most humble, as the steady focus of the American system of government. Nothing is more revealing of this modest philosophy than his request early in 1955 for authority to defend Formosa and the Pescadores, a request repeated in 1957 for similar authority in the Middle East. It is obvious that Eisenhower, quite unlike Truman, considered the President to be under stern moral obligation to ask approval of Congress—certainly when there is time to ask it—for the use of powers in the twilight zone between them. Stern morality, needless to say, may also be good politics in situations like these. Speaker Rayburn, it should be noted, took the lead among those who wondered aloud if these two requests would not cripple the striking power of the Presidency in a sudden crisis, but the point seemed to trouble Mr. Eisenhower not at all. In any case, he was much less impressed with the authority of the Presidency than were his Democratic predecessors, and if this, too, was a brake on his progress toward the stature of a great President, he did not appear to be overly worried. He may well have thought that posterity was for once ready to salute a President who saw no threat to his own position in being polite to Congress.

Eisenhower's competence as a technician is a subject of hot dispute. His supporters insist that he moved beyond Roosevelt and Truman in distributing the routine burdens of the Presidency efficiently among an industrious and loyal team. His critics reply that he learned the lesson of his army days much too thoroughly, for he delegated not only the use but the control of some of his highest prerogatives and lost his freedom of maneuver to an outsized, self-directing staff. From the very beginning, they say, he reigned too much and ruled too little; indeed, the "Eisenhower regency" began to function long before September 24, 1955.

The truth, I think, rests just about in the middle of the extreme claims of his friends and his foes. The Presidency was at least as efficiently organized as it was in the best days of Harry Truman, and by delegating responsibility on a broad and imaginative scale the President himself gained more hours for his own use than either of his predecessors enjoyed. Far more important in the light of history, his plans and methods—and a touch of Eisenhower luck—made it possible on three occasions for the Presidency to run for weeks almost without a President and almost without a hitch. At the same time, it can hardly be denied that Mr. Eisenhower came much closer than did either of the other two modern Presidents to becoming a prisoner in his own overorganized house—a house in which his press secretary often said "we" when he meant "the President," in which Sherman Adams ruled for several years as an autocrat who seemed to know the workings of the Presidency far better than the President himself, and in which "the White House" took on the dimensions of an independent center of power, most notably in the dumping of Joseph W.

Martin from his position as minority leader in the House in 1959. I shall have something to say in my last chapter of the dangers to the Presidency that lurk in the growing pattern of institutionalization, but I must say now that I had President Eisenhower specifically in mind when I wrote the words of caution that appear on pages 243-244. There are many levelheaded students of the Presidency who think of him as a man who was spared, who allowed himself to be spared, a little too much of the suffering and glory of democratic leadership. I myself would still think that the main fire of his critics should be directed against the use he made of all those extra hours which Governor Adams and General Persons gave him, although some might also be directed against his too ready reliance on his own team for information and advice. He should have tried a little harder to keep the back door open to callers of his own choosing, and he should have devoted a few more of those pleasant evening hours to reading the newspapers, especially the ones that criticized him. Be all that as it may, he did himself and the Presidency a great service by carrying the process of institutionalization at least a step and a half farther than Truman. If he went too far in surrendering control of some of his powers, the next President should have no trouble recovering it.

The men around Eisenhower, like the men around Roosevelt and Truman, presented a composite picture of all the virtues and most of the faults (if not the sins) of public life. In these years of gradualism there was a clear reduction in vision and daring and humor among the men who ran the country, but there was also a clear expansion in probity and frugality and attention to the business at hand. In the still of the night and with the eye of his mind Mr. Eisenhower must have often looked back sheepishly to his campaign promise of 1952 to mobilize "the best brains of America," for it is one promise he did not even come close to keeping, even on his own terms. Yet how could he, a career soldier, have known that his freedom of choice would be narrowed so drastically

by Republican politics and American folkways? Not only was
he pledged in ways he could barely understand to concentrate
on "jobs for the boys" rather than "boys for the jobs"; his, after
all, was a businessman's government, and businessmen are
understandably more reluctant than, let us say, professors to
drop everything and rush to their President's call. It seems
plain that Eisenhower will not be especially remembered for
the talents he assembled about him. He was clearly more successful in finding the right men for his immediate staff than
for the great offices of state. James C. Hagerty, Arthur Burns,
Gabriel Hauge, Gerald D. Morgan, Robert E. Merriam, Ber-
nard M. Shanley, General Goodpaster, General Persons, Roger
Jones, Robert Cutler, and, yes, the unlamented Sherman Adams
were a far better team in their league than the department
heads were in theirs. Of the nineteen men and one woman who
headed the executive departments, a good deal less than one-
third, notably John Foster Dulles, Marion Folsom, James P.
Mitchell, and William P. Rogers, turned in first-class performances, and a roughly equal number, notably Charles E.
Wilson and Mrs. Hobby, were unrelieved disasters. In the
offices that really count—the Secretaryships of State, Defense,
and Treasury, the positions on the Joint Chiefs of Staff, the
chairmanship of the Atomic Energy Commission, and the key
embassies—Mr. Eisenhower was content, indeed seemed well
content, with a team that will never, I am certain, be mentioned
in the same breath with that wonderful band of stalwarts who
helped see Lincoln through to glory: Seward, Chase, Stanton,
Welles, Charles Francis Adams, Sherman, and Grant. Only
Secretary Dulles may have been in their class, but that is a
judgment I prefer to leave to the future. For only the future
can tell whether his obdurate but not fanatical anti-Communism
was the correct policy for our times, and whether his fame
will therefore prosper. If it does, it will very possibly be at
the expense of the fame of that President for whom Dulles
ran the diplomatic show as no Secretary of State had run it for

generations, certainly not for any President with a claim to distinction. The amazing relationship between Eisenhower and Dulles brought far more credit to the servant than it did to the master, and in this relationship future historians may very well find conclusive evidence of Eisenhower's refusal to make his own rendezvous with history. An important bit of the evidence in this matter will be the apparent shift in our policy toward the U.S.S.R. that followed the death of Mr. Dulles. One is bound to ask whether the Khrushchev visit would have taken place if Dulles had been alive and healthy—and bound to answer that it is not very likely. Who, then, we must go on to ask, was the effective molder of our foreign policy between 1953 and 1959?

One final point can be made emphatically in Eisenhower's favor: his appointments to the Supreme Court were vastly superior to Truman's. Indeed, I think it altogether possible that the future may salute him as the unwitting and perhaps unwanting molder of one of the great Courts in American history. Mr. Eisenhower did his work; the rest is up to Chief Justice Warren and his colleagues.

About the man himself there is nothing to say that has not been said a thousand times, except that despite his unique hold on the people of this country, or perhaps because of it, he is less likely than Roosevelt to project his personality forcefully on the consciousness of history. A President who is adored by a little more than half the people and despised by the rest is a more probable candidate for immortality than a President who is liked by all those in the center, which means most Americans, and disliked only by those on the fringes. The very qualities of decency and affability that made him exactly the man the American people wanted at a restful stage in their pilgrimage may be woven by time into a curtain of indifference that will hang darkly between our posterity and our most popular President. He aroused his fair share of enthusiasm but not of anger, and I can think of no memorable President after Washington who did not arouse both to a pronounced degree. (Washington aroused pure awe, but that is a feeling in which, for better or worse, modern men do not indulge.)

President Eisenhower's public character was not above criticism. He was a dogged anti-intellectual in an age when intellect alone stands between us and annihilation, a man of hot temper who boiled over at the wrong times and for the wrong reasons, a rather poor judge of the qualities of mind and heart that are needed in high places. Even his admirers were troubled by the gap that often yawned between what the President said and what he did about reducing tariffs or protecting our natural heritage or playing fair with those accused of disloyalty or educating the white South in the ways of tolerance. Yet it cannot be doubted that his character, like his life, was an amazingly accurate projection of much of what is best in the American dream. He had been a small-town boy with a job in the local dairy, a West Point halfback with a trick knee, a soldier who stood close to Marshall and MacArthur, a commander with a genius for molding diverse spirits into a fighting force, a grandfather with a small but active crew of appealing descendants, a man known to swear because he missed a two-foot putt. He was manly, brave, charming, honest, capable, friendly, fair-minded, and incredibly lucky—and who, except for the Muse who keeps the rolls of true greatness, could have asked for anything more?

Eisenhower's influence on the Presidency passed through three fairly distinct stages. During his first year it often seemed that his incumbency would prove a disaster for the office. It was not so much his unwillingness to exercise his legitimate prerogatives that troubled students of the Presidency, but rather his indifference to an unruly Congress celebrating the end of twenty years of "executive encroachment" with some encroachments of its own. Sometime in 1953 Eisenhower came to a clearer understanding of the modern Presidency, and for

the next two years he was, if not a "strong" President, certainly
a firm one. The manner of his tenure throughout those most
vigorous of his years was, in point of historical fact, a huge
blessing for the office, for in his own quiet way he introduced
many of the precedents of Roosevelt and Truman, about which
the touch of crisis or partisanship still lingered, into the normal
pattern of the Presidency. To put the matter another way,
the Presidency called loudly for a Republican in 1952, for not
until the Republicans had learned by experience that Whiggery
was obsolete could the modernization of the Presidency be
considered complete. Eisenhower proved himself a strong
enough President to hold the line that his predecessors had
staked out, but not too strong to lose touch with the Whigs
in his party and thus miss a wonderful chance to educate them.
We may go beyond this general observation to give him credit
for these specific actions: his decisive opposition to the Bricker
Amendment, his efforts to save the Cabinet from further decline, his reinvigoration of the National Security Council, his
further refinement of the press conference, his personal solution
to the problem of disability (of which more in Chapter 7), and
his gallant attempt to do something with the Vice-President if
not with the Vice-Presidency. All in all, it was a long journey
uphill from 1953 and his needless surrenders to "the courtesy of
the Senate" to 1955 and his bold announcement that he would
ignore a provision of an act he had just signed—because he,
the President, thought the provision unconstitutional.

The three successive illnesses of 1955 and 1956 ushered in
the third stage of Mr. Eisenhower's influence on the Presidency.
He never forgot the painful lessons of 1953, and he kept the
power and prestige of the office intact against the forces in
Congress and country that wanted to "cut the President down
to size." If he reduced the effectiveness of the Presidency
itself, it was only because he let his staff bear more than its
proper share of his political burden. The "White House," I
repeat, took over a little too much of "the Presidency" in Mr.

Eisenhower's second term. But that, I insist, is an imbalance that his successors should be able to correct with no difficulty. Mr. Eisenhower once told his Cabinet, according to Robert Donovan, that he did not want to "become known as a President who had practically crippled the Presidency," and certainly he need have no fears on this score. His new show of vigor in 1959, which was not entirely a figment of the wishful imaginations of Henry Luce and Arthur Krock, was a genuine boon to the Presidency. Indeed, historians may record, although I remain somewhat doubtful, that Eisenhower's last two years—the years without Humphrey, Dulles, and Adams—were a fourth and generally more successful stage in his presidential career.

To speak of Eisenhower's influence on history is to soar on wings of brass into the realms of fantasy. History plays malicious tricks, especially on historians with a penchant for prophecy, and I am well aware that before I am gathered to my fathers I may have to eat all these words without benefit of spice or sauce. But having come this far I cannot turn back, and so I make bold to predict that Mr. Eisenhower will finally be judged to have been a faithful if not farsighted son of his own time; and the time, as I said before, was the kind in which a President could win gratitude but not immortality.

His total performance in the Presidency will be assessed, I think, at two levels, which even now seem to match up fairly closely with his two terms. At the first level, that is to say, in his first term, he gave us just about the most satisfactory dose of conservatism we have taken since the administration of Rutherford B. Hayes—or would it be John Quincy Adams? He not only kept the shop but put it back in order; he not only offered us a rest but made us take it. He "widened the vital center" so steadily that the American people enjoyed a climate of unity that they had not known for thirty years or more. Mr. Eisenhower did all this largely through his leadership of that difficult but essential minority, the Republican party. He did not succeed as much as he might have liked in remolding it in his own image of moderate conservatism, but he did persuade most of its leaders to follow him into the twentieth century. By a route that often seemed much too circuitous but had a final logic of its own, he brought the Republican party, and with it the business community, very near to accepting once and for all the ground rules of the New Economy and the burdens of the New Internationalism. He did a job the American people wanted to have done—not an exciting job, to be sure, but one for which history, too, had been calling— and history ought to make a special effort to remember him for it. I cannot emphasize too strongly that it usually prefers to ignore the President who promises peace rather than prog- ress. Yet Eisenhower's conservatism was obviously of a newer and higher order than that of McKinley or Taft or Coolidge, and it is possible that he may be richly honored for it. It is possible, too, that the credentials of presidential greatness may be revised in the next generation to permit an occasional earth-smoother to sit in glory with the earth-shakers. Knowing what I do of history and historians and, for that matter, of the American people, I doubt it strongly, but for a man like Mr. Eisenhower the knowledge of a job well done is a reward more precious than any premonition of immortality.

By 1957, I would think, we had had our fill of moderate conservatism. Even as most of us went on catching our own breaths, we began to feel the breaths of countless others upon us—of Soviet scientists and Chinese steelmakers, of angry Latins and even angrier Virginians, of American men unable to find work in a booming economy. The times had begun to run ahead of our will and imagination, and they called for a leader who would rouse us from the lethargy of "fat-dripping prosperity" and point out the hard road we would have to travel into a demanding future. Mr. Eisenhower, I repeat, was not that kind of leader. The temper of the times was against him, and so were many circumstances—the nature of his

mandate, the division in the ranks of his party, the new constitutional provision that rendered him a "lame duck" at the very
moment of his smashing re-election, the three illnesses in a
row, the general loss of vigor. But most serious of all as a
factor in a performance that failed to shake history was his
whole approach to life—his character, his methods, his cast of
mind. His character was that of the peacemaker, the man who
wants to like everyone and wants everyone to like him. "Eisenhower's personal inclination," James Reston has written, "always has been to try to talk and conciliate. It was the talker
and the conciliator in him that brought him to the pinnacle of
American public life in the first place." It would have been
a far different Eisenhower who could have acted consistently
on the memorable advice of Herbert Bayard Swope: "I don't
have a formula for success, but I know the sure formula for
failure; try to please everybody." His methods were those of
a man with a distaste for aggressive politics and a horror of
administrative detail. "He has never been willing," Walter
Lippmann has written, "to break the eggs that are needed for
the omelet." His cast of mind was that of the genuine conservative. He seems to have been made aware of the magnitude
of the impending crisis, but he acted, however bravely he
may have talked from time to time, like a man who preferred to let problems solve themselves. Unfortunately for
his future reputation, he was President in the age in which it
finally came home to most Americans that the problems of
the modern world are of a different order of nastiness and
urgency. It would have been enough for him to have pointed
them out with a harsh finger, as did Theodore Roosevelt in his
last two years, or to have chalked up a gallant failure in a
premature effort to solve one of them, as did Woodrow Wilson.
But the best he could do in the years in which we first reached
into space—and found the Russians there to greet us—was to
talk like a Coolidge of a balanced budget and a reduction in
taxes. If we find a new road to peace, if we make a mockery of

Khrushchev's promise to "bury" us, if we win new opportunity and respect for the Negro, if we get control of the population explosion, if we win something more than cheap glory in our explorations in space, it will not, alas, be thanks to him. He will be remembered, I fear, as the unadventurous President who held on one term too long in the new age of adventure. Like Washington, he was already a legend when he entered the White House, and it helped to make him the best Chief of State since our very first President. Unlike him, he gained no added luster from his service as President. I make bold to predict that the historians of a century hence, and the people who learn from them, will rank him outside the first eight, even outside the first ten of the Presidents who went before him. He was a good President, but far from a great one. If our descendants judge him finally to have been a truly great man, it will be the General rather than the President who has taken their fancy.

It may appear to some of my readers that I have been too hard on Eisenhower and too easy on Truman. To this indictment I return two pleas: First, I have tended to be more negative in the case of Eisenhower and more positive in the case of Truman because popular opinion appears to hold exactly the reverse of my predictions. And second, I have tried to anticipate the judgments of posterity with all the objectivity I can command. In so doing I have surprised even myself, and I trust that my readers will give me credit for having risen at least a few feet above my own political prejudices. I must come back in the end to take refuge in the simple truth that popularity in one age does not guarantee fame in another. The examples of Truman and Eisenhower may conspire to prove that the combative, unpopular President is the fellow with the head start to glory. I am left with the prickly suspicion that history, after all, is wiser than the people.

It would seem useful to conclude by drawing a few impersonal lessons from this exercise in personality. I propose, therefore, with only the barest comment, to list certain qualities that a man must have or cultivate if he is to be an effective modern President. In this instance I am more concerned with success than with greatness, with the needs of our contemporaries than with the judgments of our descendants. This is not a catalogue of every habit and talent we should hope for in our President. Like most Americans, I should be delighted if he would practice, faithfully but not self-righteously, all those virtues celebrated in the New Testament, *The Compleat Gentlemen, The Way to Wealth,* and the handbook of the Boy Scouts of America. It can go without my saying that we like our President to be brave, clean, kind, industrious, frugal, and honest. My list of stocks is short, but each item on it pays rich dividends:

Bounce: Not only must the President be healthy, in the sense of freedom from ailments; he must have that extra elasticity, given to few men, which makes it possible for him to thrive on the toughest diet of work and responsibility in the world. This quality, I would suppose, is to be found in full measure only in those Presidents who really enjoy themselves in the White House, who welcome the challenges of the office as delightedly as they do the privileges. Franklin Roosevelt learned at first hand about the importance of being bouncy. As a small boy he had stood before Grover Cleveland, who hoped out loud that he would never be so unfortunate as to grow up and become President. As a young man he had heard someone ask his cousin Theodore what kind of time he was having in the White House, whereupon the Colonel replied with a roar, "Ripping, simply ripping!" I leave it to my readers to decide what sound moral the second Roosevelt drew from this experience.

Affability: The President's heart must be not only stout but warm. He must care deeply about people in the flesh, show an unfeigned interest in everything from dogs to the Dodgers, be willing to live his private life publicly, and have the sure instincts of the democrat. The Presidency is a people's office, and there is no room in it now for a man with ice in his veins.

Political skill: We used to hear a lot of wailing about men who were "too high-minded ever to be nominated and elected" but who none the less "would make excellent Presidents." If this was ever true, it is true no longer. The man who lacks the little arts to be elected President lacks the little arts to be President. How can he persuade people to do "what they ought to do without persuasion" if he cannot persuade them first of all to give him the job?

Cunning: We do not openly admire this quality, and too much of it can destroy the most dedicated man. Yet a President cannot get the best out of the dozens of able figures around him or keep them under his command unless he is a master in the delicate art of manipulating men.

A sense of history: This cast of mind raises him above all those around him, sobering yet exalting him with the thought that he sits in Lincoln's seat. No man or combination of men can match his power to influence history, and his grasp of this stark truth can save him from going astray into the fields of petty strife. It can save him, too, when he must act arbitrarily, from the backlash of opinion. There is practically nothing a President may decide to do in a moment of crisis that Washington or Jackson or Lincoln, or often Harding and Coolidge, did not already do in a similar spot.

The newspaper habit: The modern President must be on guard lest he be cut off from harsh reality. He needs badly to know what people are thinking about events and about his handling of them. If he values his independence, he must have clear channels to the outside, and there is no substitute —certainly not a one-page digest of news and opinion prepared by his own secretaries—for a front page of the New York *Times* or the Chicago *Tribune,* an editorial in the St. Louis *Post-Dispatch* or the New York *Daily News,* a cartoon by Herblock or Fitzpatrick, a column by Alsop or Pearson, or a magisterial lecture on the Constitution by Lippmann or Krock. An occasional half-hour in the appendix of the *Congressional Record* is another experience no President should miss.

A sense of humor: If he reads the *Record* and the *Tribune* at all faithfully, he will need a thick skin and a light heart. At least two recent Presidents have testified convincingly that they could not have survived in office if they had been unable to laugh at the world and themselves. It is remarkable how many of our admitted failures in the Presidency were men who could not chuckle at an unfriendly cartoon, much less frame the original for hanging in the President's study—a happy practice engaged in by several of our admitted successes.

Any one of these habits or talents can be a snare to a President who turns to it too often and confidently, but so, too, can almost every virtue in the American catalogue. The most we can hope for is a man who blends self-confidence and self-restraint in the balanced attitude that all our successful Presidents have struck. In the end, perhaps, it is essential (if far from enough) for him simply to look the part. Woodrow Wilson took hold of a momentous truth when he remarked in awe: "The office is so much greater than any man could honestly imagine himself to be that the most he can do is look grave enough and self-possessed enough to seem to fill it."

CHAPTER

THE HIRING OF PRESIDENTS

★

The air of satisfaction with which most Americans gaze upon the Presidency turns suddenly chilly when they shift their attentions to the patched-up machinery for nominating and electing a man to fill it, even chillier when they look around and fail to find any machinery at all with which to replace a President who has lost the physical or mental capacity to govern. The problem of choosing an able President is one about which we have been disturbed almost without rest since the election of 1796; the problem of removing or sequestering a disabled President is one about which we have got heated up only occasionally, that is, on every occasion a President has appeared to be disabled. Popular unrest with the whole question of the selection and tenure of Presidents has reached a new peak in the years since World War II; almost every week of every session of Congress some member (as often as not a would-be President) rises to propose an amendment to the Constitution that would spare us the real or imagined horrors of a minority President or a sick President or no President at all.

In the next two chapters I intend to take serious note of this unrest, in particular to judge whether it is justified by the realities and probabilities of American politics. My opinion is that most of it is not, but I would not want to state such an opinion with conviction until I had reviewed the evidence. Let me therefore turn to consider four specific issues of selection and tenure that have been widely discussed, and in two instances acted upon, during the past fifteen years: in this chapter, nomination and election; in the next, disability, succession, and re-eligibility.

The framers of the Constitution, who were obsessed with the notion that all men are real or potential fools, devoted an unusual amount of thought to devising a foolproof system of filling the office of President with a man whose authority to govern would be recognized as legitimate. "The subject has greatly divided this House," James Wilson observed on the floor of the Convention. "It is in truth the most difficult of all on which we have to decide." Not until the framers had slogged their way through more than thirty votes did the Committee of Eleven come up with the general method finally laid out in Article II, Section 1, clauses 2-4 of the Constitution.

I would ask my readers to turn to Appendix II and study these clauses. They should pay particular attention to the federal character of the electoral process (for example, the unrestricted power of the state legislatures to determine the manner of choosing electors); to the total exclusion of national legislators and officeholders from participation in the activity of the electoral college; to the contingent role of the House of Representatives; and to the ingenious provision through which each elector was to vote for *two* men as President, "of whom one at least shall not be an inhabitant of the same State" as himself.

One reason for this double vote was to guarantee the presence of a first-class man in a second-class office, the Vice-Presidency; but far more important a consideration was the certainty that the electors would be forced to look beyond the boundaries of their own states to search for men with national reputations. The framers of the Constitution were genuinely concerned with the persistence of provincialism in the politics of the new republic. They assumed that the electors in each state, with or without the directions of the people, would almost always vote for a native son for President. The double vote, they thought, would be the one sure way in which to raise "continental characters" above the dull herd of native sons. I would ask my readers to bear this fact in mind as they study the original electoral system, and I would ask them to read into these clauses four other expectations shared by the most perceptive of the framers: that the electors, in Hamilton's straightforward words, would be "chosen by the people"; that, once assembled "in their respective States," they would exercise discretion but not independence in casting their double vote for President; that the whole process would operate in a decentralized and largely unorganized way; and that, as the chief result, many elections would be settled finally in the House of Representatives. In general, then, they meant to remove the entire process of electing the President, or at least a key stage, to a point outside the legislature, and to mingle in this process both the will of the people and the judgment of the gentry. And once they had made their intentions known, they began to think rather highly of them. Hamilton spoke for most of the framers in *The Federalist* when he "hesitate [d] not to affirm that if the manner" of electing the President "be not perfect, it is at least excellent."

So long as Washington was available for the Presidency, the original system operated well enough to justify Hamilton's confidence. But the retirement of the one truly continental character, the rise of the Federalist and Republican parties, and the establishment of the congressional caucus to nominate candidates for the Presidency all conspired to bring this system to an early demise. Perhaps the most serious blow to the sanguine hopes of the framers was the natural insistence of the electors on discriminating in their minds (as they could not in their ballots) between the man they really wanted to make President and the man they intended to be Vice-President. The result of all these new departures was the election of 1800, and the result of that fiasco (and of some shameless Federalist "politicking") was the

Twelfth Amendment, which I also invite my readers to study with care. I trust they will note the one major change it worked in the original plan of election: henceforth each elector would cast one vote for one man as President and a distinct vote for a second man as Vice-President.

More than 150 years have passed since the adoption of the Twelfth Amendment, and still it continues to govern our manner of choosing the President. But it operates within a context of national custom and state law that has converted the election into a process of decision-making far more centralized, direct, protracted, hot-blooded, and popular, one might even say *plebiscitary,* than the framers could have imagined in their most restless nightmares. Almost every major feature of this context of law and custom was in full operation in the fabled election of 1840 between Harrison and Van Buren. The question ignored by the framers—how to nominate candidates for consideration by the people and the electors—had been answered once and for all by the collapse of the congressional caucus and the emergence of the nominating conventions. The first such convention met in Baltimore in September 1831 to nominate William Wirt for President on the Anti-Masonic ticket, and the two major parties, who have never scrupled to steal our third parties blind, held their first nominating conventions before the passage of another year. The question answered gingerly by Hamilton—how to "appoint" the electors in each state—had been answered resoundingly by the rise of American democracy. Only South Carolina still held out against white manhood suffrage in the choice of electors in the election of 1840. The people had been moving toward the last step to a truly popular system of electing the President—the conversion of the electors into "mere agents" for registering the wishes of the voters— almost from the beginning, and the abandonment of the double vote in 1804 wiped out any lingering hope (or worry) that the electors would be anything more elevated than "mere agents" or "mouthpieces" or "puppets on a string." In 1796 an elector in Pennsylvania had ignored a pledge to vote for Adams and had voted instead for Jefferson. The complaint of a Federalist voter still rings through our political consciousness: "Do I choose Samuel Miles to determine for me whether John Adams or Thomas Jefferson is the fittest man for President of the United States? No, I choose him to act, not to think."

To these three extraconstitutional changes in the method of electing a President yet a fourth was added in these years of the upsurge of democracy: by 1840 every state except South Carolina had adopted the so-called "general-ticket" system of choosing electors or, more exactly, of casting the state's electoral vote. Under this arrangement the total electoral vote in each state went to the candidate with the highest popular vote. Once some of the states had adopted it, all of them had to, and since 1892 it has prevailed throughout the Union. The people and politicians even of Nevada and Alaska are apparently convinced that their influence in a presidential election is a good deal larger because they give all their electoral votes in one lump to one lucky candidate. As to New York and California, their larger-than-life importance in the calculation of those who nominate candidates and conduct their campaigns depends almost entirely on the maintenance of the general-ticket system. Finally, most of the paraphernalia of the nationwide popular election were on full display throughout the Union in the battle between "Old Tippecanoe" and "Van, Van, the used-up Man," and in some regions well before then. The appeal of each candidate for the Presidency was henceforth and forever to be directed to the people, and it was to be an appeal to their fears and fancies as much as to their powers of rational decision.

Our machinery for electing a President, which has been functioning virtually without change for a century and a quarter, operates today in five successive stages:

1) In the period from March to June of each presidential election year, delegates are chosen to the nominating conven-

tions of the two major parties. In roughly one-third of the states the voters of each party have a voice in this process, in two-thirds the delegates are chosen by party machinery.

2) In the period between mid-June and late July (or even as late as August if one of the parties is running a popular President for re-election) the nominating conventions meet to choose their candidates for President and Vice-President. So familiar is the sight and sound of these quadrennial extravaganzas to all Americans who own TV sets (perilously close to *all* Americans) that I hardly think it necessary to describe the events that take place. I will confine myself to the observation that they fill a yawning void in the electoral system designed for us by the framers and their immediate successors.

3) On the first Tuesday after the first Monday in November, a day fixed uniformly by law of Congress (November 8 in 1960, November 3 in 1964), the people of the United States go to the polls to vote—in fact and fancy for President and Vice-President, in law and Constitution for electors for these two offices. By midnight in San Francisco, if not hours before, they almost always know the results of their part in the election, which they correctly consider the only part that really counts.

4) On the first Monday after the second Wednesday in December, a day also fixed by law (December 19 in 1960, December 14 in 1964), the electors of the successful candidates in each state meet and cast their solemn and meaningless votes for the men to whom they have been pledged. For those who care about such details, I should point out that in some states the electors are chosen by party conventions, in others by party primaries, in still others by party organizations, and in hardheaded Pennsylvania by the party's candidate for President. In more than half the states the names of the electors never even appear on the ballot; in only two (California and Oregon) are they commanded directly by law to follow the custom of the country and honor their pledges to the people who chose them.

5) On January 6 of the following year, just two weeks before inauguration day, the Senate and House sit as one body to count the electoral votes of the states. A certification of the validity of each state's votes by its "executive" is declared by law to be "conclusive." Except in unusual circumstances, which need not concern us in a survey as general as this, Congress acts simply as a recording machine. When the count has been completed, the President of the Senate rises to announce the results, and then proclaims the winner "President-elect of the United States." A President of the Senate named John Adams was once put in the embarrassing position of proclaiming himself President-elect; being an Adams, he performed this task with courage if not with relish.

Twice in our history there has been one further stage to pass through before we could be certain of the identity of our rightful President. The ironic and almost tragic tie in 1800 between Jefferson and Burr and the failure in 1824 of either Jackson or John Quincy Adams to secure a majority of the electoral vote both set the contingent machinery of the Constitution into operation; and the House of Representatives was called upon to make the final choice. To bring the continued possibility of this contingency closer to home, many of my readers will remember the morning hours of November 3, 1948, when it appeared that neither Truman nor Dewey, thanks to Thurmond and Wallace, would achieve the necessary constitutional major- ity. If such had been the outcome of the popular election in November, the House of Representatives would have moved immediately after the inconclusive count of January 6, 1949, to ballot for President. In keeping with the straightforward command of the Constitution, the members of the House would have been restricted in their choice to the three leaders— Truman, Dewey, and Thurmond—and the vote of each state delegation would have been counted as one. Twenty-five would have been the magic number for election in 1949; it is, of course, twenty-six today.

This machinery operates within the climate of opinion and expectation known as the American way of life. At least three features of this climate, three notable characteristics of the American people, pervade and shape the whole process of electing a President.

First, we are a political people, and it is therefore a highly political process, one in which all our units of public decision— from the biggest party to the smallest interest group, from the broadest ethnic minority to the most exclusive clique in "the power elite"—play a lively part. The importance of the Presidency for the character and very existence of our parties is even greater than the importance of the parties for the support and control of the Presidency. Arthur Macmahon comes close to the truth of the matter when he remarks that the two great parties "may be described as loose alliances to win the stakes of power embodied in the Presidency." The one persistent purpose of their existence on a national scale is to elect a President.

Second, we are a rich people, and the bill for all the fun and frolic and hard labor of seating a President in the White House now runs into tens of millions of dollars. No man for whom other men are unwilling to spend vast sums of money has much right to think about nomination as candidate for President in the affluent society. If he is the kind of man who can and should be nominated, he will have little trouble gathering it together. In any case, at least one sizable stretch of the path to the White House is paved with greenbacks.

Third, we are a modern, industrialized people, citizens of a mass society, and we rely heavily on the instruments with which we communicate with one another—newspapers, periodicals, books, the mails, opinion polls, advertising media, radio, and above all television—to keep the machinery of election in purposeful motion. The election of the President is truly a mass experience; it is the one great national ritual in which all Americans, whether they vote or not, have no choice but to

join with shouts of glee or despair. The media of communication have helped mightily to make it such a ritual—like all
public rituals (like all men, for that matter) a fantastic blend
of the solemn and the silly. Yet, to tell the truth, the election
has been a mass experience since as far back as 1840, perhaps
even 1828. The paving of Madison Avenue and the triumph
of television added a new quality but not a new dimension to
the workings of the Twelfth Amendment.

Let me conclude this brief survey as dramatically as I can:
no power of the Presidency is more fateful and symbolic than
its power to force all thinking Americans to speculate constantly about the identity of the next man to occupy it. I go
most of the way with Professor Binkley, who wonders "how
else the electorate as a whole could be made so acutely aware
of the very existence of our national state," and all the way
with Walt Whitman, who wrote in *Democratic Vistas,* "I know
nothing grander, better exercise, better digestion, more positive proof of the past, the triumphant result of faith in human
kind, than a well-contested American national election." The
American people are rightly convinced that they have no more
solemn task to perform and gripping melodrama to enjoy than to
elect a President every four years. Hamilton engaged in one of
his keenest displays of prophecy when he foretold a time "when
every vital question of state will be merged in the question,
'Who will be the next President?' " That time has come, and
it is a time that has no stop. The next election for President
now begins the day the last election ends.

In the light of the significance, both rational and emotional,
we attach to placing the best of all Americans in the presidential
office, it is hardly surprising that we should feel so uneasy
about the machinery with which we are asked to do it. It is
complicated and costly, a weird design of bits and pieces put
together by countless hands, and no one starting out to construct a new method of election would dream of copying it.

Many years have passed since anyone has commented upon the electoral system with the smugness of Hamilton. Committee after committee, text after text, editorial after editorial have paraded before us the dangers and injustices of the system, especially those of the nominating conventions and the electoral college, and most Americans now assume that there is something terribly wrong with it.

The case against the nominating convention is almost too familiar to bear repeating. I doubt that I need rehearse the cultural sins of which it is accused by sensitive observers. It should be enough to remind ourselves that this windy, vulgar circus is met to nominate a candidate for the most powerful office on earth, and to wonder if there could be any gathering of men that seems less in character with its high purpose, that seems more unhappily to express what Henry James called "the triumph of the superficial and the apotheosis of the raw." The convention is certainly a gross distortion of that picture of intelligent men reasoning together which we carry in our heads as the image of free government. It was the sight of an American convention that led a famous European scholar (Ostrogorski) to observe, first, that "fifteen thousand people all attacked at once with Saint Vitus' dance" was not his idea of democracy; and, second, that God in His infinite wisdom watches benevolently over drunkards, little children, and the United States of America.

And yet the case against the convention as a cultural abomination is itself a distortion. It is, indeed, a barrage directed through clouded sights at the wrong target. For the plain truth is that most criticisms of this noisy, plebeian, commercial institution are really criticisms of the noisy, plebeian, commercial civilization within which it operates. We see our follies as a people in the follies of the convention, and unless we reform ourselves, which I know we will not and suspect we dare not do, the convention will continue to disturb the reasonable, shock the fastidious, and fascinate all of us. In any case, it is yet to be proved that men who act like deacons can make a better choice of candidates for the Presidency than men who act like clowns, and that—the kind of choice the convention makes—is the meaningful test of its value as an institution of American life.

The more technical charges against the nominating convention are that it is undemocratic, since it cuts the rank and file of the party out of the process of selecting a candidate; unreliable, since it ignores or distorts the real sentiment of the party in making the selection; and corrupt, since it puts a premium on the kind of horse trading in which men cannot expect to succeed unless they unlearn every rule of public and private morality. The convention, we are told, offers us a man we neither want nor deserve, and it offers him on a platter of corruption and cynicism. Those who make these charges usually go on to advocate some sort of nationwide presidential primary. The convention would become a pep rally to shout approval of the people's choice or, quite possibly, would be abolished altogether.

These charges, it seems to me, are a caricature of reality. The first and third might just as easily be leveled at Congress as at the nominating convention, while the second, which is most often and earnestly advanced, simply cannot stand up under the scrutiny of history. When in the twentieth century, except perhaps in the Republican convention of 1912, has a majority of the voters of either great party been handed a candidate it did not want? When, except in the nomination of Harding in 1920, did a convention pass over several first-rate men to choose an acknowledged second-rater? Quite to the contrary of accepted legend, the convention has done a remarkable job over the years in giving the voters of each party the man whom they, too, would have selected had they been faced with the necessity of making a responsible choice. The convention is anxious to satisfy, not frustrate, the hopes of the members of the party; if the latter give an unmistakable sound, the former will echo it gladly and faithfully. If they speak in a babble of voices, if they cannot agree on a clear choice, the convention will choose their man for them, even if it take a hundred ballots, and the choice, moreover, will be made finally with near or complete unanimity. One of the undeniable merits of the convention, as opposed to the primary, is that it heals most of the wounds that are inevitably laid open in the rough process of making so momentous a political decision.

There is something to be said, I suppose, for the efforts of Senator Douglas and his friends to encourage the growth of presidential-preference primaries. In more than one-third of the states of the Union the voters of each party are now given some chance to elect or instruct their delegation to the convention, and no one would argue that professional politicians should be protected against such expressions of the public mood or choice. Yet it would be a mistake to make these exercises in public opinion much more uniform in pattern or binding in effect than they are at present. Reformers should be careful not to upset the nice balance that history has struck between the hard responsibilities of the professionals at the convention and the vague wishes of the voters at home. The real question about our presidential primaries, it seems to me, is not whether they should take over completely the key role of the convention, which is an academic question at best, but whether they are worth all the fuss they cause in the minds of the public and all the strain they put upon even the most hard-shelled candidates. The active campaign for the Presidency becomes much too long drawn out a process; money becomes much too decisive a factor in the hopes and plans of any one candidate; some of the best candidates are torn between the responsibility of the important positions they already fill and the lure of the one after which they hunger and thirst. Under the system as it now operates, even the most popular candidates are hostages to whim and accident, especially to the whim of the "favorite sons" who sprout quadrenially and to the accident of the timetable of the primaries. The Democrats of New Hampshire, where the first primary is usually held, are all fine people, I am sure, but neither so fine nor so wise that they should be able to make or break a presidential aspirant all by themselves. I am inclined to agree with Adlai Stevenson, who speaks to the point with matchless authority, that the presidential primaries are a "very, very questionable method of selecting presidential candidates." Rather than have a handful of primaries spread carelessly over the months between February and July, it might be the wiser and even more democratic thing to have none at all. I for one would be happy to see our strongest candidates take the advice of the publisher of the *Adirondack Daily Enterprise,* James Loeb, Jr., and join in boycotting the present system entirely. It is, by almost any standard, one of the failures of our political system.

The convention, to the contrary, is a clear if not brilliant success. It meets the one test to which we like to put all our institutions: it does the job it is asked to do, and does it remarkably well. Indeed, one can be more positive than this in defense of the convention, for it performs several tasks that no other institution or arrangement can perform at all. Not only does it serve as the major unifying influence in political parties that are decentralized to the point of anarchy; it is, as Professor V. O. Key has written, "part and parcel of the magic by which men rule." And Americans, I again insist, are far from that enlightened condition in which political magic has lost its usefulness. The nominating convention fills a constitutional void; it unites and inspires each of the parties; it arouses interest in the grand plebiscite through which we choose our President. We will have to hear more convincing charges than have hitherto been pressed against the convention before we tamper with this venerable instrument of American democracy.

The case against the electoral system is much more impressive, so impressive indeed that it led two-thirds of the Senate in 1950 to propose an amendment to the Constitution, the Lodge-

Gossett amendment, abolishing the electoral college, retaining the electoral vote, and dividing it within each state in exact proportion to the percentages of the popular vote cast for candidates for the Presidency. Not satisfied with this compromise between the old federal republic and the new continental democracy, former Senator Lehman and friends would like to institute a national plebiscite, that is, to sweep away the whole machinery of the electoral college in favor of direct election by all eligible voters without regard to state boundaries. Former Representative Coudert, on the other hand, has stated the case for the district system, which was much used in the early years of the republic. Under this system each state would be divided into as many electoral districts as it has representatives in the House. The voters in each district would choose one elector; the voters in all the districts together would choose the two additional electors to which they are entitled by reason of their representation in the Senate.

All these men, whatever their particular panacea, unite in condemning the present system, concentrating most of their fire on those injustices and inconsistencies that arise out of the tyranny of the general ticket. And these are the criticisms in which they join most insistently:

1) The electoral vote distorts, often radically, the real sentiment of the country; a close election can have the appearance of a landslide.

2) Millions of votes go practically uncounted, and many Americans, at least in Vermont and Georgia, are doomed indefinitely to cast their presidential ballots in vain. As a result, many voters do not even bother to turn out.

3) The system, in the words of Lucius Wilmerding, one of its most effective critics, "puts a premium on accident." It is entirely possible for us to elect (indeed we have several times elected) a "minority President," a man who has not received even a plurality of the popular vote.

4) The parties are forced to concentrate much too heavily

and corruptly on the large and unsure states, and the system becomes an invitation to fraud. Moreover, minorities in these states swing political power out of all proportion to their size and importance.

5) The small states, even though overrepresented in the electoral count, are ignored as sources of presidential and even vice-presidential talent.

Harsh criticisms have also been aimed at other parts of the system. Some feel it potentially dangerous for the electors to retain, constitutionally and legally, their freedom of choice. Others argue that the House of Representatives, with each state delegation casting one vote, is about the last place in which a President should be chosen in the event that no one candidate secures an electoral majority. And we can all imagine the crisis that might develop if a President-elect were to die between the election in November and the casting of the electoral vote in December. There is no provision whatever, in Constitution or in law or in custom, for such a situation.

Distortion, injustice, apathy, accident, fraud, sectionalism— these are powerful arguments against our system of choosing the President, and yet the system, having survived the challenge of 1950, bids well to endure in unreconstructed glory for years to come. The case against either the Lodge-Gossett or Coudert proposals, which like the proposals themselves is now largely political in inspiration, has been stated with refreshing frankness on the floors of both houses. The decisive obstruction to reform is the general expectation that various minorities outside the South (in particular, labor unions and ethnic groups) would lose much of their present hold over both parties, especially over the Democrats, if the presidential vote were to be divided in proportion to the popular vote of each state. This explains why the chief sentiment for rewriting the Twelfth Amendment is now centered in the conservative South, the chief sentiment for holding fast in the progressive North. There can be no doubt that the one-party South, where the electoral margin for the victorious candidate would be not much less than it has been in most elections in the past, would gain in political power at the expense of the two-party North, where the margin in the large states would often be shaved as thin as a wafer. Men who already decry the disproportionate power of the South in Congress can hardly be expected to welcome such a shift in the power base of the Presidency. Many continue to advocate direct election of the President by the whole nation, but they couple their advocacy, as well they should, with a condition that has no hope of realization in the face of old history and new politics: that qualifications for the presidential suffrage be fixed by national law.

There is innate wisdom, if not always reasoned delicacy, in the stand of those who oppose drastic revision of the present system. One may take this stand for either or both of two solid reasons. The first is essentially conservative in mood and essence, for it is the argument of those who, recognizing that constitutional perfection is a cruel will-o'-the-wisp, would simply leave well enough alone. Such men, if I understand them rightly, are not unmindful of the defects of our electoral system. Yet they are sincerely convinced that a reformed system, from which all present dangers and injustices had been eliminated, would soon enough develop dangers and injustices of its own; some of these might be far nastier than any we are asked to suffer at present. They argue, further, that many of the dangers in the present system are hypothetical, many of the injustices not unjust at all. There is, for example, no indication that our political life has been hurt by distortions such as those registered in 1860 and 1936, and the American people should be given credit for ability to recognize an obvious distortion when they see one. There has been no convincing instance, certainly not in 1824 and 1876 and probably not even in 1888, in which a candidate was cheated out of the Presidency in spite of a clear plurality in the popular vote. A single elector might exercise his alleged freedom of choice, as James Russell Lowell was vainly implored to do in 1876, but the chances that it could make any difference are one in ten thousand. Only twice in more than 150 years has an elector clearly voted for someone other than the candidate to whom he was pledged—William Plumer of New Hampshire for John Quincy Adams instead of James Monroe in 1820, W. F. Turner of Alabama for Judge Walter B. Jones instead of Adlai Stevenson in 1956—and each instance was a show of harmless eccentricity. As to the point pressed vigorously by Senator Lodge—the way in which men from the small states are passed over abruptly as candidates for the Presidency—I doubt seriously that his scheme would change our political folkways. We turn to the large states for a dozen reasons, not least because they are far more likely than the small states to produce the kind of large-calibered men we need in the American Presidency.

And so it goes with the whole attack on the present system: men who are understandably unsettled by the fantasy of our machinery for electing a President are determined to replace it with one that is simple and rational, no matter what new and unsuspected problems they may raise in the process. Such men, say defenders of the present system, are digging into the foundations of the state—always a dangerous thing to do, but especially in a time of watchful waiting.

The second reason for opposing change is directed, at least in terms of current party politics, to liberal ends. The men who make it are frank to concede that the present electoral system is gerrymandered in favor of the urban vote, but this distortion, they assert, is a necessary counterbalance to the overrepresentation of rural interests in the House and Senate. The various proposals to eliminate the general ticket of electors in each state would upset the balance of representation in our total political system, and it would be even more difficult than at present for the forces of reform to come to grips with the problems of our industrial society. The Presidency, like Congress, would fall into the hands of the standpatters rather than the progressives in each party. Indeed, the character of the Presidency as a great democratic office might well be jeopardized were its constituency thus altered. These men are not so much concerned about the system of electing the President as about the kind of President it produces. An urban civilization, they argue forcefully, deserves at least one urban-oriented institution in the complex of effective power at the national level.

Each of these arguments has much to be said for it, and for the present at least we should be content to rest upon them and contemplate the electoral system with wry tolerance. I would certainly favor abolishing the electoral college. If the electors are puppets, they are useless; if they are free agents, as several Southern states have tried to make them, they are 175 years out of date. I see no reason why we should not take steps to plug the gap between November 8 and December 19. It is absurd for us to rely on the party of the successful candidate to choose a man in his place, even his running mate, if he were to die in these six weeks. This would put a strain on the "old pros" in the party, not to mention the semipros in the electoral college, that neither we nor they could be at all happy about. There is even less reason to go on ignoring the problems that might arise between December 19 and January 6. The Twentieth Amendment lists several rude possibilities in Sections 3 and 4, but Congress has thus far refused to accept its flat invitation to "provide" against them "by law." And the only reason I have ever heard raised against having the House and Senate meet jointly (with each member casting one vote) to decide inconclusive elections is that the small states would never permit it, which is not a reason at all but a sigh of despair.

There are several reasons, all of them convincing, why we should hesitate a long time before replacing a humpty-dumpty system that works with a neat one that may blow up in our faces. All the arguments for the system are practical; most of those against it are theoretical. Until we are sure that the Presidency itself will not suffer from a radical change in the method of election, we had best stand fast on tradition and pre-scription.

So much for the machinery, but what about the products? What kind of men does it give us to be President of the United States? The answer, as I tried to show in Chapters 3 and 5, is all manner of men—men of the twentieth century, for example, so different in belief and style and competence as Theodore Roosevelt and Calvin Coolidge, Herbert Hoover and Harry S Truman, Woodrow Wilson and Warren G. Harding, Franklin D. Roosevelt and Dwight D. Eisenhower. At the same time, we should not make too much of these differences, for these men also had important qualities in common. They all had to meet certain tests to which the American people like to subject candidates for the Presidency. Not all of these tests are polite or even reasonable; they are none the less a formidable part of our electoral system. The question they raise in my mind, and which I pose in conclusion to this chapter on nomination and election, is this: What kind of man is most likely to be nominated as a candidate for President of the United States? What kind of man can never hope to be nominated? To put the question another way, how large is the pool of men who are really eligible for the Presidency? I have already mentioned some of the qualities a man must have or cultivate if he is to be an effective modern President. Now I am concerned with the attributes he must have, many of which are impossible to cultivate, before he has a right to think of being President at all. I am no less concerned with those attributes—physical, political, ethnic, religious, cultural, social—that disqualify a man no matter how noble and talented he may be.

Let me put the answer to this question of who can and who cannot hope for the lightning to strike in the form of a list that may not seem very scientific but is loaded with hard fact. If my reading of American history and understanding of Ameri-

can mores is at all correct, then we may say of a man who
aspires to the Presidency:

He must be, according to the Constitution:
    at least 35 years old,
    a "natural born" citizen,
    "fourteen years a resident within the United States," what-
        ever that means.
He must be, according to unwritten law:
    a man,
    white,
    a Christian.
He almost certainly must be:
    a Northerner or Westerner,
    less than sixty-five years old,
    of Northern European stock,
    experienced in politics and public service,
    healthy.
He ought to be:
    from a state larger than Kentucky,
    more than forty-five years old,
    a family man,
    of British stock,
    a veteran,
    a Protestant,
    a lawyer,
    a state governor,
    a Mason, Legionnaire, or Rotarian—preferably all three,
    a small-town boy,
    a self-made man, especially if a Republican,
    experienced in international affairs,
    a cultural middle-brow who likes baseball, detective stories,
        fishing, pop concerts, picnics, and seascapes.
It really makes no difference whether he is:

a college graduate,

a small businessman,

a member of Congress,

a member of the Cabinet,

a defeated candidate for the Presidency, providing that he
emerged from his defeat the very image of the happy
warrior.

He ought not to be:

from a state smaller than Kentucky,

divorced,

a bachelor,

a Catholic,

a former Catholic,

a corporation president,

a twice-defeated candidate for the Presidency,

an intellectual, even if blooded in the political wars,

a professional soldier,

a professional politician,

conspicuously rich.

He almost certainly cannot be:

a Southerner (for more reasons than one, I am at a loss to
know whether Texas is in the South or West),

of Polish, Italian, or Slavic stock,

a union official,

an ordained minister.

He cannot be, according to unwritten law:

a Negro,

a Jew,

an Oriental,

a woman,

an atheist,

a freak.

He cannot be, according to the Constitution:

a former President with more than a term and one half of
service,

less than thirty-five years old,
a naturalized citizen,
an expatriate.

Several things should be noted about this list. First, I have purposely left out a number of intangibles—achievement, friendliness, moral repute, presence, eloquence, intelligence, moderation in views and tastes, rapport with the current mood of the country, willingness to serve faithfully (and, before that, to run hard), the look of a winner—that are obviously factors of decisive importance in transforming men who are merely "available" into serious contenders for nomination. What I have tried to list here are those self-evident qualifications and disqualifications which act almost automatically to dry up the pool of available men to probably not more than seventy-five to one hundred Americans, less than one out of every million adults.

Second, any rule in the fourth and sixth categories, if not exactly made to be broken, can certainly be broken with relative impunity by a man who scores high on the other self-evident tests of availability, especially if his intangibles are all in working order. Wendell Willkie was a corporation president, Adlai Stevenson was divorced, William Jennings Bryan was a twice-defeated candidate, Al Smith was a Catholic, and yet they were nominated by hardheaded men who hoped they would win. None of them did win, be it noted, and we are left with the almost certain feeling that each of them lost a sizable number of votes by reason of his particular disqualification. I need hardly point out that the pluses and minuses on this list apply even more forcefully to the two candidates for election than to the many candidates for nomination.

They do not apply quite so forcefully, however, to aspirants for the Vice-Presidency. No man born and living in the South has been nominated for the Presidency on a major party ticket since the Whigs came up with Zachary Taylor in 1848, but the nomination of John Sparkman of Alabama in 1952 is proof enough that the Democrats will give second place on their ticket to a man ineligible for first. So, too, will the Republicans, who could not have dared nominate a man as young as Richard Nixon for President in 1952, but who gave freshness to their ticket by putting him up for Vice-President.

I hasten to proclaim that I cannot guarantee the applicability of every item on this list, especially those in the middle categories, any longer than the next quarter-century. Although many of our common tastes and expectations (and, alas, our prejudices) are constant to the point of obduracy, many, too, are likely to change, as they have changed in the past, under the pressures of social progress and readjustment. If men of Italian or Polish descent are not eligible today, they may very well be in the year 2000. Catholics were certainly not eligible in 1900, but they have become more eligible with every new census of religious affiliation in the United States. Indeed, we may very well have reached the point at which a party, especially the Democratic party, would hurt itself more by refusing nomination to a Catholic otherwise fully available and qualified than by defying an ancient taboo that is slowly losing its force. Assuming that their qualifications are otherwise identical, however, a Protestant is still more likely than a Catholic to be nominated and elected President.

In conclusion, I would call attention to the special problem of each of our two great parties. It is an established fact, the kind of fact that tough-minded men take fully into account, that the Democrats are now the majority party and the Republicans the minority party in the American political system. What the Republican party enjoyed from 1896 to 1934 the Democratic party enjoys today: the allegiance at the polls, where allegiance pays off, of a clear majority of the voters of this country. Other things being equal, which they are perhaps more often than not, the Democrats should win every presidential election they contest. Their special problem, therefore, is to nominate a candidate who can bring the party's own voters to the polls. It is important to find a man who can appeal to the floaters in the center and to the deviants in the Republican party, but it is even more important to find one who can hold together the squabbling legions of this astounding coalition, who can please both the United Automobile Workers and the United Daughters of the Confederacy, the Irish of Boston and the Jews of Brooklyn, the professors and the professionals, the farmers and the factory-workers, the white supremacists of Georgia and the Negroes of Harlem. An unwritten law governs the proceedings of the Democratic national convention, commanding the delegates to nominate a candidate for President who is 1) a loyal son of the party, a warrior with scars, 2) not too closely identified with any of the major elements in the coalition, and 3) not openly hostile to any one of them. If anyone doubts the force of this law, let him try to account in any other way for the nomination of so reluctant a man as Adlai Stevenson in 1952. If Stevenson had been from Missouri, and had not been divorced, he would have been the almost perfect candidate of the modern Democratic party.

The trouble was, of course, that he ran head-on into the absolutely perfect candidate of the Republican party—and in a year, when, thanks to "Communism, Corruption, and Korea," all other things were far from equal. The special problem of the Republicans, needless to say, is to nominate a candidate who can bring the party's voters to the polls and, further, attract several million persons who normally vote Democratic or not at all. A man like Eisenhower was designed in heaven for just such a purpose, and I have always thought that there was something a little unreal about the savagery of the struggle between Eisenhower and Taft at the Chicago convention in 1952. Senator Taft, I am certain, would know what I mean when I say that if he had been as good a Democrat as he was a Republican, he would have been the candidate of "that other party" at least twice in his life. Unfortunately for him, he went down more than twice to what now seems a preordained defeat because his party was driven by the logic of its minority position to seek a candidate with more appeal for that bogey of all good Republicans, the "independent vote." So long as the tides of politics run as they are running today, the Republicans, like the Democrats from Buchanan to Roosevelt, choose suicide if they choose a party stalwart with no visible appeal beyond the ranks of the faithful. A man who aspires seriously to the Republican nomination for the Presidency must be (or appear to be) a "modern Republican."

These, if not the laws, are at least the axioms of presidential politics in the United States, and I do not expect to see them ignored with impunity for some years to come.

CHAPTER

THE FIRING, RETIRING, AND EXPIRING

OF PRESIDENTS

★

Once settled in office, a President can look forward confidently
to four years of power and service. If he chooses, and we choose,
too, his course can run eight years. We may refuse him re-
election, but his party is rarely in a position to refuse him
renomination. (Taft in 1912, Hoover in 1932, and Truman in
1948 all demonstrated the power of even the most whipsawed
President to insist on a second shot at the grand prize.) Beyond
eight years not even the most popular and dominant President
can now go—but of that I shall have more to say in a few
pages.

The prospect of a full term should fill a President with
confidence, but not with serenity. Nothing in life is that certain,
and every incumbent knows perfectly well that there are at
least four ways in which his tenure can be cut short. All of
them are openly contemplated in the Constitution.

The first is conviction by a vote of two-thirds of the Senators
"present" on impeachment by the House on charges of "treason,
bribery, or other high crimes and misdemeanors." I have
already said most of what needs to be said about "the extreme
medicine of the Constitution." I would call fresh attention only

to the point that impeachment is not a *political* process, an
inquest of office by the House and Senate acting as legislative
bodies, but a *judicial* process, a trial of the President for crimes
known to law in which the House acts as prosecutor, the Senate
as jury, and the Chief Justice as presiding judge. Despite what
I said in jest on page 53 about "the next President to be impeached," I do not think we are likely ever again to witness
such a trial.

The second is death, which comes to Presidents perhaps more
easily than it does to other men of their years. Many of our
political calculations—for example, our choices of candidates
for Vice-President—would be differently made if we were to
face the fact that seven of the twenty-nine elected Presidents,
just about one in four, have died in office. For those who care
about such details, this little table should prove interesting.

President who died	Date of death	Cause of death	Unexpired portion of term
William H. Harrison	April 4, 1841	pneumonia	3 years, 11 months
Zachary Taylor	July 9, 1850	cholera morbus (acute indiges- tion)	2 years, 7 months, 23 days
Abraham Lincoln	April 15, 1865	assassination (lingered 9 hours)	3 years, 10 months, 17 days
James A. Garfield	Sept. 19, 1881	assassination (lingered 80 days)	3 years, 5 months, 13 days
William McKinley	Sept. 14, 1901	assassination (lingered 8 days)	3 years, 5 months, 18 days
Warren G. Harding	Aug. 2, 1923	embolism (on top of bron- cho-pneumonia, on top of a gas- trointestinal at- tack)	1 year, 7 months, 2 days
Franklin D. Roosevelt	April 12, 1945	cerebral hemor- rhage	3 years, 9 months, 8 days

Those who think that our Constitution is all written provision and no unwritten precedent should take a good look at what happened upon the occasion of each of these deaths, for what happened on the first occasion and has been happening ever since is in clear if sensible disregard of the wording of Article II, Section 1, clause 6 of the Constitution (which was not, to be sure, its most precise admonition) and of the intentions of the framers (which are not, to be sure, binding upon us). Constitutional historians are in unanimous agreement that the framers intended the Vice-President to act as President but not to be President whenever the office should fall vacant. Yet, when the office did fall vacant for the first time, upon the death of Old Tippecanoe, his Vice-President, John Tyler, strengthened in resolution by the tough-minded support of Secretary of State Daniel Webster, took over the power, duties, emoluments, residence, status, *and* title of the President almost without opposition. Except for eight Senators, a handful of editors, and, as one might expect, crusty old John Quincy Adams, no one was disposed to challenge Tyler's description of the event as "my accession to the Presidency."

The next time the office fell vacant, upon the death of Zachary Taylor, this shaky precedent hardened into a rock against which no one has been disposed to butt his head from that day to this. The Cabinet dispatched official notice of Taylor's death to Vice-President Fillmore in a message addressed to "the President of the United States," and Fillmore took the oath of office as President the very next day before a joint session of Congress. Despite the introduction of a resolution in the House describing Andrew Johnson as "the officer now exercising the functions pertaining to the office of President of the United States," he was finally accorded the signal honor of being impeached as President.

The last four Vice-Presidents to succeed to the Presidency have done so without challenge or even question. One of these, Calvin Coolidge, took the oath of office as President of the

United States from his own father, a notary public in Plymouth, Vermont, and in his father's house. The story had every prop for which a sentimental nation could have asked, from an old man "standing like a ramrod" to an old kerosene lamp with "etched sides," but that did not stop Coolidge from quieting his own doubts about the legality of this ceremony by taking a second oath from a federal judge in Washington two weeks later. The judge was sworn to secrecy by the Attorney General, and the secret was kept until 1932, by which time the elder Coolidge was safely past all caring.

No President has ever chosen the third and only voluntary way out of office, resignation, although one, Woodrow Wilson, seems to have contemplated it seriously. (I assume that every President with a skin less than six inches thick contemplated it half-seriously at least once in his term of office.) Just before the election of 1916 Wilson wrote a letter to Secretary of State Lansing suggesting that, if he were to lose to Charles Evans Hughes, he would appoint Hughes to Lansing's position and then, along with Vice-President Marshall, whose advice in the matter had not been asked, resign abruptly. Under the succession law as then written, Hughes would have become acting President almost four months before his elected term was scheduled to begin, and thus, in Wilson's words, the country would be "relieved" of the "perils" of a President "without such moral backing from the nation as would be necessary to steady and control our relations with other governments." Unfortunately for this story if not for history, Wilson was re-elected, and we shall never know if he really meant it. Two days after the election of 1920 Williams Jennings Bryan called on Wilson publicly to appoint the victorious Harding as Secretary of State, and then do manfully what he had promised to do in 1916. Bryan's proposal was greeted with icy silence.

So, too, was Senator Fulbright's well-meaning but ill-considered call for Truman's resignation after the Republican victory in the congressional elections of 1946; so, too, were the calls, just as well-meaning and not much more carefully considered, for Eisenhower's resignation issued from time to time in his second term. I question the essential wisdom of all such appeals for a President's resignation, principally because they seem to ignore the solemn nature of the mandate he holds from the people. We elect our Presidents on the assumption that, barring death or disability, they will go the whole way. A President-by-election proceeding at three-quarters speed is still preferable to a President-by-succession going full blast. The Presidency is indeed a kind of "republican kingship" which a man would abdicate rather than resign if he were to throw it over. Be all that as it may, resignation is contemplated by the Constitution and provided for in a law of 1792. By "an instrument in writing" signed and then "delivered into the office of the Secretary of State," a President or Vice-President may consummate an intention to resign or, for that matter, may refuse to accept election. One Vice-President, John C. Calhoun, did resign with two months of his term still to run. The Senate called him back, and he answered eagerly.

The Constitution points to a fourth way out of the Presidency, whether for a short time or for good, in a passage that speaks cryptically of "inability to discharge the powers and duties of said office." The word "disability" is used later in the same clause and may be regarded as exactly interchangeable with this phrase. John Dickinson asked his colleagues on the floor of the Convention to tell him what was meant by "disability" and who should decide that it existed, but no one found it necessary or possible even to hazard a guess. We will never know what the framers had in mind. This is clearly an instance in which we must find our own way, something we have hitherto done with no success whatever.

There have been two occasions in the history of the United States on which a President was unquestionably in no condition for a considerable length of time "to discharge the powers and duties of said office." From the day Garfield was shot until the day he died, a period of more than eleven weeks, he was unable to put his mind to a single issue of importance for the country; his one official act was to sign an extradition paper. In the last few weeks his mind seems to have deteriorated along with his wounded body. From the day of Wilson's breakdown of September 25, 1919 (followed by a paralyzing stroke a few days later) until well into 1920, he, too, was at his best only a fragment of a President. Acts of Congress became law because of his failure to pass on them; he did not meet his Cabinet for eight months, nor did he learn for four months that it was meeting without him; requests for information by the Senate Committee on Foreign Relations went unanswered. Wilson's disability was, in an objective sense, more acute than Garfield's because the times called more loudly for a show of presidential leadership. His collapse took place during a nationwide tour designed to win friends and influence Senators in the history-making debate over the League of Nations.

There have been other occasions on which the Presidency was, in effect, a fully paralyzed office (if not institution)— the last few days of Harrison, Taylor, McKinley, and Harding, the last few hours of Lincoln and Franklin Roosevelt, and the first few hours or days after each of Eisenhower's three sudden illnesses—but all were self-resolving crises of short duration which, except perhaps for the instances in which Eisenhower was the stricken protagonist, no one wanted to complicate further by insisting upon a heavy-footed interpretation of the Constitution. To these should be added two potential cases of disability that tease the historian's imagination almost to distraction: the chaotic situations that would have arisen if either Madison or Lincoln, as was altogether possible, had been captured by enemy forces. Quite needless to add, except that we have a habit of ignoring it, is the plain truth that every day of his life every President has faced, like everyone else in the country, the chance that accident or disease would strike him helpless or even unconscious without striking him dead.

The problem of disability is, then, a real problem, real in history and even more real in the threat of demoralized chaos it constantly poses. Perhaps the single most pressing requirement of good government in the United States today is an uninterrupted exercise of the full authority of the Presidency. We need a man in the Presidency at all times who is capable of exercising this authority; we need one, moreover, whose claim to authority is undoubted. No man should be expected or permitted to wield the power of the Presidency without the clearest of titles to it. Whatever arguments may exist for the grand doctrine that all power must be first of all legitimate apply twice as severely to the power that is lodged in the American Presidency. For this reason, if for no other, the problem of disability in the Presidency presses hard upon us, and we have a right to expect our men of decision, which in this instance means the men who lead Congress, to do their statesmanlike best to provide the most workable solution of which American ingenuity and common sense are capable. We have done a lot of talking about this problem in the years since September 24, 1955, just as we did in the first years after July 2, 1881 and September 25, 1919, but thus far the only acting has been done by Dwight D. Eisenhower. Our continued failure to come to grips with it is not, I am sure, a product of carelessness or petty politics. It is, rather, our left-handed way of acknowledging how slippery a problem it really is.

The road to a workable solution must be built out of reasonable answers to four questions raised directly or obliquely, and answered not at all, in the Constitution.

1) What is "disability" in the Presidency?

2) Who decides that disability exists?

3) In the event of a clear-cut case of disability, what does the Vice-President assume—"the powers and duties of the said office" or the office itself? Is he acting President or President pure and simple?

4) If he is only acting President, that is to say, if the Presidency is recoverable, who decides that disability, in the words of the Constitution, has been "removed"?

After all the hearings and editorials and learned commentaries of the past few years, there is nothing new to be said on any of these questions. Let me sum up the present consensus on each (or where no consensus exists, the most important points of disagreement) and see if we can make a good start down the road to that "workable solution."

1) Most persons who have done any sound thinking at all on the subject would now agree with Professor Ruth Silva, who has done more sound thinking on it than all the members of Congress put together, that the words of the Constitution contemplate "any *de facto* inability, whatever the cause or the duration, if it occurs at a time when the urgency of public business requires executive action." Since the state of the President and the state of the Union must both be considered in any judgment of disability, it would be the height of folly to define disability any more precisely than this. A detailed law imagining all possible cases of disability would prove, as Emerson said of all "foolish legislation," a "rope of sand" that would "perish in the twisting." It might be pointed out in passing that, thanks respectively to Andrew Johnson and Woodrow Wilson, neither impeachment nor voluntary absence from the country falls within the definition of disability.

2) No one has ever doubted the President's right to decide and proclaim his own disability; few have doubted the Vice-President's duty—in a situation so obvious that even the inner circle at the White House would be anxious to give way—to initiate a determination of disability in the absence or even defiance of the President's express wish. But what of situations in which some doubt exists? What, in particular, of a Vice-President as reluctant as Vice-Presidents Arthur, Marshall, and Nixon all proved to be? How could he be persuaded to assume the powers of the Presidency? And how could we be persuaded

that his assumption was constitutionally and morally legitimate? The answer that appeals to most persons who have thought about it at all is: a decision of disability by an organ so legitimate in its own right, so laden with power and prestige, that the nation would be disposed to accept its judgment without hesitation. Congressmen, editors, lawyers, and professors of political science have had a field day trying to imagine the identity or composition of such an organ in the last few years, and their imaginations have stretched as far as all these possibilities:

The Vice-President alone, who would act according to his conscience and take his chances with Congress, the Supreme Court, public opinion, and history.

The Cabinet, whether a) with or b) without the consent of the Vice-President, and with the concurrence of a) an ordinary or b) an extraordinary majority of its members.

The Secretary of State, with the advice and consent of the Cabinet.

Congress, which would act by concurrent resolution a) on its own initiative, b) on application of the Cabinet, c) on application of the Vice-President, or d) on application of both. The vote in Congress would be a) by a simple majority in each house, b) by a two-thirds majority, or c) by a three-fourths majority. (If my readers are beginning to see spots before their eyes, so did I in reading through the hearings and debates on this subject in the seven Congresses that have discussed it seriously.)

The Supreme Court, acting a) in its capacity as a court or b) as a special tribunal, and by margins ranging from a simple majority to unanimity.

The governors of all or some of the fifty states.

A panel of leading physicians.

A panel of eminent private citizens, including all former Presidents of the United States.

Any one of the several dozen combinations that can be

constructed out of the officers and institutions listed above.

A special tribunal composed of great officers of state—for example, the Chief Justice, two senior Associate Justices, the Speaker of the House, the President pro tem of the Senate, the minority leaders in both houses, and the Secretaries of State, Treasury, and Defense. Some of those who propose such a privy council would make its decision binding; others would limit its role to giving advice to Congress or the Cabinet or the Vice-President, as the case might be. At least one learned publicist would reserve a place on this tribunal for the President's wife.

I do not wish to render this problem even more confusing than it must now appear, but it should be pointed out that there is a serious division of opinion between those experts (and who is not one in this matter?) who think it can be settled by statute and those who insist upon an amendment to the Constitution.

3) We have already noted that the framers of the Constitution never intended the Vice-President to become President except by election in his own right. If John Tyler and his associates had paid heed to these intentions (or, to be fair to Tyler, if the intentions had been proclaimed in unmistakable language), this third question would never have arisen. And if it had never arisen, the question of disability would not have been half so difficult to answer. Neither Arthur nor Marshall could have been persuaded to take over from his ailing President because too many men whose co-operation was needed were certain that such a transfer was irrevocable. A President who moved or was pushed aside, they argued, was no longer President at all; indeed, it was constitutionally impossible to have two Presidents at the same time, one acting and one mending on the shelf. For every one person who was certain that this was the meaning of the Constitution as it had developed through precedent, there were another ten who were at least in doubt. Under these circumstances of doubt, neither Arthur nor Marshall could have been permitted to take over. These doubts have been largely but not entirely laid to rest in recent years, and so long as a man, even a cranky

man, in a position as central as that of Speaker of the House expresses them, they will continue to plague all honest efforts to solve the problem of disability.

4) Although almost every method proposed for determining that disability exists has also been proposed for determining that it has come to an end, once again the chief responsibility is pinned on the President himself. His announcement that he was ready to reassume his powers would, in the nature of things political and constitutional, be conclusive. I am assuming, of course, that a deranged President would not be permitted to announce anything to anyone who would dare or care to "leak" it to the press. I could be wrong.

What then should be our solution to the problem of disability? Before I try to answer this question, let me record the circumstances and details of the only arrangement for a transfer of power that has ever been given formal expression. I speak, of course, of the Eisenhower-Nixon agreement, which was revealed in outline by the President February 26, 1958, and in detail (by popular demand) five days later. For months Mr. Eisenhower had been asking Congress to bring some order out of the confusion raised in all our minds by his three illnesses, and, then, despairing of legislative action, he decided to do the best he could simply as President. This he did by coming to a "clear understanding" with his Vice-President, which was announced to the nation in these words:

The President and the Vice-President have agreed that the following procedures are in accord with the purposes and provisions of Article 2, Section 1, of the Constitution, dealing with Presidential inability. They believe that these procedures, which are intended to apply to themselves only, are in no sense outside or contrary to the Constitution but are consistent with its present provisions and implement its clear intent.

(1) In the event of inability the President would—if possible— so inform the Vice-President, and the Vice-President would serve as Acting President, exercising the powers and duties of the Office until the inability had ended.

(2) In the event of an inability which would prevent the President from communicating with the Vice-President, the Vice-President, after such consultation as seems to him appropriate under the circumstances, would decide upon the devolution of the powers and duties of the Office and would serve as Acting President until the inability had ended.

(3) The President, in either event, would determine when the inability had ended and at that time would resume the full exercise of the powers and duties of the Office.

Speaker Rayburn and Mr. Truman raised objections to this arrangement that can be described only as "talmudic," and that made sense only as one more way for them to express their well-known contempt for Vice-President Nixon. Otherwise there was nothing but praise, warm or cool according to the political allegiance of the man who spoke it, for this simple and sensible arrangement. It remains to be seen whether Mr. Eisenhower has set a precedent for future Presidents, but at least he did all that he could have done to solve the problem for the duration of his own Presidency.

In my own opinion, we need something more than this arrangement, however compelling a precedent it may be for future Presidents, and something less than one of the grandiose schemes presented for our consideration in the past few years. I say "something more" because there are simply too many people of influence who remain in doubt about this question, "something less" because it would be either feckless or reckless to lay out an elaborate plan to solve a problem that in one sense is not much of a problem at all and in another is quite insoluble.

I would agree with those Congressmen and scholars who think that most of what we can reasonably hope to do can be done by a simple concurrent resolution of Congress. Such a resolution could end debate on at least five doubtful issues; the rest could properly be left to the men of good will and good sense we expect to govern us in the years to come. And these are the points it could make with conviction, principally because they express what has always been the most thoughtful opinion on the matter:

1) The President of the United States has the right to declare his own disability and to bestow his powers and duties upon the Vice-President or, in the event there is no Vice-President, upon the next officer in line of succession.

2) If the President is unable to declare his own disability, the Vice-President is to make this decision on his own initiative and responsibility.

3) In the event of disability, the Vice-President shall only act as President; his original oath as Vice-President shall be sufficient to give full legitimacy to his orders, proclamations, and other official actions.

4) The President may recover his powers and duties simply by informing the Vice-President that his disability no longer exists.

5) Disability, to repeat Professor Silva's words, means "any *de facto* inability, whatever the cause or the duration, if it occurs at a time when the urgency of public business requires executive action."

I am not a lawyer, and I would expect that these points could be made with a good deal more precision than I have given them. They are, in any case, the common sense of the matter, conformable alike to the intentions of the framers, to the assumptions of those who initiated the Twentieth and Twenty-second Amendments (which teem with men "acting as President"), and to the foreseeable needs of the nation. They add exactly nothing, in my opinion, to the situation as it now exists, and as it was so honestly put by President Eisenhower; but if a resolution incorporating them would help clear the air of doubt, let us by all means have it. And for the benefit of those who would still have doubts, let us at the same time move to declare these principles in an amendment to the Constitution.

Let us be careful to do no more than that. Let us not write a law that tries to provide for all the eventualities that might arise, lest we trap our descendants in a snare of technicalities. Let us not go beyond the President and Vice-President in search of machinery to decide doubtful cases of disability, lest we construct a monstrosity that raises more doubts than those it is supposed to settle. I see almost nothing to give us confidence, rather a great deal to give us pause, in the dozens of schemes that would drag Congress or the Cabinet or the Supreme Court or former Presidents into the picture. A judgment of presidential disability would be, in both great senses of the word, a *political* decision—a determination of high policy, and thus a task for men who can be held accountable to the country; a demonstration of "the art of the possible," and thus a task for men (the same men, I would think) who are permitted to practice their art under the most favorable circumstances. The men who count politically, whether in Congress or in the Cabinet, will have their say in any case, and I think we should leave it to them to decide how best to have it. The men who do not, among whom I would include all governors, physicians, private citizens, former Presidents, presidential spouses, and Justices of the Supreme Court, should speak only when spoken to— and, in the case of the Justices, not even then. It is comforting to learn that all members of the present Court are said to agree with this argument. They want no part of any of the schemes that would incorporate them, whether as Court or as individuals, into the machinery of decision in this delicate area.

As to the proposal of a special tribunal, a Presidential Disability Commission, the notion that it could lay our doubts to rest seems quite unsubstantial. The last thing we should do is to provide a method that resembles a trial, complete with expert witnesses and cross-examination. In circumstances that called for action it would use up too much time; in a crisis that called for unity it would open up needless wounds. The next to last thing is to provide a method that would make it too easy for a President to surrender his powers temporarily. We have labored for generations to preserve the unity of the Presidency, and I

for one would tremble to see us open the door even a little way
to pluralism in this great office. All suggestions that an indisposed President can, like an indisposed corporation executive
or union chief or general or even Secretary of State, hand over
his powers formally to his first deputy betray a lack of understanding of the qualitative difference between this office and
all others in or out of the government of the United States.
They ignore, too, the harsh fact of history that the Vice-President is very seldom the President's "first deputy," that he is as
likely as not to be someone who stands well outside the President's inner circle. This was certainly one of the difficulties of
Arthur's position, for he was a "Stalwart" who had been placed
on the ticket to heal the wounds opened by the nomination of
a "Half-Breed" (we would call him a Modern Republican)
like Garfield. Marshall, too, was an outsider whom the President
had never taken into his confidence. Worse than that, he was
Thomas R. Marshall and the President was Woodrow Wilson;
the contrast between their relative standings in the eyes of
Congress, the Cabinet, the American people, and the world
was so sharp that the notion of the one acting for the other
in any important way still seems ridiculous. Marshall might
have signed a few laws and made a few appointments, but he
could hardly have done anything to influence the debate over
the League of Nations. The one thing we could not expect
an acting President to do would be to commit his disabled
chief to a policy or bargain which the chief would never have
made himself.

I am led by all these considerations to repeat my observation
that in one sense, probably the most important sense, the problem of disability is quite insoluble. We may yet solve it legally
by framing an understanding in law and custom that leaves
no doubt about the terms on which power is to be transferred
from an ailing President to a healthy Vice-President; we can
even do away with the practical difficulties we have already met
in the Vice-President who is an outsider or the President who is

a giant, not to mention the President who is mentally alert but physically confined. A period of clearly established presidential disability will always be a messy situation, one in which caution or even timidity must mark the posture of the acting President.

A period of doubt, a time in which a Roosevelt declines or an Eisenhower recovers, will be even messier, and it is really no help at all to ask why a Truman or a Nixon should not take over in such a situation. The answer is that he *cannot,* that the Presidency is an office governed by none of the ordinary rules, that a wise custom of the American people commands us at all reasonable costs to guard the unity of the Presidency and the dignity of any man who holds it. This, in any case, is what has troubled the people, the professors, and the politicians over the past few years: not the memory of Garfield or the phantom of another Wilson, but the disturbing sight of the partial paralysis that stole over the White House during the confused days after each of Eisenhower's three illnesses. We had a right to be troubled, and at least one ingredient of our discomfort was the realization that we were caught up in a situation that had no easy solution, perhaps no solution at all except patience, prayer, and improvisation. To expect any neater solution than we got on each of those occasions is to ask something of our political institutions that they cannot give. Putting aside the plain fact that Eisenhower was not disabled except for a few hours or days, that not a single piece of routine business failed to get done, we might ask just what it was that Nixon could have done any better or would have done any differently during the weeks in which, on each of these occasions, the President was recovering. And the answer is: exactly nothing. As acting President he would have done just what he and the other members of the Eisenhower team did so well in so painful a pause: he would have kept the shop. Let us be entirely clear on this point: the only thing a Vice-President can do, so long as there is the slightest chance that the President will recover, is to keep the shop. All the machinery in the world cannot alter that fact, which is inherent in the status and functions of all great offices of state, and most especially in the unique case of the American Presidency.

I conclude by expressing my own modest hope that Congress will move in good time to enact a law expressing "the common sense of this matter" as I tried to describe it a few pages back. Armed with such a declaration, with our compelling instruments of publicity, and with the knowledge that decency and patriotism and political maturity still pervade the upper reaches of our government, we can face this problem with as much confidence as we can ever expect to muster in the face of chance. I would call special attention to those "instruments of publicity," for they have already gone far, in my opinion, to correct the unpleasant situation that arose in the illnesses of Garfield and Wilson. We have long since reached and passed the point of no return in our journey toward what I would call "the public Presidency." The American people now assume that nothing of this nature is to be kept from them, and they would expect and surely get daily, if necessary hourly, reports on the condition of a stricken President. The palace guard now exists to feed information, not to withhold it.

For those who entertain doubts on this score, I would recommend thoughtful study of the sharp contrast between the way things were done in Cleveland's day and the way they have been done in Eisenhower's. Grover Cleveland underwent an operation for cancer of the jaw in 1893, and the first credible news the nation had of it was in 1917, nine years after his death, twenty-four after the fact. Dwight D. Eisenhower had a heart attack in 1955, and the news, which was both credible and full, started to gush forth within a couple of hours. In less than forty-eight hours, with an explanation that it would be "good for the morale of the people," Dr. Paul Dudley White and James Hagerty were telling us all about the President's bowel movements. I mention this with no relish, because I think it was a show of vulgarity rendered even more vulgar by White's remark that "the country is so bowel-minded anyway," but simply to clinch my argument that henceforth and forever we will be informed directly of every bit of information on a stricken President's condition necessary for us to make our own judgment about his ability to bear the burden of his office. If we cannot have confidence in our ability to make such a judgment as men of sense and decency, then what in heaven's name can we have confidence in at all?

The problem of succession is in some ways stickier than the problem of disability. The Presidency is an office that can never, so to speak, be left empty for a moment; the authority of the man who wields its mighty powers must be recognized as constitutionally and morally legitimate by Congress, the courts, the people, and history. It is therefore imperative, especially under conditions of modern existence, that a line of succession be marked out clearly, that the line be extended downward through a number of persons, and that these persons be men of standing in the national community.

The framers of the Constitution handled this problem in characteristic fashion. They designated the Vice-President, whom they expected to be a man of genuine standing, as heir apparent, and then invited Congress to guard against the calamitous event of a double vacancy (or a vacancy combined with a disability, or even a double disability) by enacting a law "declaring what officer shall then act as President." Congress has responded to this invitation on three occasions—1792, 1886, and 1947— each time with a law that has pleased just about no one who studied it with a lawyer's care or a historian's imagination. Fortunately, we have thus far been spared the necessity of doing anything more than study these three laws for imperfections. In the course of 170-odd years we have lost seven Presidents and eight Vice-Presidents during their terms of office, which comes to a total of fifteen occasions when the heir apparent to the authority if not the office of the Presidency was marked out by law. But never yet, thanks, I suppose, to the same luck of which Ostrogorski spoke, have we lost both men whom we had elected to serve us for four years. This is no guarantee for the future.

There are two obvious pools of talent and prestige upon which the nation can be expected to draw for an acting President: the heads of the executive departments and the leadership in Congress. Those notable pools that spawn generals, Justices, and state governors are all, for one sound reason or another, a little too muddy to be tapped with confidence, and Congress has refused to look beyond the Cabinet and its own leadership for men to entrust with the powers of the Presidency in the event of a double vacancy.

Congress came up with its first shaky solution to the problem of succession in 1792; the solution, be it noted by those who like to make bloodless gods of the founding fathers, was a product of political animosity rather than of creative statesmanship. Instead of designating the Secretary of State as first in line after the Vice-President (the sensible solution, except that the Secretary of State was Thomas Jefferson), the conservative leadership in Congress picked on the President pro tempore of the Senate and, after him, the Speaker of the House. Neither of these officers was to be President, but was only to act the part. Further, if the double vacancy were to occur during the first two years and seven months of any given presidential term, the Secretary of State was to proceed "forthwith" to call a special election.

Despite many doubts about both the constitutionality and practicality of this law, Congress did not make a real attempt to improve upon it until 1886. Then, for motives so mixed that I beg to be excused from deciphering them, the two houses turned abruptly to the other great pool of talent and prestige, the President's own Cabinet. Henceforth, in the event of a double vacancy, the succession was to run down the line from Secretary of State to Secretary of the Interior. Upon such a child of fortune only the "powers and duties" of the Presidency were to devolve, but he was to hold them all the way to the next regular election. The provision for a special election in the law of 1792 was consigned to oblivion—and with it another clear but never clearly stated expectation of the framers of the Constitution.

Just before leaving for Potsdam in 1945, Harry S Truman asked Congress to reconsider the succession established in 1886. As an old legislative hand he had been strongly impressed by the argument that it would be more "democratic" to have an elected rather than an appointed official in line right after him. When this argument was first put forward for Truman's consideration, Edward R. Stettinius was Secretary of State, and the chance to replace him as crown prince with Sam Rayburn, Speaker of the House, was enough to get the wheels of Congress in motion. After James F. Byrnes had taken over from Stettinius, however, the wheels ground to a halt. The victory of the Republicans in the congressional elections of 1946 provided Mr. Truman with a matchless opportunity to act the statesman; this he did by once again asking Congress to recast the succession in favor of the Speaker, who had now been transformed by the alchemy of politics from a man named Sam Rayburn to a man named Joseph W. Martin. Congress responded with the law of 1947, which we are likely to carry on the books for some time to come, praying all the while that we shall never have to use it.

The Presidential Succession Act of 1947 draws primarily on the legislative pool, keeping the Cabinet in reserve for the most contingent of contingencies. It is a complicated piece of legislation, and I will limit this exposition of it to those provisions designed to produce an acting President in the event both the Presidency and Vice-Presidency have fallen vacant. In such an unhappy event, "the Speaker of the House of Representatives shall, upon his resignation as Speaker and as Representative in Congress, act as President." If there is no Speaker, or if "the Speaker fails to qualify as Acting President, then the President pro tempore of the Senate shall, upon his resignation as President pro tempore and as Senator, act as President." If there is no Speaker or no President pro tempore, or if neither is qualified (for example, neither is a natural-born citizen), the line of succession then runs down through the Cabinet to the first of its members "not under disability to discharge the powers and duties of the office of President," which is to say that he must be "eligible to the office of President under the Constitution," must hold his office "with the advice and consent of the Senate," and must not be under impeachment. Such a man would be an acting President twice over, for he would serve only until a Speaker or President pro tempore had qualified to take over. As in the law of 1886, no provision at all is made for a special election.

A number of substantial objections have been raised against this latest arrangement for the succession to the Presidency. For one thing, it is a quite unsettled question whether either the Speaker of the House or the President pro tempore of the Senate is an "officer" within the meaning of the Constitution. For another, as Professor Silva points out, the Succession Act of 1947 perversely requires the man upon whom the powers and duties of the Presidency devolve to resign the very office— the one he is already holding—to which these powers and duties are attached by law. Congress, that is to say, has power to attach the authority of the Presidency to an office, but not to decide what officer shall become President, which is exactly what it has done in the Act of 1947. Even if these are technicalities that we could overcome with a show of common sense, would it not be more sensible to return to the Act of 1886 and designate the Secretary of State as statutory heir apparent and to line up the other members of the Cabinet behind him? At least three reasons can be mustered in support of the contention that the Act of 1886 is superior to the Acts of 1792 and 1947: first, that we have several times been without a Speaker or President pro tempore; second, that the Secretary of State (or Treasury or Defense) would be more likely to provide continuity in the executive branch; and third, to be as realistic as possible, that more men of presidential stature have presided over the Department of State than over the House of Representatives. If the Speaker of the House is a more "democratic" choice than the Secretary of State, it is not by a very substantial margin, certainly not while most Speakers rise to the top by way of the "safe district," seniority, and faction.

The problem of succession as it has existed up until now is, all things considered, one over which we cannot be expected to lose much sleep. It is pleasant to speculate about alternative solutions, and I think we should debate the possibility of a special election in the event of a double vacancy during the first year and a half of a regular term. But here, too, I think we can trust to common sense and patriotism to carry us through a crisis which could never, by means of any conceivable solution, be made a happy time for the nation.

What I am concerned about is the problem of succession as it will exist from now on. If we are only poorly prepared for a double vacancy, we are not prepared at all for a multiple vacancy; and it is this kind of vacancy, so I am told by colleagues who deal in the laws of probability, that we are most likely to be faced with during the next hundred years and beyond. One well-aimed bomb, or at the most three or four, could leave us with no one to exercise the authority of the Presidency and, perhaps worse, with several persons to claim it —and all this at a moment in history when, as in April 1861, our future would rest in the capacity of the Presidency to provide autocratic leadership. How are we to provide against this ghastly contingency? By placing still other executive offices in the line of succession? By insisting that several men at the top live and work in other parts of the country? By dragging in the Governor of New York or the Commanding General of the Sixth Army? Or by trusting in Providence or, as some would prefer, providence? I leave this question to a posterity which, I pray, will never have to answer it. If we can hold off the great cataclysm, we need worry no more than we have worried in the past. If we cannot, if we are bombed in full force by the Soviet Union or China (or in time by Egypt or Ghana or Andorra), we may be past all worrying. How thoroughly smashed can a nation be and still remain a salvageable political entity? This may not be the place to raise such a question, but I raise it none the less.

The other problem of selection and tenure that has been acted upon formally in recent years has to do with the number of terms for which any one man can be elected to the Presidency. The framers of the Constitution gave the most serious consideration to limiting each President's tenure to one term or at most to two consecutive terms. In the end, they decided to make him re-eligible for election to any number of terms. Hamilton laid out all the rational arguments for indefinite re-eligibility in *The Federalist,* but one suspects that the real reason for the absence of any restriction in the Constitution was the strong hope that George Washington would be willing to serve as first President and the even stronger expectation that the people would want to keep him in command until the day he died.

If Washington was only indirectly responsible for the absence of all restrictions on re-eligibility in the Constitution, he was directly responsible for initiating the wholesome custom that made it possible for the American people to live calmly for more than 150 years with this "open door to dictatorship" and to shrug off all attempts (and there have been hundreds) to close it with the aid of a constitutional amendment. I refer, of course, to the two-term tradition, which he and the three other Virginia Presidents of the early days made a compelling if not compulsive precedent of our political system. More than one man in the long line of two-term Presidents between Washington and Franklin D. Roosevelt was tempted by his vanity, his ambition, or his train of friends, or by all three in concert,

to ask for a third helping of glory. More than one kept his
hand firmly on the great lever of political power by refusing to
back off from the possibility of a third term until the last
possible moment. But there was never much doubt in the
popular mind that this was an almost sacred tradition that
could never be suspended except in the most unusual circumstances.

We would still be sailing along calmly under the terms of
the casual arrangement in the Constitution had it not been for
the circumstances of 1940, the most unusual of which was the
emergence of the first President in history who was ready to
brave the storms of a violated tradition and seek a third term
in office. Franklin D. Roosevelt got his third term, and at least
part of a fourth term, too, and we got the Twenty-second
Amendment. History may yet judge it a fair bargain, and I
mean both the history written by his friends and the history
written by his foes.

Congress proposed the Twenty-second Amendment in 1947,
with not a single dissenting vote in the Republican majority in
either house, and it was ratified by the requisite number of state
legislatures in 1951. There can be no mistaking the intention
of its key passage:

No person shall be elected to the office of the President more
than twice, and no person who has held the office of President, or
acted as President, for more than two years of a term to which
some other person was elected President shall be elected to the
office of the President more than once.

This amendment is apparently designed, in contrast to com-
parable restrictions in state constitutions, to impose *permanent*
ineligibility for re-election on any person who has been President of the United States for six years.

The case for the Twenty-second Amendment was stated with
eloquence in both the House and Senate in 1947. Senator Revercomb of West Virginia went to "the real heart" of the matter

by insisting, in effect, that the longer any one man held on to the Presidency, the closer this country drew to "autocracy," to "the destruction of the real freedom of the people." A clever and ambitious President, Senator Wiley agreed, was in an ideal position to increase and perpetuate his authority: by dispensing the many favors in his possession to men willing to do his bidding, whether in the administration, the armed forces, the judiciary, or even in Congress; by buying the extra votes necessary to secure his repeated re-election; and by posing at all times as "the indispensable man" whom the people should support and Congress never thwart. David Lawrence has recently echoed the key argument of these men by describing the proposal to repeal the Twenty-second Amendment as the "dictatorship amendment." If a "dictatorship" were ever "to arise in America," he writes, it would probably "come out of the tremendous powers derived by a President from the right to continuous office." This fear of presidential dictatorship was and still remains the surface logic of the Twenty-second Amendment.

The case against the amendment was stated by men like Representatives Sabath and Kefauver and Senators Kilgore, Pepper, and Lucas. Although they fought in a losing cause, their appeal to history was forceful, and their cause has been slowly attracting new converts over the intervening years. President Eisenhower several times described the flat ban on a third term as "not wholly wise," although he reversed himself obliquely in 1959 by permitting Attorney General Rogers to advise Congress to "defer any legislative action in regard to the amendment to permit further experience thereunder"—in other words, to wait and see how it works over a sizable period of time. Former President Truman, with whom Speaker Rayburn agrees, puts the Twenty-second Amendment in a class with the Eighteenth. And such doughty characters as Senator Neuberger and Representatives Celler and Udall have offered resolutions designed to do away with it. The arguments of all these men, and of the political scientists who support them, are summed up in this indictment of the Twenty-second Amendment:

1) It bespeaks a shocking lack of faith in the common sense and good judgment of the people of the United States, who apparently cannot be trusted to decide for themselves when an extraordinary situation demands an extraordinary break with the customary pattern of politics.

2) As a corollary to the first point, it should be noted that this amendment was not, like the Twenty-first, submitted to ratifying conventions elected by the people. Suspecting that the voters who elected Roosevelt for two extra terms would resent this oblique rebuke, the Republican leaders in Congress went back to the old method of seeking ratification from the state legislatures, which were then worked over one by one while most people were looking the other way.

3) It puts a new element of rigidity in a Constitution whose flexibility has been one of our most precious possessions, and thus subjects future generations of Americans needlessly to "government from the grave."

4) Although we may have to wait many years to see this critical weakness reveal itself fully, sooner or later we will find ourselves trapped in a severe national emergency and be anxious to keep the incumbent President in office. Against our own will, and in submission to the will of men who acted hastily and vindictively far back in 1947, we will have to put aside the man to whom we would otherwise choose over-whelmingly to recommit our destiny. Then we will be sorry that we did not pay heed to the advice of Washington, who, in writing to Lafayette about this very matter, professed to see no sense at all "in precluding ourselves from the services of any man who on some emergency shall be deemed universally most capable of serving the public."

5) We already have evidence before our eyes that the second term of even the most popular President will henceforth be an especially unhappy time for executive leadership. No second-

term President except Jackson, not even Jefferson or the two Roosevelts, finished his eighth year as strong a leader as he had been in his seventh or sixth year or especially in his fourth, and his decline began the day when he admitted, or his friends and foes could assume, that he was not a candidate for re-election. As William Plumer, of New Hampshire, put it in 1806:

It seems now to be agreed that Mr. Jefferson is not to be a candidate at the next Presidential election. The disclosure of this fact, thus early, is an unnecessary and imprudent letting down of his importance. Most men seek the rising rather than the setting sun.

Now that every President's sun starts to set forever the day he begins his second term—to be less poetic, now that he is a "lame duck" a full four years before his certain demise—we must expect to see a steady deterioration in his capacity to persuade people "to do what they ought to do without persuasion." This is not a serene prospect for the second half of the twentieth century, years in which we will be in no position to afford the old luxury of having Presidents who have lost their political grip. We have dealt the modern Presidency a grievous blow by depriving the second-term President of that notable political weapon, his "availability," with which men as different as Coolidge and Truman, not to mention Jackson and Grant, kept their troops in line by keeping them guessing.

6) Finally, the Twenty-second Amendment disfigured the Constitution with words that still express the sharp anger of a moment of reaction rather than the studied wisdom of a generation. It was, indeed, although the fact may no longer be relevant, an undisguised slap at the memory of Franklin D. Roosevelt. No one can ever question the inalienable right of Americans to be critical of dead Presidents as well as of the living, but the Constitution is not the place to engage in a display of rancor. A concurrent resolution of Congress redirecting our attention to the rectitude of the two-term tradition would have accomplished the purpose just as well.

The fourth and fifth particulars in this bill of indictment are the essence of the case against the Twenty-second Amendment, and I am bound to say that I find them convincing. To the fourth there is no rebuttal except that there may never be so desperate a crisis combined with so badly needed a man, to which I can only reply grimly: Just wait and see. To the fifth there are two rebuttals, which arise out of different theories of the Presidency and are rarely joined together. The first is the argument that the President who cannot hope for re-election is uniquely situated to rise above politics and to act, as no President since Washington has acted, the noble role of "leader of all the people." As one hopeful citizen, Mr. William B. Goodman, of Flushing, New York, framed this argument in a letter to the New York *Times* just after President Eisenhower's re-election:

He has nothing to lose. He cannot be re-elected. He may reconsider foreign and domestic policies he could not politically afford to suggest were less than adequate during his first term. He no longer need consider what, for example, the Senatorial opposition in his own party can do to him. He can do more to them if he will organize Congressional support of his policies solely around agreement to them rather than to the membership in a party over which he has steadily decreasing control. His appeal to the people on issues need no longer carry the mark of party.

Thus to free the President from mere partisanship, while not the intent of the Twenty-second Amendment, may well be its result. Freeing the President for truly national leadership as it does, the amendment also makes him a lonelier figure—but his freedom is worth such isolation for the freedom of action it confers. He can maneuver, wheel, and fight, as no President has ever been able to before.

I confess that my own spirit rouses to the note of antique patriotism in this message, but I do not see how we can escape the blunt lesson of history that a President "free" from "mere partisanship" is a *roi fainéant,* a man commanded to "maneuver, wheel, and fight" with a blunted sword in hand. Any second-term President who tried seriously to abdicate his role as leader of his party would be worse than a lame duck: he would be a dead one. And as if that were not a cruel enough fate, some men might also consider him an ingrate or even a renegade. The party that elected him twice to the Presidency would have every right to expect him to "go all out" for the party's candidate in the next election. While the vision of the nonpartisan President will always beckon us, it is fated to remain no more than a vision.

The second rebuttal is simply that, if the hard choice must be made, it is more important to guard against the pretensions of a third-term President than to strengthen the hand of a second-term President. In point of fact, most of those who support the Twenty-second Amendment do not consider this a hard choice at all. If this amendment has served to weaken the Presidency, they argue, so much the better for the health of our democracy. The real logic of the Twenty-second Amendment is, then, that it helps to shift the balance of power in our government away from the executive and back toward the legislature, thus reversing a trend that had appeared irreversible by any ordinary exertion of the will of Congress. Senator Revercomb came near to expressing this inarticulate major premise when he said:

It may be argued that the Congress, the membership of which is elected from term to term, might well be sufficient assurance of safety against individual power in the Executive. I submit that the Congress cannot stop the growth of Executive powers which may be gained by an individual through long tenure in so powerful an office as that of President of the United States. There are immense innate powers in that office. They can be mushroomed fast or gradually grown until the strength of thorough despotism may be in the hands of one man, or a group of individuals, for that matter, to rule the people by his will and not by laws. If such a situation should be brought about it would be, in summary, the very destruction of government by free and independent people and a move toward the creation of dictatorship in fact.

And I submit that it was not the possibility of dictatorship but the reality of the strong Presidency, not the shadow of a third-term President but the substance of any President, that gave force to the successful drive for the Twenty-second Amendment. When all the arguments and rebuttals and prophesies of doom have been mustered by each side, the fact remains that those who take pride and comfort in the amendment are Whigs, men who fear the Presidency and put their final trust in Congress, and that those who propose to repeal it are Jacksonians, men who respect Congress but look for leadership to the Presidency. Since this whole book is a salute to the modern Presidency, I doubt that I need to explain any further why the Twenty-second Amendment should be stricken from the Constitution. (I doubt that it will be, but that is no reason to think it should not be.) I would be sorry to see it stricken, however, without a dramatic reaffirmation, by Congress and the President then in office, of the essential wisdom of the two-term tradition. Let it thereafter be left to the American people to decide whether, in the event of another 1940, this tradition should be honored in the observance or in the breach.

CHAPTER 8

THE FUTURE OF THE PRESIDENCY

★

We need no special gift of prophecy to predict a long and exciting future for the American Presidency. There are those who dream of a President in the image of Calvin Coolidge; there are those who fear that the Presidency will be sapped by "the assaults of ignorance and envy." Neither the dream nor the fear is likely to find much substance in coming events. All the great political and social forces that brought the Presidency to its present state of power and glory will continue to work in the future. Our economy and society will grow more rather than less interdependent, and we will turn to the President, anxiously if not always confidently, for help in solving the problems that fall thickly upon us. Our government will become more rather than less involved in the affairs of "mankind, from China to Peru," and the peoples of the world will look to its head for bold and imaginative leadership. Emergencies will grow nastier; Congress will become more unwieldy; politics will take on more and more the spirit of a vast town meeting. And one of the few things we can say for certain about the next war is that it will convert our form of government overnight into a temporary dictatorship of the President of the United States.

Another thing we can say for certain is that we have not seen our last great man in the White House. The people of the United States are no longer interested in presidential aspirants who promise only to be meek and mild. In the foreseeable future, as in the recent past, they will expect and get a full measure of presidential leadership. Even the Republicans, who have always been distinctly less enamored of the strong Presidency than have the Democrats, are coming to realize that the scales of power have tipped drastically and probably permanently toward the White House and away from Capitol Hill. There is a Presidency in our future, and it is the Presidency of Jackson and Lincoln rather than of Monroe and Buchanan, of Roosevelt and Truman rather than of Harding and Coolidge.

If any of my readers doubts the validity of this prediction, let him make a list of the gravest social problems we now face in this country, and then let him ask himself whether a single one of them is ever going to be solved to the satisfaction of the American people without a persistent and vigorous display of presidential leadership. My own list, for what it is worth, would begin with four—the crisis in race relations, the intolerable incidence of crime and delinquency, the lag in education, and the blight of our cities—and would end with the observation that the first step toward the solution of each of these and of many other problems must be the determination of the President to bring all his power and prestige to bear upon them. These problems call for state and local action, but such action now seems doomed to failure in the absence of co-ordination, stimulation, and even direction from the federal government. They call for bold legislation by Congress, but for a complex of historical, sectional, and political reasons Congress seems powerless to move forcefully against them. As a result, we have never been in more obvious need of presidential manipulation of all the techniques that are available to him to mold opinion, goad Congress, and inspire public officials at all levels.

Within the federal government itself the need for presidential leadership is no less pressing. We have talked ourselves dizzy in recent years about the steps we ought to take toward more effective co-ordination and supervision of the government's wide-ranging and costly activities in the rapidly expanding realm of science. I have no intention of aggravating this state of dizziness, but I would like to point out that a good deal of it would disappear quickly if all participants in this great conversation, especially the scientists themselves, were to recognize the paramount position the President must occupy in any reasonable solution. He is Commander in Chief, and fully eighty per cent of the four billions of dollars we now spend annually on scientific research and development is devoted to purposes of national security; he is Chief Executive, and science, like every other activity in the government, reduces in the end to questions of budgeting, reporting, and the choice and supervision of personnel; he is, above all, the President of the United States, and we have a national habit of sooner or later bringing our major problems to focus in the office of Washington, Lincoln, and Roosevelt. I do not know what the solution is to this complicated problem, or whether, indeed, there is any solution that can ever satisfy all the many constituencies that must be satisfied. I know only that the Presidency is the peg on which we will surely have to hang all co-ordination and supervision, not to mention inspiration and direction, of scientific endeavor under the auspices of the federal government. And I know, too, that Eisenhower's appointment of James A. Killian, Jr., in November 1957 to the post of Special Assistant to the President for Science and Technology was only a first timid step toward the kind of bold solution—perhaps a new unit in the Executive Office, perhaps a Department of Science, perhaps a tightly reined group of interdepartmental committees—to which we must surely come in time. My own preference would be for a combination of the first and third of these loudly voiced proposals, not least because it would acknowledge the President's central position and draw authority directly from his prestige. If we have to have a "czar of science" in Washington in the years ahead, the only candidate I can imagine our swallowing would be the President himself.

I trust that no one will interpret this last remark as a plea for central direction of our scientific effort from the White House. The President already has far too many other eggs to watch without asking him to take immediate command of the race into space or the search for new sources of energy or the attempt to control the weather; and, in any case, that is not the way we get great things accomplished in our society. But I would still insist that whatever hope we have for a more alert, rational, economical management of the human and financial resources our government contributes to research and technology depends to a large degree on the capacity of the Presidency to co-ordinate the kind of activity in which dozens of federal agencies must necessarily be involved. I am not nominating the President for the role of Chief Scientist; neither he nor science nor the American cause would profit from such a development. I am merely expressing what seems to be the common sense of the matter: that every President from now on must give considerable time and thought to the serious problem of how to make the government of the United States a benevolent force in our advance into the wonders of the future, and that he must serve consciously as the center of gravity around which the scientific endeavors of the federal government revolve in a multitude of orbits. Science demands a pattern of pluralism, inside as well as outside our government, but pluralism is anarchy without a common point of reference. For the National Science Foundation, the Atomic Energy Commission, the National Aeronautics and Space Administration, the Advanced Research Projects Agency, and all other major agencies and committees that we may in time create, this point of reference can only be the President of the United States.

Since the Presidency of the future will grow out of the Presidency of the present, it is imperative to go one step farther with this appraisal. The total picture of the office drawn in this book has been perhaps more cheerful than it should be. In attempting to point up sharply the elements of strength and reliability in the Presidency, I have passed too lightly over problems and weaknesses to which some of our most useful public servants and astute political scientists have addressed themselves with fervor and ingenuity. Let me now turn to examine the most pressing of these. This is not, be it noted, an appraisal of the American system of government, even less of American society. I must assume that we have the society we deserve; I do assume that it would be neither possible nor sensible to alter the main outlines of our government. I propose to concentrate on the Presidency as it is and might be constituted, and to call attention to those defects, real or alleged, about which men of good will and good sense are most earnestly agitated. I will also have something to say about the wisdom and feasibility of current proposals to eliminate these defects.

To the worst of these, the patched-up machinery for electing an able President and the missing machinery for relieving a disabled one, I have already devoted most of two full chapters. I have nothing to add except one fearless prediction: Barring a calamity that frightens us half out of our wits, nothing will be done about them for years to come, if ever.

A third major defect that men find in the Presidency is the intolerable burden laid upon him who holds it. I am not talking here about the great functions of state he discharges in our behalf, for I cannot imagine how a single one of these could be transferred safely and effectively to some other officer in the national government. It would be a constitutional disaster if the President were even to attempt to surrender his final responsibility in the areas of war, peace, politics, opinion, ceremony, and management. I am talking, rather, of the routine of these functions: of the mechanical tasks he is required to perform by law and custom; of the briefings, appointments, speeches, conferences, and appearances; of the letters he must answer and signatures he must affix. Much has been done in recent years to relieve him of his petty burdens without relieving him of his great responsibilities, and we can be grateful to Franklin Roosevelt and his successors for having taken the lead in improving their own lot. Yet much, too, remains to be done. We should expect future Presidents, Congresses, and Executive Offices to co-operate in guarding the Presidency against the paralysis of detail. Considerable authority is already in the President's hands. For example, in 1950 Congress enacted a brief provision permitting the President to delegate functions vested in him by statute, and it is comforting to learn that Mr. Eisenhower used this authority to rid himself of hundreds of petty duties we had no business laying upon the President in the first place. We may be sure that every President from this time forward will press the search for functions to delegate to his chief lieutenants.

In seeking to lighten the President's burden, we would do well to recall the warning of Woodrow Wilson: "Men of ordinary physique and discretion cannot be Presidents and live, if the strain be not somehow relieved. We shall be obliged always to be picking our chief magistrates from among wise and prudent athletes—a small class." At the same time, we should also recall that a long list of routine tasks, each of which appears "nonessential" when viewed by itself, may well add up to an inspired performance of a great function of state. The President cannot be a successful Chief of State if he turns all the little ceremonies and visits over to the Vice-President. He cannot lead Congress if he is unwilling to spend hours listening to Congressmen. And he cannot be a vigorous Commander in Chief unless he studies the defense budget item by item. For him as for all of us there is no final escape from hard and pedestrian labor. And as the gentlemen of Congress warned in the law of 1950 I have just mentioned: "Nothing contained herein shall relieve the President of his responsibility" for the acts of those "designated by him to perform [his] functions." As Mr. Truman would say, the President may pass the details but not the buck.

The Executive Office itself presents a number of problems, although it, too, is a huge improvement over the haphazard machinery on which our Presidents had to rely before 1939. For one thing, the President still lacks complete control over the organization of this machinery; he should be completely free to establish, regroup, or eliminate the components of the Executive Office on his own order, and to experiment with the internal structure of each component. For another, there has never been a satisfactory arrangement within the Executive Office to assist him in handling his numerous duties as chief personnel officer of the national government. And for a third, he still lacks adequate assistance, in the form of a single staff agency or perhaps of several agencies, in co-ordinating the many elements in his total program.

The real problem of the Executive Office is potential rather than actual: the danger that the President might be buried under his own machinery. The institutionalization of the Presidency could be carried so far that the man who occupies it would become a prisoner in his own house, a victim of too much and too rigid organization. I doubt very much that such a situation could last for long if it did develop. Andrew Jackson proved once and for all the capacity of a determined President to burst the bonds of restrictive custom and legislation and to beat a retreat to the plain words of Article II. Yet rather than make it necessary for another Jackson to blow across Washington like a "tropical tornado," we should be alert to steps that might weaken or smother the President's position of dominance over his own auxiliaries. Much depends, of course, on his intimate advisers. It is their unrelenting duty to protect the President against all but the most essential problems in their designated areas, to present these in such form that they can be readily mastered, and especially to preserve the President's freedom of choice among competing alternatives. Needless to say, the President himself must set the tone for the operations of the Executive Office. He must insist that he be spared routine but not thought and decision, for he is, after all, the responsible head of government. He must be careful not to rely too heavily on the briefings and opinions of his own staff, for he will soon find himself out of touch with harsh reality. Above all, he must leave channels open to the political and social pressures that excite imagination and breed sensitivity. Unfriendly visitors, hostile newspapers, and free-swinging press conferences are three such channels he must have the insight and bravery not to block off. The Presidency must not become so highly mechanized that the President himself is spared the "suffering and glory of democratic leadership."

The Executive Office never will or should take on a permanent pattern of organization. Each President must feel free to tinker with it; no part of it, not even the Bureau of the Budget, should be considered too sacred to touch. The President, like the Red Queen, must run as fast as he can to stay in the same place. He must make a half-dozen adjustments in the course of his incumbency simply to keep pace with the rising tempo of his duties. The need in this vital area is for change and experiment, for an Executive Office that is not so much a perfect design as a plastic mosaic of formal and informal arrangements. There is, however, an outer limit beyond which it would be unwise to expand the Executive Office. It must be big enough to make it possible for the President to supervise the administration, but not so big that he has trouble supervising it. It must have enough officers and agencies and committees to make it possible for him to make up his mind, but not so many that his mind is made up for him. In the White House itself, as in the administration that sprawls all around it, we have quite possibly reached the limit of "government by committee."

The Cabinet has been a problem for at least a generation— in George Graham's words, "a bleeding and anemic patient." Only tough custom and past glory have kept it from sliding noiselessly into oblivion. It is no longer a body upon which the President can rely for sage advice on great issues of state; it is not even, in its formal composition, a gathering of his most important and intimate associates. It is at best a relic of a simpler past when department heads were thought to be men of broad interests and held in their own hands the whole power of administration.

Mr. Eisenhower, to be sure, did his best to restore the Cabinet to full duty. He invited such key officials as the Director of the Budget and the Chairman of the Civil Service Commission to attend regularly. He went ahead to institute what other Presidents had only talked about vaguely: a formal Cabinet secretariat to organize its work, keep the necessary records, and follow through on decisions. In addition to setting up a subcabinet to support the Cabinet itself, he continued the practice of authorizing Cabinet-level committees to deal with special problems, which in his incumbency ranged all the way from the co-ordination of foreign-aid activities to a drive on narcotics. He even reminded us of the existence of the Cabinet by staging one of its sessions on television, although the chief result of this exercise in the "soft sell" was to dramatize the unimportance of a council whose proceedings could be tuned in (and tuned out) by an entire nation. Eisenhower followed Truman in the practice of using the National Security Council (which has *not* appeared on television) as a functional cabinet in matters of military and foreign policy, leaving the Cabinet to devote itself narrowly to domestic, administrative, and political affairs. A group that takes no real part in making and co-ordinating policy in the area of national survival can hardly be considered a great council of state in the image of the Cabinets of our past.

It remains to be seen whether any efforts to revive the Cabinet prove successful. Eisenhower bucked an ebb tide that has been running for a long time, and it is just possible that his successors could ride this tide to a happier solution. The President needs conciliar advice, in national as in international affairs; he needs agencies to co-ordinate executive policy, in the government at large as in the White House. Yet it is clear that the Cabinet cannot serve these two high purposes as well as other groups and agencies that exist already or could be set up without too much difficulty. What would probably serve the President best is a series of functional cabinets and Cabinet-level committees, each with a secretariat of its own and each recognizing him or his deputy as chairman. The Cabinet itself, which has been around too long to be allowed to disappear entirely, might well be doubled in size and raised to the status of a privy council. It would meet only at moments of solemn decision; it would be a dignified holding company for the several subcabinets to which pertinent members of the parent body would belong. Though I tread here in fields of fancy, I think it altogether possible that the Cabinet's future lies in this direction.

Perhaps the softest spot of all in the general health of the Presidency lies in the gap between responsibility and authority, between promise and performance, in the area of public administration. The President, as I pointed out in Chapter 1, is held primarily responsible for the ethics, loyalty, efficiency, frugality, and responsiveness to the public's wishes of the two million and more Americans in the national administration. He is the Chief Executive, the general manager of the business of government, the one officer designated by the Constitution to "take care that the laws be faithfully executed." Yet his authority over the administration is in no way equal to his responsibility for its performance. Many executive functions are placed by statute beyond his reach in the independent commissions; many are carried on by bureaus and offices upon which time, tenure, and politics have bestowed an autonomy he challenges at his peril. Committees of Congress, themselves practically independent of their parent bodies, maintain more intimate relations with many agencies than those enjoyed by the President and his department heads. His own subordinates are often vested by statute with direct authority to conduct important programs; at the same time, they are granted appropriations in such detailed form that neither they nor the President can administer them with the necessary freedom of maneuver. Almost everywhere the President turns to supervise and discipline, he is trapped in the toils of pluralism, tradition, politics, professionalism, and inertia.

Here, too, improvements have been wrought in recent years, although it is always a question whether these have kept pace with the careening growth of the administration. The most essential of these improvements, of course, was the incorporation of the Bureau of the Budget in the Executive Office, for without its help in both fiscal and administrative affairs the Presidency would long since have sunk without a trace. And here, too, much remains to be done, as the first Hoover Commission reminded the nation forcefully. Most of those who have lived with the problem and gone home to write about it agree that the President would benefit most as Chief Executive from these steps, no one of them easy to take:

The President should be granted full and permanent statutory power, subject to congressional disapproval within a specified time, to reorganize the internal structure of the executive branch, and then he should use this power to straighten out the lines of control throughout the administration.

Congress should help him to reduce the pockets of obstinate independence for whose existence there are not even convincing political reasons, and together they should work to cut down the number of officials whom the President is expected to supervise directly.

Congress should resist the urge to insert in the laws needlessly detailed instructions to those designated to execute them.

The President himself should experiment with groups and procedures designed to co-ordinate policy throughout the administration.

An entirely new study should be made of the independent regulatory commissions, and steps should then be taken to bring their strictly executive functions more clearly into the President's area of responsibility. To integrate the commissions completely in the executive branch would be, I think, to pile one gross mistake on top of another, but much can be done to give more purposeful direction to our celebrated "headless fourth branch of government."

The whole system of personnel administration in the national government should be overhauled. On one hand, a reformed Civil Service Commission should be located within the Executive Office; on the other, the actual selection and management of personnel should be largely decentralized to department and commission heads.

We must not be misled by counsels of perfection in this confused area; we must not expect too much of the man who is supposed to supervise it. Inertia and tradition are found in all human organizations, and as often as not they serve some good purpose. There will always be conflict of purpose between the administrator with his professional knowledge and the politician with his constituency. In the very nature of things political and administrative, many tasks of government have to be performed with little or no opportunity for the application of over-all management. The "perfect pyramid" of administration is more a delusion than a panacea; rivalry and friction have virtues of their own. As long as power is both divided and shared by Congress and President, the former must be expected to take an active role in overseeing administration, and the role, as we know, can be played usefully as well as actively. The most essential point of all is to remember that the President has responsibilities that range far beyond his formless duty "to produce a good administration," and that many of these are impossible to delegate and disastrous to ignore. He has other and more important roles to play, and if he works too hard, if he succeeds too auspiciously, as Chief Executive, this is a certain sign that he is neglecting his high duties as Chief Diplomat or Commander in Chief.

It may well be time to readjust our thinking about the President's responsibility and authority as Chief Executive. If we cannot level the latter up, perhaps we should level the former down. We should not hold him to such strict account, as we still do in the country at large, for every blunder and fraud throughout the administration. He can never surrender constitutionally, nor should he surrender effectively, the final duty to oversee the execution of the laws. But we should ask no more of him than that he set a high personal example of integrity and industry, choose able men to administer the nation's business, delegate his administrative powers broadly and support his deputies faithfully, give a clear political lead that can be transmitted downward through his chief lieutenants, and act magisterially to punish glaring breaches of decorum and democracy. Perhaps we should be more tolerant of our President, at least in his capacity as Chief Executive.

Since the opening day of Washington's administration the President's relations with Congress have been a target of criticism; the target is still being shot at with enthusiasm and at least passing accuracy. Much of this criticism is irrelevant, since it ignores the blunt truth that we long ago made our irrevocable choice of co-ordinate rather than unified government. Much is soft-headed, since it refuses to rise above the political and personal frictions that are the mark, but not the only mark, of such government. Yet much hits the target squarely, and I think we should take notice of two major areas in which the hope of improvement must never be abandoned.

In the first place, the President's leadership of Congress remains spotty and discontinuous. Although he is acknowledged widely to be the Leader of Legislation, his tools of persuasion, except his own machinery for drafting, clearing, and forwarding legislative proposals, are not one bit sharper than they were forty years ago. Here, too, as in the field of administration, there is a widening gap between what the people expect and what he can produce. He must have a program and push for its enactment, but he has no way to force a decision upon a reluctant Congress.

There have been a dozen or more proposals, some modest and others extravagant, to stabilize the President's leadership and increase his influence in Congress. Senator Kefauver has taken up Representative Pendleton's ancient plan for a question-and-answer period for department heads on the floor of either house. Professor Corwin predicts great gains for harmony if the President would choose part of his Cabinet from leading members of Congress. The La Follette–Monroney Committee of 1946 recommended a joint council of congressional leaders and Cabinet officers who would presumably work together in making and executing national policy. Some political scientists talk fondly of "responsible party government"; others put their trust in elaborate schemes for parallel organization of each major department or agency and its related committee in Congress. All these proposals are well-intentioned, and one, the establishment of an executive-legislative council by joint resolution, might be worth a try. Most, however, are not nearly so clever or feasible as they may seem at first glance, and several might have results far different from those predicted. In particular, it is not impossible that the President's leadership, which we have labored long to fix in custom, would suffer grave damage.

Is there nothing, then, that we can do to achieve a more stable relationship between the two great political branches? Nothing, I would answer, that ignores these facts, some of which I have already stated: First, superficial remedies will not cure, and may only quicken, the nervous tension between President and Congress that is endemic to our system. Second, stronger remedies, such as those proposals of a parliamentary system we have heard from Professor W. Y. Elliott and Thomas

K. Finletter and David Lawrence, are just not called for in the present situation, nor would the patients submit to them in any situation. Third, we cannot have the best of both possible worlds, the rugged safeguards of our own system and the sweet harmonies of the British. To mix the metaphor hopelessly, there is no such thing as a happy mongrel that combines the good points of both parents. And finally, the affliction of dissension and irresponsibility arises from much deeper causes in our system than the arrangements of the Constitution. Those who insist that the affliction is a disease, and also think they can cure it, must go beyond government to reform politics and beyond politics to reform society—which is another way of saying that they should take the sage's advice to "relax and enjoy the inevitable."

In the last reckoning, we will continue to make progress toward firmer and friendlier executive-legislative relations by traveling the familiar path hacked out by the successful Presidents of this century. By following this path, even when it wandered through the swamps of petty politics, we have moved to a point at which co-operation under the President's guidance is far more certain that it was before 1900. Term by term, crisis by crisis, men in and out of Congress have been educated to accept the necessity of presidential leadership, and the Presidents have gone through a cumulative learning process of their own. This process of education in statesmanship must be carried on indefinitely, for in prescriptive growth, not in clever "gimmicks," lies our best hope for the co-operation we have a right to expect.

Most political observers are now more concerned with the other side of the two-way street between President and Congress. While he is busy asserting leadership in making laws, Congress is busy asserting control over their execution, and there is evidence to support the charge that Congress has roamed farther out of bounds than the President in the past few years. It is, to be sure, an axiom of co-ordinate govern-

ment that the independent legislature must exercise oversight
of the administration. Congress, too, must be concerned with
ethics, loyalty, efficiency, frugality, and responsiveness in the
public service; it must judge for itself whether the laws are
being faithfully executed. No one can argue that it has any
less constitutional right than the President to stake its claim
to the disputed territory between them. But it does not have
the right, probably not constitutionally and certainly not morally,
to take over effective control of any part of the executive branch.
It may inquire, expose, encourage, and warn, but it may not
direct; and this—straight-out direction of various agencies and
officers—is what Congress has been doing too much of in recent
years. The result has been disorder, dissension, indecision, and
disruption of morale at key points in the public service. Needless to say, Congress as a whole is guilty only of nonfeasance.
It is the members of Congress, operating as committees, sub-
committees, or lone wolves, who have poked their inquiring
noses beyond the limits of political decorum and constitutional
practice.

Concern over improper congressional meddling in the business of the executive reached a peak of indignation in the heady
days when Senator McCarthy was asserting with implausible
gall his right of espionage in the executive branch. It did seem
for a while as if he and his friends might do permanent damage
to those vague but visible lines drawn by custom between President and Congress. The decline of the Senator, matched and
hastened by the rise of the President, did much to restore the
old condition of equilibrium in this delicate area. There are
even those who feel that the lines were made more visible by
Mr. Eisenhower's ordeal, or, rather, by the ordeal of those whom
he seemed unwilling to protect; many members of Congress are
now said to be more aware of the limits beyond which they
cannot go in their search for misconduct in the administration.
Surely we are all much clearer in our minds about the responsibility of the President and his chief lieutenants to keep Congress

out of the executive sphere. It would be pleasant to think that each of the houses would have enough sense and bravery to hold its marauders in check, but while we await the Golden Age of congressional self-discipline, we must put our trust in the truth that power alone can check power. It is up to the President, exercising his rightful power, to hold the lines of constitutional sanity against those who would break through them in reckless quest of notoriety or sincere inquest of wrong-doing. He must defend his own authority while conceding that of Congress.

He has the best chance of doing this, it seems to me, by applying prudently this tested rule: The head of a department or agency, who has the power to give orders to his subordinates, must in turn stand ready to answer for the manner of their execution. The pertinent corollary is this: The head has the right and duty to interpose his authority, as best he can, between the investigator and the subordinate and give the necessary answers himself to congressional committees. In terms of recent experience, it was not a question of Senator McCarthy's right to ask "who promoted Major Peress," which we must concede with a grimace; it was a question of who should give the answer—the responsible head and his chief deputies, or a procession of bewildered and belabored subordinates. The responsible head, not a marauding Senator, must command the loyalty of the men for whose performance he is constitutionally and legally accountable. There are limits, of course, both political and practical, to the authority of a top administrator to control, defend, and speak for the public servants under his direction. Yet not until this wise old rule is established in our constitutional thinking will peace (as much peace as we can expect under our system) reign on this side of the street between President and Congress.

It may be thought irrelevant to call attention to the defects of Congress, but it is generally conceded that a strengthening of the national legislature in terms of its own internal structure would do much to improve working relations with the President. He has nothing to fear, to the contrary, he has much to gain, from the adoption of most proposals for reform that have been pressed on Congress by some of its best friends. Congress as a whole presents no improper threat to his legitimate control over the operations of the administration. Small groups and freewheeling individuals strike illicit bargains, plant co-operative friends, and ask indecent questions; small groups and freewheeling individuals hamstring the power of legislative decision and bring Congress into disrepute. Any step, therefore, that would lead to tighter organization, to a situation in which the houses could exercise some discipline over their outlaws and control over their obstructionists, would be a blessing alike to President and Congress. Any step toward efficiency, for example, a reduction in the number of committees, could not fail to give the President satisfaction. He has no stake in an inefficient and overburdened Congress. He has a sizable stake, as do all of us, in the reform of Congress.

There is one final defect in the relations of President and Congress of which we should take careful note, especially since its correction would strengthen the President's control over the administration as well as his influence in Congress. I refer to his lack of any power to veto separate items in the overstuffed appropriations bills presented for his approval. The President often feels compelled to sign bills that are full of dubious grants and subsidies rather than risk a breakdown in the work of whole departments. While it salves his conscience and cools his anger to announce publicly that he would veto these if he could, most Congressmen have learned to pay no attention to his protests. The champions of the "item veto," who point out that forty governors have a power denied to the President, insist that nothing but great good would come from giving it to him, whether through a constitutional amendment or, failing that, a self-denying ordinance of Congress. On one hand, his leadership of Congress would be strengthened, for he would hold an efficient new weapon, one that works out in the open, for reminding Congressmen that economy in the national interest is just as important as spending in the local interest. On the other, his' work as Chief Executive would run more smoothly, since he would at last have full authority to match his responsibility for the executive budget. No agency of the government would be spending new money on a project of which he had the courage to disapprove sharply.

The loudest argument that has been raised against the item veto is that it might strengthen the President's hand just a little too much in his dealings with Congress. It would open the door to presidential pressure on individual Congressmen, and thus to bargains of the hardest kind. There is much to be said for this argument, and we might well pause before amending the Constitution to grant this new power to the President. But there is no reason why Congress itself should not experiment with an occasional appropriations bill that authorizes the President to eliminate or reduce specific items subject to congressional reversal by concurrent resolution within a specified number of days. We have the assurance of several prominent constitutionalists that such a device would violate neither the letter nor the spirit of the Constitution. If Congress could once give this power outright to the governors of several territories, it can certainly give it now under wraps to the President of the United States. If we learn through these experiments that the power is one he ought to have, and is unlikely to abuse, we could then catch up with the Confederate States of America by writing it into the Constitution. We should hesitate much longer to grant him power to veto items in ordinary bills. Although the practice of attaching "riders" may often set our teeth on edge, Congress, too, needs weapons for the perpetual struggle, and we have no right to expect it to surrender this ancient blunderbuss.

★

Many Americans, not all of them Miniver Cheevys, would insist that I have thus far passed over with intent or in ignorance the gravest defect in the Presidency: the high concentration of power that rests in the President's hands, the startling expansion of this power over the past generation, the frustrations that face Congress in the attempt to regain its share and thereby to "restore the balance of the Constitution." This was not my intent, nor am I ignorant of this charge and the supporting evidence. No one who pays even passing attention to American politics can fail to know the full particulars of the case against the strong Presidency and the proposed steps to restore the old balance. Senator Taft's challenge to Truman's initial action in Korea, Representative Coudert's attempt to limit Eisenhower's power to station troops in Europe by "rider," Senator Bricker's campaign to reduce any President's power to negotiate treaties and agreements with other nations, Judge Pine's restatement of the Whig or "errand-boy" theory of the Presidency in the District Court decision in the Steel Seizure case, Senator McCarthy's riotous assault on the first principles of the Constitution—all these are straws, or whole bales of hay, in a wind that beats relentlessly on the White House. Challenges arise in every Congress to the scope if not the existence of the President's power to adjust tariffs, issue ordinances, make appointments, and influence the passage of legislation. And in persuading the country to adopt the Twenty-second Amendment, the opponents of the strong Presidency struck a mighty blow for their cause.

Their cause, I am bound to say, is ill-considered and ill-starred. It is ill-considered because any major reduction now in the powers of the President would leave us naked to our enemies, to the invisible forces of boom and bust at home and to the visible forces of unrest and aggression abroad. In a country over which industrialism has swept in great waves, in a world where active diplomacy is the minimum price of survival, it is not alone power but a vacuum of power that men must fear.

It is ill-starred because the Whigs, who may win skirmishes

and even an occasional battle, cannot win a war against American history. The strong Presidency is the product of events that cannot be undone and of forces that continue to roll. We have made our decisions for the New Economy and the New Internationalism, and in making them we have made this kind of Presidency a requisite for the effective conduct of our constitutional system. No government can exercise the supervision that ours does over the economy at home or honor the bargains that ours has made abroad unless it has a strong, unified, energetic executive to lead it.

I do not mean to say—I have not meant to say throughout this book—that "strength" in the Presidency is to be equated with "goodness" and "greatness." A strong President is a bad President, a curse upon the land, unless his means are constitutional and his ends democratic, unless he acts in ways that are fair, dignified, and familiar, and pursues policies to which a "persistent and undoubted" majority of the people has given support. We honor the great Presidents of the past, not for their strength, but for the fact that they used it wisely to build a better America. And in honoring them we recognize that their kind of Presidency is one of our chief bulwarks against decline and chaos.

In point of fact, the struggle over the powers of the Presidency, fierce though it may seem, is only a secondary campaign in a political war, now pretty well decided, over the future of America. Few men get heated up over the Presidency alone. Their arguments over its powers are really arguments over the American way of life and the direction in which it is moving. The strong Presidency is an instrument and symbol of the 1960's; the weak Presidency is an instrument and symbol of the 1920's. Those who truly yearn to "go home again," like John T. Flynn and Clarence Manion and the Daughters of the American Revolution, are right in thinking that a reduction in the powers of the Presidency would be an excellent first step to the rear, although it would be only a first step. It should be clearly understood that an attack on the Presidency like the Bricker amendment is aimed beyond the Constitution at America's position in the world. The backers of this amendment may be greatly worried about the potential dangers of "presidential autocracy," but they are even more worried about the present consequences of the New Internationalism. Conversely, many voices that are raised for an even stronger Presidency are really raised for an even bigger government with even more control of society.

We should not look with equanimity on the Presidency and its huge arsenal of authority. We should be careful about giving the President additional powers, alert to abuses of those he already holds, cognizant that the present balance of the Constitution is not a cause for unlimited self-congratulation. But we can look on it with at least as much equanimity—each of us according to his own blend of blood, bile, phlegm, and melancholy—as we do upon the present state of the Union. For the strength of the Presidency is a measure of the strength of the America in which we now live. Those who reject this America and are alarmed by the course we are taking reject the strong Presidency angrily. Those who accept this America and do not fear the one that is coming accept the strong Presidency soberly.

As I look back through this book, I detect a deep note of satisfaction, although hardly of complacency, with the American Presidency as it stands today. A steady theme seems to have run all through this final review of its weaknesses and problems, a theme entitled (with apologies to the genius of Thurber) "Leave Your Presidency Alone!" This feeling of satisfaction springs, I am frank to admit, from a political outlook more concerned with the world as it is than as it is said to have been by reactionaries and is promised to be by radicals. Since this outlook is now shared by a staggering majority of Americans, I feel that I am expressing something more than a personal opinion. If we accept the facts of life in the 1960's, as we must, and if we shun the false counsels of perfection, as we do, then we are bound to conclude that we are richly blessed with a choice instrument of constitutional democracy. Judged in the light of memory and desire, the Presidency is in a state of sturdy health, and that is why we should not give way easily to despair over the defects men of too much zeal or too little courage claim to discover in it. Some of these are not defects at all; some are chronic in our system of government; some could be cured only by opening the way to others far more malign.

This does not mean that we should stand pat with the Presidency. Rather, we should confine ourselves to small readjustments—I have noted a dozen or more that might be worth a try—and leave the usual avenues open to prescriptive change. We should abolish the electoral college but leave the electoral system to pursue its illogical but hitherto effective way. We should plan carefully for mobilization in the event of war but take care that the inherent emergency power of the President— the power used by Lincoln to blockade the South, by Wilson to arm the merchantmen, and by Roosevelt to bring off the Destroyer Deal—be left intact and untrammeled. We should experiment with a joint executive-legislative council and the item veto but be on our guard against the urge to alter radically the pattern of competitive coexistence between Congress and President. We should give the President all the aides he can use but beware the deceptively simple solution of a second and even third Vice-President for executive purposes. And we should tinker modestly with the President's machinery but wake from the false dream of perfect harmony in high places, especially in the highest place of all. For if the Presidency could speak, it would say with Whitman:

> Do I contradict myself?
> Very well then I contradict myself.
> (I am large, I contain multitudes.)

"Leave Your Presidency Alone": that is the message of this chapter, and I trust I have made clear in all these chapters why I transmit it so confidently. To put the final case for the American Presidency as forcefully as possible, let me point once again to its essential qualities:

It strikes a felicitous balance between power and limitations. In a world in which power is the price of freedom, the Presidency, as Professor Merriam and his colleagues wrote in 1937, "stands across the path of those who mistakenly assert that democracy must fail because it can neither decide promptly nor act vigorously." In a world in which power has been abused on a tragic scale, it presents a heartening lesson in the uses of constitutionalism. To repeat the moral of Chapter 2, the power of the Presidency moves as a mighty host only *with* the grain of liberty and morality. The quest of constitutional government is for the right balance of authority and restraint, and Americans may take some pride in the balance they have built into the Presidency.

It provides a steady focus of leadership: of administration, Congress, and people. In a constitutional system compounded of diversity and antagonism, the Presidency looms up as the countervailing force of unity and harmony. In a society ridden by centrifugal forces, it is, as Sidney Hyman has written, the "common reference point for social effort." The relentless progress of this continental republic has made the Presidency our one truly national political institution. There are those who would reserve this role to Congress, but as the least aggressive of our Presidents, Calvin Coolidge, once testified, "It is because in their hours of timidity the Congress becomes subservient to the importunities of organized minorities that the President comes more and more to stand as the champion of the rights of the whole country." The more Congress becomes, in Burke's phrase, "a confused and scuffling bustle of local agency," the more the Presidency must become a clear beacon of national purpose.

It is a priceless symbol of our continuity and destiny as a people. Few nations have solved so simply and yet grandly the problem of finding and maintaining an office of state that embodies their majesty and reflects their character. Only the Constitution overshadows the Presidency as an object of popular reverence, and the Constitution does not walk about smiling and shaking hands. "The simple fact is," a distinguished, disgruntled Briton wrote at the end of the "Royal Soap Opera" of 1955, "that the United States Presidency today is a far more dignified institution than the British monarchy." In all honesty and tact we must quickly demur, but we can be well satisfied with our "republican king."

It has been tested sternly in the crucible of time. Our obsession with youth leads us to forget too easily how long our chief instruments of government have been operating in unbroken career. The Presidency is now the most venerable executive among all the large nations of the earth, and if one looks back beyond 1787 to "times of ancient glory and renown," he will find that the formula has worked before. "The truth is," Henry Jones Ford wrote with grace and insight,

that in the presidential office, as it has been constituted since Jackson's time, American democracy has revived the oldest political institution of the race, the elective kingship. It is all there: the precognition of the notables and the tumultuous choice of the freemen, only conformed to modern conditions. That the people have been able . . . to make good a principle which no other people have been able to reconcile with the safety of the state, indicates the highest degree of constitutional morality yet attained by any race.

It is, finally, an office of freedom. The Presidency is a standing reproach to those petty doctrinaires who insist that executive power is inherently undemocratic; for, to the exact contrary, it has been more responsive to the needs and dreams of giant democracy than any other office or institution in the whole mosaic of American life. It is no less a reproach to those easy generalizers who think that Lord Acton had the very last word on the corrupting effects of power; for, again to the contrary, his doctrine finds small confirmation in the history of the Presidency. The vast power of this office has not been "poison," as Henry Adams wrote in scorn; rather, it has elevated often and corrupted never, chiefly because those who held it recognized the true source of the power and were ennobled by the knowledge.

The American people, who are, after all, the best judges of the means by which their democracy is to be achieved, have made the Presidency their peculiar instrument. As they ready themselves for the pilgrimage ahead, they can take comfort and pride in the thought that it is also their peculiar treasure.

Appendix I

THE PRESIDENTS OF

THE UNITED STATES

	Date of Inauguration	Age at Inauguration	State of Residence	Politics	Date of Death
George Washington	1789	57	Va.	Fed.	1799
John Adams	1797	61	Mass.	Fed.	1826
Thomas Jefferson	1801	57	Va.	Dem.-Rep.	1826
James Madison	1809	57	Va.	Dem.-Rep.	1836
James Monroe	1817	58	Va.	Dem.-Rep.	1831
John Q. Adams	1825	57	Mass.	Dem.-Rep.	1848
Andrew Jackson	1829	61	Tenn.	Dem.	1845
Martin Van Buren	1837	54	N. Y.	Dem.	1862
William H. Harrison	1841	68	Ohio	Whig	1841
John Tyler	1841	51	Va.	Whig	1862
James K. Polk	1845	49	Tenn.	Dem.	1849
Zachary Taylor	1849	64	La.	Whig	1850
Millard Fillmore	1850	50	N. Y.	Whig	1874
Franklin Pierce	1853	48	N. H.	Dem.	1869
James Buchanan	1857	65	Pa.	Dem.	1868
Abraham Lincoln	1861	52	Ill.	Rep.	1865
Andrew Johnson	1865	56	Tenn.	Dem. (Union)	1875
Ulysses S. Grant	1869	46	Ill.	Rep.	1885
Rutherford B. Hayes	1877	54	Ohio	Rep.	1893
James A. Garfield	1881	49	Ohio	Rep.	1881
Chester A. Arthur	1881	50	N. Y.	Rep.	1886
Grover Cleveland	1885	47	N. Y.	Dem.	1908
Benjamin Harrison	1889	55	Ohio	Rep.	1901
Grover Cleveland	1893	55	N. Y.	Dem.	1908
William McKinley	1897	54	Ohio	Rep.	1901
Theodore Roosevelt	1901	42	N. Y.	Rep.	1919
William H. Taft	1909	51	Ohio	Rep.	1930
Woodrow Wilson	1913	56	N. J.	Dem.	1924
Warren G. Harding	1921	55	Ohio	Rep.	1923
Calvin Coolidge	1923	51	Mass.	Rep.	1933
Herbert Hoover	1929	54	Cal.	Rep.	—
Franklin D. Roosevelt	1933	51	N. Y.	Dem.	1945
Harry S Truman	1945	60	Mo.	Dem.	—
Dwight D. Eisenhower	1953	62	N. Y. (Pa.)	Rep.	—

THE PRESIDENCY IN THE

CONSTITUTION

Those passages in the Constitution that touch directly upon the Presidency run as follows:

Article I
Section 3:

6. The Senate shall have the sole power to try all impeachments. When sitting for that purpose, they shall be on oath or affirmation. When the President of the United States is tried, the Chief Justice shall preside; and no person shall be convicted without the concurrence of two-thirds of the members present.

7. Judgment in cases of impeachment shall not extend further than to removal from office, and disqualification to hold and enjoy any office of honor, trust, or profit under the United States; but the party convicted shall, nevertheless, be liable and subject to indictment, trial, judgment, and punishment, according to law.

Section 7:

2. Every bill which shall have passed the House of Representatives and the Senate shall, before it becomes a law, be presented to the President of the United States; if he approve he shall sign it, but if not he shall return it, with his objections, to that house in which it shall have originated, who shall enter the objections at large on their journal and

proceed to reconsider it. If after such reconsideration two-thirds of that house shall agree to pass the bill, it shall be sent, together with the objections, to the other house, by which it shall likewise be reconsidered, and if approved by two-thirds of that house it shall become a law. But in all such cases the votes of both houses shall be determined by yeas and nays, and the names of the persons voting for and against the bill shall be entered on the journal of each house respectively. If any bill shall not be returned by the President within ten days (Sundays excepted) after it shall have been presented to him, the same shall be a law, in like manner as if he had signed it unless the Congress by their adjournment prevent its return, in which case it shall not be a law. 3. Every order, resolution, or vote to which the concurrence of the Senate and House of Representatives may be necessary (except on a question of adjournment) shall be presented to the President of the United States; and before the same shall take effect, shall be approved by him, or being disapproved by him, shall be repassed by two-thirds of the Senate and House of Representatives, according to the rules and limitations prescribed in the case of a bill.

Article II

Section 1:

1. The executive power shall be vested in a President of the United States of America. He shall hold his office during the term of four years, and, together with the Vice-President, chosen for the same term, be elected as follows:

2. Each state shall appoint, in such manner as the legislature thereof may direct, a number of electors, equal to the whole number of Senators and Representatives to which the State may be entitled in the Congress; but no Senator or Representative, or person holding an office of trust or profit under the United States, shall be appointed an elector.

[3. The electors shall meet in their respective States and

vote by ballot for two persons, of whom one at least shall not be an inhabitant of the same State with themselves. And they shall make a list of all the persons voted for, and of the number of votes for each; which list they shall sign and certify, and transmit sealed to the seat of the government of the United States, directed to the President of the Senate. The President of the Senate shall, in the presence of the Senate and House of Representatives, open all the certificates, and the votes shall then be counted. The person having the greatest number of votes shall be the President, if such a number be a majority of the whole number of electors appointed; and if there be more than one who have such majority, and have an equal number of votes, then the House of Representatives shall immediately choose by ballot one of them for President; and if no person have a majority, then from the five highest on the list the said House shall in like manner choose the President. But in choosing the President the votes shall be taken by States, the representation from each State having one vote; a quorum for this purpose shall consist of a member or members from two-thirds of the States, and a majority of all the States shall be necessary to a choice. In every case, after the choice of the President, the person having the greatest number of votes of the electors shall be the Vice-President. But if there should remain two or more who have equal votes, the Senate shall choose from them by ballot the Vice-President.]

4. The Congress may determine the time of choosing the electors and the day on which they shall give their votes, which day shall be the same throughout the United States.

5. No person except a natural born citizen, or a citizen of the United States at the time of the adoption of this Constitution, shall be eligible to the office of President; neither shall any person be eligible to that office who shall not have attained to the age of thirty-five years, and been fourteen years a resident within the United States.

6. In case of the removal of the President from office, or of his death, resignation, or inability to discharge the powers and duties of the said office, the same shall devolve on the Vice-President, and the Congress may by law provide for the case of removal, death, resignation, or inability, both of the President and Vice-President, declaring what officer shall then act as President, and such officer shall act accordingly until the disability be removed or a President shall be elected.

7. The President shall, at stated times, receive for his services a compensation, which shall neither be increased nor diminished during the period for which he shall have been elected, and he shall not receive within that period any other emolument from the United States or any of them.

8. Before he enter on the execution of his office he shall take the following oath or affirmation:

"I do solemnly swear (or affirm) that I will faithfully execute the office of President of the United States, and will to the best of my ability preserve, protect, and defend the Constitution of the United States."

Section 2:

1. The President shall be Commander-in-Chief of the Army and Navy of the United States, and of the militia of the several States when called into the actual service of the United States; he may require the opinion, in writing, of the principal officer in each of the executive departments, upon any subject relating to the duties of their respective offices, and he shall have power to grant reprieves and pardons for offenses against the United States, except in cases of impeachment.

2. He shall have power, by and with the advice and consent of the Senate, to make treaties, provided two-thirds of the Senators present concur; and he shall nominate, and, by and with the advice and consent of the Senate, shall appoint ambassadors, other public ministers and consuls, judges of the Supreme Court, and all other officers of the United States,

whose appointments are not herein otherwise provided for, and which shall be established by law; but the Congress may by law vest the appointment of such inferior officers, as they think proper, in the President alone, in the courts of law, or in the heads of departments.

3. The President shall have power to fill up all vacancies that may happen during the recess of the Senate, by granting commissions which shall expire at the end of their next session.

Section 3:

He shall from time to time give to the Congress information of the state of the Union, and recommend to their consideration such measures as he shall judge necessary and expedient; he may, on extraordinary occasions, convene both houses, or either of them, and in case of disagreement between them with respect to the time of adjournment, he may adjourn them to such time as he shall think proper; he shall receive ambassadors and other public ministers; he shall take care that the laws be faithfully executed, and shall commission all the officers of the United States.

Section 4:

The President, Vice-President, and all civil officers of the United States shall be removed from office on impeachment for and conviction of treason, bribery, or other high crimes and misdemeanors.

Amendment XII

The electors shall meet in their respective States and vote by ballot for President and Vice-President, one of whom, at least, shall not be an inhabitant of the same State with themselves; they shall name in their ballots the person voted for as President, and in distinct ballots the person voted for as Vice-President, and they shall make distinct lists of all persons voted for as President and of all persons voted for as Vice-President, and of the number of votes for each; which lists they shall sign and certify, and transmit sealed to the seat of the government of the United States, directed to the President of the Senate. The President of the Senate shall, in the presence of the Senate and House of Representatives, open all the certificates and the votes shall then be counted. The person having the greatest number of votes for President shall be the President, if such number be a majority of the whole number of electors appointed; and if no person have such majority, then from the persons having the highest numbers not exceeding three on the list of those voted for as President, the House of Representatives shall choose immediately, by ballot, the President. But in choosing the President the votes shall be taken by States, the representation from each State having one vote; a quorum for this purpose shall consist of a member or members from two-thirds of the States, and a majority of all the States shall be necessary to a choice. And if the House of Representatives shall not choose a President whenever the right of choice shall devolve upon them, before the fourth day of March next following, then the Vice-President shall act as President, as in the case of the death or other constitutional disability of the President.

The person having the greatest number of votes as Vice-President shall be the Vice-President, if such number be a majority of the whole number of electors appointed; and if no person have a majority, then from the two highest numbers on the list the Senate shall choose the Vice-President; a quorum for the purpose shall consist of two-thirds of the whole number of Senators, and a majority of the whole number shall be necessary to a choice. But no person constitutionally ineligible to the office of President shall be eligible to that of Vice-President of the United States.

Amendment XX

Section 1:

The terms of the President and Vice-President shall end at

noon on the 20th day of January, and the terms of Senators and Representatives at noon on the 3d day of January, of the years in which such terms would have ended if this article had not been ratified; and the terms of their successors shall then begin.

Section 2:

The Congress shall assemble at least once in every year, and such meeting shall begin at noon on the 3d day of January, unless they shall by law appoint a different day.

Section 3:

If, at the time fixed for the beginning of the term of the President, the President elect shall have died, the Vice-President elect shall become President. If a President shall not have been chosen before the time fixed for the beginning of his term, or if the President elect shall have failed to qualify, then the Vice-President elect shall act as President until a President shall have qualified; and the Congress may by law provide for the case wherein neither a President elect nor a Vice-President elect shall have qualified, declaring who shall then act as President, or the manner in which one who is to act shall be selected, and such person shall act accordingly until a President or Vice-President shall have qualified.

Section 4:

The Congress may by law provide for the case of the death of any of the persons from whom the House of Representatives may choose a President whenever the right of choice shall have devolved upon them, and for the case of the death of any of the persons from whom the Senate may choose a Vice-President whenever the right of choice shall have devolved upon them.

Amendment XXII

No person shall be elected to the office of the President more than twice, and no person who has held the office of President, or acted as President, for more than two years of a term to which some other person was elected President shall be elected to the office of the President more than once. But this Article shall not apply to any person holding the office of President when this Article was proposed by the Congress, and shall not prevent any person who may be holding the office of President, or acting as President, during the term within which this Article becomes operative from holding the office of President or acting as President during the remainder of such term.

Appendix III

A BIBLIOGRAPHY OF THE

PRESIDENCY

The Presidency has been the subject of a vast amount of writing both good and bad. What I have tried to do in the following list is to separate the wheat of the fifty or so most rewarding books on the Presidency from the chaff of the hundreds that one would have to read to exhaust the subject. The ones I have starred are, if I may be pardoned the expression, the cream of the wheat. Some of the best writing on the Presidency, of course, is to be found in general histories of the United States, treatises on the national government, and the dispatches of such perceptive observers as James Reston and Walter Lippmann.

I. GENERAL WORKS

Wilfred E. Binkley, *The Man in the White House,* Baltimore, 1958
*Edward S. Corwin, *The President: Office and Powers,* 4th Edition, New York, 1957
Edward S. Corwin and Louis W. Koenig, *The Presidency Today,* New York, 1956
*Sidney Hyman, *The American President,* New York, 1954
Sidney Hyman (ed.), *The Office of the American Presidency,* in *The Annals of The American Academy of Political and Social Science,* Vol. 307, 1956
*Harold J. Laski, *The American Presidency,* New York, 1940, also issued in paperback
J. Francis Paschal (ed.), *The Presidential Office,* in *Law and Contemporary Problems,* Vol. 21. 1957

Robert S. Rankin (ed.), *The Presidency in Transition*, in *The Journal of Politics*, Vol. 11, 1949

II. SPECIAL STUDIES

*Lawrence H. Chamberlain, *The President, Congress and Legislation*, New York, 1946

Richard F. Fenno, Jr., *The President's Cabinet*, Cambridge, Mass., 1959

*Joseph P. Harris, *The Advice and Consent of the Senate*, Berkeley, Calif., 1953

Pendleton Herring, *Presidential Leadership*, New York, 1940

Edward H. Hobbs, *Behind the President*, Washington, 1954

W. H. Humbert, *The Pardoning Power of the President*, Washington, 1941

Harry S. Learned, *The President's Cabinet*, New Haven, Conn., 1912

Richard E. Neustadt, *Presidential Power*, New York, 1960

Bennett Milton Rich, *The Presidents and Civil Disorder*, Washington, 1941

Clinton Rossiter, *The Supreme Court and the Commander-in-Chief*, Ithaca, N. Y., 1951

Glendon A. Schubert, Jr., *The Presidency in the Courts*, Minneapolis, 1957

Norman J. Small, *Some Presidential Interpretations of the Presidency*, Baltimore, 1932

Ruth C. Silva, *Presidential Succession*, Ann Arbor, Mich., 1951

Irving G. Williams, *The Rise of the Vice-Presidency*, Washington, 1956

*Lucius Wilmerding, Jr., *The Electoral College*, New Brunswick, New Jersey, 1958

III. PRESIDENTIAL POLITICS

Paul T. David, Malcolm Moos, and Ralph M. Goldman, *Presidential Nominating Politics*, 5 vols., Baltimore, 1954

Malcolm Moos, *Politics, Presidents, and Coattails*, Baltimore, 1950

Eugene H. Roseboom, *A History of Presidential Elections*, New York, 1957

IV. HISTORIES

*Wilfred E. Binkley, *President and Congress*, New York, 1947

George Fort Milton, *The Use of Presidential Power*, Boston, 1944
Charles C. Thach, Jr., *The Creation of the Presidency, 1775-1789*, Baltimore, 1922
*Leonard D. White, *A Study in Administrative History*, 4 vols., New York, 1947-1958. The titles of the volumes are *The Federalists, The Jeffersonians, The Jacksonians, The Republican Era.*

V. AUTOBIOGRAPHIES, DIARIES, INSIDE GLIMPSES

Grover Cleveland, *Presidential Problems*, New York, 1904
Herbert Hoover, *Memoirs*, 3 vols., New York, 1951-1952
David F. Houston, *Eight Years with Wilson's Cabinet*, New York, 1926
*James K. Polk, *The Diary of a President*, Allan Nevins (ed.), New York, 1929
W. C. Redfield, *With Congress and Cabinet*, New York, 1924
*Theodore Roosevelt, *Autobiography*, New York, 1913
*Robert E. Sherwood, *Roosevelt and Hopkins*, New York, 1948
William Howard Taft, *Our Chief Magistrate and His Powers*, New York, 1916
William Howard Taft, *The Presidency*, New York, 1916
Harry S Truman, *Memoirs*, New York, 1955-1956
*Gideon Welles, *Diary of Gideon Welles*, Boston, 1909

VI. BIOGRAPHIES

Irving Brant, *Madison the President*, Vol. V, New York, 1957
*James M. Burns, *Roosevelt: The Lion and the Fox*, New York, 1956
Robert J. Donovan, *Eisenhower: The Inside Story*, New York, 1956
Douglas S. Freeman, *George Washington*, Vols. VI-VII, New York, 1954-1957
*Burton J. Hendrick, *Lincoln's War Cabinet*, Boston, 1946
*Herbert Hoover, *The Ordeal of Woodrow Wilson*, New York, 1958
*Marquis James, *Andrew Jackson: Portrait of a President*, New York, 1937
*Margaret Leech, *In the Days of McKinley*, New York, 1959
Robert J. Morgan, *A Whig Embattled*, Lincoln, Neb., 1954
Allan Nevins, *Grover Cleveland: A Study in Courage*, New York, 1932

Roy F. Nichols, *Franklin Pierce: Young Hickory of the Granite Hills,* Philadelphia, 1931

*Henry F. Pringle, *Theodore Roosevelt,* New York, 1931, also issued in paperback

Henry F. Pringle, *The Life and Times of William Howard Taft,* New York, 1939

*J. G. Randall, *Lincoln the President,* 4 vols. (fourth volume by Randall and Richard N. Current), New York, 1945-1955

Arthur M. Schlesinger, Jr., *The Crisis of the Old Order,* Boston, 1957

Arthur M. Schlesinger, Jr., *The Coming of the New Deal,* Boston, 1959

INDEX

277